Yellen

Yellen

The Trailblazing Economist Who Navigated an Era of Upheaval

JON HILSENRATH

HARPER
BUSINESS

An Imprint of HarperCollins*Publishers*

HarperCollins books may be purchased for educational, business, or sales promotional use. For information, please email the Special Markets Department at SPsales@harpercollins.com.

FIRST EDITION

Designed by Bonni Leon-Berman

Library of Congress Cataloging-in-Publication Data has been applied for.

ISBN 978-0-06-316246-4

22 23 24 25 26   LSC   10 9 8 7 6 5 4 3 2 1

For my mother, Elaine, who taught me to think critically and that history turns like a kaleidoscope; and for my father, Joseph, who taught me to embrace every day with hope and purpose and to love the meanings, sounds, and rhythms of words.

Contents

Contents

Introduction

Janet Yellen followed her routine on the way to Washington, DC. She packed her bags carefully and arrived at the San Francisco airport early. She didn't like mishaps and she wasn't one to hurry while traveling, so she always left hours in advance to be the first person at the gate. There she sat, waiting for her long-haul flight to the East Coast while thumbing through briefing books prepared by her staff and playing Brick Breaker on her phone.

Yellen was a worrier, and she moved methodically. Her approach to life was to plan and prepare for all contingencies. For a woman making her way in a man's business, preparation was especially important. She worked details over in her head, reading up, thinking through scenarios, calculating probabilities for different outcomes, and sizing up strategies for how to respond should worst-case scenarios become actual problems.

She had picked up an exacting attention to detail from her mother, Ruth. When Yellen was a girl growing up in Brooklyn in the 1950s, Ruth often sent Yellen's older brother, John, down the street to fetch the day's newspaper. Then the children watched their mother sit with the paper, in a dress with her feet up on a couch, meticulously writing down daily stock prices she tracked on the back of envelopes in neat square handwriting.

Do your homework, Yellen learned. Don't be caught off guard by outcomes you could have foreseen. Eliminate worries. Reduce unnecessary risk. Prepare.

In December 2009 the United States was emerging from more than two years of shocking financial crisis. The economy was growing again. Janet Yellen, however, still had a great many worries.

Yellen was a central banker, sixty-three years old, one of twelve presidents of Federal Reserve banks spread around the country, two of which were run by women. Their job was to monitor the economy and the banking system, look out for problems like inflation or banks struggling with bad loans, and then work with the powerful Federal Reserve Board in Washington to figure out how to respond. When banks were failing, the Fed was called in to help sort their problems out. When the economy careened toward recession, the Fed had to rescue it.

The San Francisco Fed, which Yellen ran, was mandated to monitor a vast piece of the US economy covering 1.4 million square miles, from frigid mountain peaks in northern Oregon to dusty Native American tribal lands in the Arizona desert. In between were the nation's hotbed tech market in Silicon Valley and pockets of some of its most unstable real estate markets, including Los Angeles, Las Vegas, and Phoenix. In all it had a greater land mass than India and was home to sixty-nine million people and thirty-one million workers, about a fifth of the nation's population and a large part of the national economy.

During the preceding two years, a succession of big financial institutions had teetered or collapsed. Their top executives, typically the most confident of men, spent long weekends begging competitors and the Fed to save them during fraught rescue negotiations as frightened investors and depositors in their institutions fled for safety from the storm.

The list of casualties was long, diverse, and astonishing: Countrywide Financial, Bear Stearns, Fannie Mae, Lehman Brothers, Merrill Lynch, American International Group (AIG), Citigroup, General Electric, and many others.

Their problem was a mortgage meltdown. Americans had binged on mortgage debt in an era of low interest rates and financial innovation. They took out loans with unusual terms and used the cash to bid up the prices of homes, to pay for vacations and cars, or simply to cover their regular bills. Wall Street encouraged the frenzy, buying many of these mortgages and selling them to investors around the world in complicated financial packages. For a while this boosted profits and executive pay. Then overburdened households delayed or defaulted on debts. When mortgage delinquencies piled up, the financial system was starved of funds and nearly collapsed.

Some of the most aggressive mortgage writing happened in the West, which Yellen was monitoring. That meant she saw problems brewing early, though not early enough nor with the authority in a diffuse regulatory system to stop it.

As mortgages went bad, lenders panicked for funds, which in turn set off a frenzy inside the Fed to stop a potentially catastrophic crisis. The Fed's healing medicine was money. It provided loans to banks when funds were nowhere else to be found. It tried to work in an orderly manner. In this case it administered its medicine as slews of patients crashed at its doors, convulsing and near death.

Yellen foresaw the panic before many of her colleagues at the Fed and urged them to move swiftly to stamp it out. The Fed's responses prevented a financial collapse, but the nation was still left with something terrible. After two years of exhausting bank rescues, a recession had cascaded out of the canyons of Wall Street to communities across America, leaving more than fifteen million people unemployed.

In December 2009, Yellen didn't think jobs would be coming back anytime soon. As she saw it, this was the next crisis.

It all seemed so unfair. Wall Street got bailouts, and for good reason; the crisis revealed that the economy couldn't work if banks stopped making loans. But while the banks got support, millions of Americans were left behind to pick up the pieces of their lives with part-time jobs, food stamps, and disability claims. Two Princeton professors would later use the term *deaths of despair* to describe lives lost to depression, drug addiction, alcoholism, and suicide, a long-running trend that further signaled a nation where elites and everyone else were on two different tracks.[1]

After landing in Washington, DC, that December evening, Yellen gathered with the eleven other regional bank presidents for an informal dinner in a hotel a few blocks from the Fed's austere Depression-era building on Constitution Avenue. The next day the regional bank presidents met formally with five Washington-based Fed board governors and an army of PhD-trained staff to discuss the grim economic outlook and what to do about it. Technically economic output was growing again, which meant a recovery had started. Yet the unemployment rate had recently risen to 10 percent.

They sat in a cavernous boardroom with two-story-high ceilings, its tall windows decorated with elegant light drapes. Above the large mahogany table at its center hung a dark, pointed chandelier that hovered above their heads like the tip of a missile that had crashed through the building, poised to detonate.

Yellen, who stood around five feet tall, wore modest dark pantsuits to meetings, sometimes dressed up with a silk scarf. Ben Bernanke, an introverted and socially awkward genius who had written books on the Great Depression, conducted the proceedings as the Fed's chairman. As a young academic, Bernanke had concluded that the Fed's hesitation to act had made the Great Depression much worse than it needed to be. He was a quiet man with bold views and the burden of orchestrating the Fed's response. Bernanke had been in the job less than four years, having taken over from Alan Greenspan, a legendary central banker who led the institution through nearly two decades of rising prosperity and then retired just before the cracks in the economy were becoming apparent.

Fed staff sat along walls in a periphery of stiff chairs around the boardroom table, deciphering results from computer models they used to track the economy and predict where it would go next. One model had its own odd-sounding name: "Ferbus," for FRB/US. This model had been created in the 1990s with great ambition and internal fanfare to simulate how the economy would behave under different scenarios. Punch in an oil price jump, and Ferbus would estimate how much less consumers, hit by higher gasoline costs, would spend, say, on cars or restaurant meals. Punch in a stock price boom, and Ferbus would say how many jobs would be created.

There was one big problem with Ferbus, though. Nobody had thought to program it to calculate the effect on the economy if the entire financial system almost collapsed.

Bernanke turned to Yellen when it was time for the regional bank presidents to share their views about what they were seeing back home. The bailouts were over, and officials believed a recovery had started, but Yellen warned that it didn't actually feel like one. She pulled out a prepared statement and read it carefully, sticking to her script. Business executives she knew in the West, "shell-shocked and traumatized from recent events," continued to lay people off. Because they had little confidence about the outlook, they still weren't considering investing or hiring, she said: "They remain focused on ensuring their survival."[2]

Fed officials were exhausted and uncertain after two years of crisis fighting. During recessions the central bank pumped money into the financial system, which helped to lower interest rates. Those lower borrowing costs in turn spurred the economy by helping businesses and households to refinance loans or take out new loans to invest and spend. But the Fed had already pushed its benchmark interest rate to near zero. How could it go any lower? What else could it do to help the damaged economy? It experimented with other strategies, including a program to buy mortgage bonds and US government bonds in an effort to bring down an even wider array of interest rates. But the costs and benefits of that unusual therapy were unknown, and many Fed officials wanted to stop before the central bank caused some new problem.

Yellen was restrained, courteous, and deliberate in these formal meetings, but her message to her colleagues was forceful: their work wasn't done. "I continue to see a persuasive case for further policy easing," she told them.

Back in San Francisco, her colleagues were seeing an even bolder Janet Yellen emerge, animated and urgent about confronting an economic crisis that she was sure wasn't close to being over. "These are fucking people!" she exclaimed during a San Francisco staff briefing about the jobs problem, pounding the table with her fist. She didn't want the economists reporting to her to look at the high unemployment rates they were projecting as just a bunch of statistics. The human suffering that persisted after the financial crisis was enormous, and they needed to work at that problem with the same sense of purpose and urgency that they had brought to repairing banks.

It was in these moments, after the fires of financial crisis had been extinguished and the enormity of rebuilding a damaged economy had sunk in, that Janet Yellen emerged as the most powerful woman in American economic history. She was two years away from the normal retirement age, and her most important and complex years of work still lay ahead of her.

Yellen had already served as the chair of the White House Council of Economic Advisers for President Bill Clinton in the late 1990s. In that role she was a top economic adviser to the president in a rough-and-tumble White House. In 2009 she wasn't yet aware that she was on course to become chair of the Federal Reserve, the nation's central bank, charged with managing interest rates, containing inflation, and stamping out financial panics. Then she would become secretary of the Treasury, charged with overseeing the tax system, the federal government's debt, and sanctions programs aimed at adversaries abroad. No person in American history to that point had ever had all three of these jobs. Yellen held each in a period of confounding and unprecedented economic upheaval.

The nation's elites—its political leaders, business titans, and esteemed academics—had begun the new millennium thinking they were marching into a new era of global prosperity, driven by advancing technology, widening international trade, Wall Street savvy, and wise central banking. In the year 2000, they had projected budget surpluses, rising incomes, and a new economy charged up by life-changing technology. This new era also seemed to promise peace and freedom. Soviet rule over Russia and Eastern Europe had ended. China was coming on the scene. They thought that would be good too.

But something else happened. By 2009 the United States was already several years into a period of stagnating household incomes, slowing job growth, rising inequality, and waning economic mobility. A bursting stock bubble, then terror attacks, war in Afghanistan and Iraq, and the emergence of China as a global trade leviathan had already thrown the United States off course. The financial shock meant the worst of a tectonic shift in the American economic landscape was yet to come. Shock waves unleashed by trade, technology, high finance, and an aging population had already altered the economic story. The long, slow recovery from financial crisis was the next blow, catching the institutions of government and society off guard. Social backlash became intense and divisive. After all of that, an economic beast that policy makers had long thought they had vanquished, inflation, resurfaced.

It became Yellen's job—over and over again—to clean up the mess from inside the very institutions that many people blamed for the crises. First she moved from San Francisco to Washington to serve as Bernanke's number two, where she surprised Fed staff with a feistiness and focus that rubbed some of them the wrong way. Then she beat out one of her former students—Lawrence Summers, a giant in economics, the nephew of two Nobel Prize winners, and an engineer of the booming 1990s—in a contest to become Fed chair.

Donald Trump, though he admired Yellen, kicked her out of the job two years into his presidency because, as a Democrat, she wasn't philosophically aligned with his economic agenda. Yellen thought her public life was done and enjoyed getting to bed early again. But by the time Joe Biden was elected president, the United States found itself in the throes of yet another economic crisis, a pandemic that shut down the economy for a year. Biden asked Yellen to come back, this time to run the US Department of the Treasury and revive the economy from what amounted to a self-induced coma. She said no at first, but then changed her mind. She felt she had a duty to take the job.

Once again Yellen had to steer a damaged economy back to safer shores. It turned out to be the hardest job she'd ever had. Her challenges started with a revival of inflation, which in this new economy many thought had disappeared. Key lessons that she had learned in the previous decades turned out to be ill suited for managing the next crisis, which likely paved a path toward the inflation revival. Then in her second year she was called upon to confront another once-vanquished foe, orchestrating a global sanctions program to punish Russia for its military incursion into Ukraine.

. . .

As Janet Yellen's influence rose over three decades, two brilliant and eccentric economic theorists, George Akerlof and Robert Shiller, had long-running conversations about strange things happening in markets. Two financial bubbles had grown and burst—first an internet stock bubble in the 1990s and then a housing bubble in the 2000s. Each ended in recession. In the latter bubble, the whole housing market, bedrock for the economy and the fortunes of households and communities, was built up on scaffoldings of unreasonable expectations, shady mortgages, and outright fraud. Then it collapsed.

How could this be?

Many economists had arrived at the view that markets gravitated toward some elegant equilibrium—that, left to their own devices, individuals and organizations acting in free markets would distribute goods and jobs and capital effectively and to their best uses, making people better off in the long run. This idea went all the way back to Enlightenment-era economist Adam Smith, who in 1776 marveled at the workings of an invisible hand guiding markets toward the best outcomes for all in his book *An Inquiry into the Nature and Causes of the Wealth of Nations*.

A foundational belief in the efficacy of markets was especially important at the University of Chicago. Professors there hatched theories in the 1960s and 1970s that fueled the rise of President Ronald Reagan and Prime Minister Margaret Thatcher and the boom-boom 1980s. Several of Chicago's economists, led by a feisty theorist named Milton Friedman, won Nobel Prizes for work that transformed the functioning of societies across the planet, from Chile to China. Government needed to stand back and let markets work independently, these economists believed. The alternative, socialism, was a failure, as proven by the collapse of the Soviet empire in the late 1980s and early 1990s. Its socialist experiment induced misery and strangled human liberty.

Akerlof and Shiller were skeptics of the orthodoxies of modern economics. They were part of a new generation of technical economists who came of age during the 1960s and 1970s. Many of them studied and taught at the Massachusetts Institute of Technology, and others at Harvard, Yale, Princeton, Berkeley, and other top institutions. Even outside Chicago, many professors saw the economy as a machine with markets at its core that could be analyzed and calibrated with mathematical precision. Akerlof and Shiller came to believe that markets weren't always efficient and that the real world didn't always work the way mathematical formulas predicted. Human behavior was more complicated than economics assumed.

Akerlof took one of the first cracks at the foundations of modern economics in 1970, when he published a paper about cars, "The Market for 'Lemons,'" just thirteen pages long.[3] The giant car market wasn't efficient, Akerlof wrote, particularly when it came to selling used cars. Sellers placed classified advertisements in newspapers or lined up old cars in dirty lots, knowing much more about what was under the hoods of their cars than prospective buyers. They might know of a broken tooth on a flywheel that was costly to replace, or a belt that was dry and cracking and might fall apart at any moment, destroying the entire engine. Maybe the sellers were getting rid of their cars simply because they knew something was wrong with them. The buyers, reluctant to fork over good money for potential lemons, stayed away. Their suspicion left good used cars unsold or underpriced, and buyers gravitated to the new car market instead.

Economists saw efficiency in markets. Akerlof looked under the hoods of cars and saw a world of complex skepticism and deceit that made the market inefficient and spoke broadly to the true nature of human behavior and how it affected economic life. Mistrust was a variable economists forgot to put in their formulas.

Robert Shiller was fascinated by financial bubbles, a phenomenon that traced back centuries, plaguing markets for Dutch tulip bulbs in the 1600s, water canals in England and America in the 1800s, and then internet stocks. Back in the mid-1990s, in the middle of an economic boom, Shiller said stock prices couldn't be sustained at such high levels. Stock prices kept rising, but he was right in the end: in 2000 the tech bubble burst, stoking a recession in 2001. That bust marked the beginning of a longer-running unraveling in American economic fortunes, small at first, then gathering force and fury in the decades that followed.

The books Akerlof and Shiller published together had an underlying message: most of what you think you know about economics is probably wrong. Along the way, Akerlof moved toward examining his next puzzle: What is the nature of social division? It turned out to be another question that he would ask decades before others realized that underneath it lurked dangerous problems—in this case not for capitalism but for democracy.

. . .

The theories of two airy academics might not have been all that remarkable had it not been for one extraordinary fact: George Akerlof was Janet Yellen's husband. Akerlof was launching his book on social division when Barack Obama nominated Yellen to become vice chair of the Fed; he was finishing another book on market breakdowns when Yellen became Fed chair. By then Akerlof was a Nobel Prize winner. "The Market for 'Lemons,'" initially dismissed by major academic journals as trivial, would eventually be recognized as a seminal work that uncovered the true complexity of economic activity.

In his Nobel lecture before an audience of luminaries in 2001, Akerlof warned, "Economies, like lions, are wild and dangerous."* He saw long before most others that the economy's enduring tendency to wander off track had not been fixed in modern times. A bold and creative thinker, he was also, like his wife, a bit of a worrier. While Akerlof was crafting theories with his friend Shiller and others, Yellen was taking on the job of fixing the very system that her husband had seen all along as prone to breaking.

Janet and George met at the Fed in 1977. They were both coming off life-changing disappointments: George had been denied a promotion at the University of California at Berkeley, and his first marriage had failed. Janet, a perfectionist who had been trying to write an economics textbook with her Yale mentor, James Tobin, had dropped the project because some of Tobin's ideas seemed to be getting outdated. The profession was also turning out to be a tough place for a woman to make her mark. It was filled with men who had big egos and were prone to shooting down the ideas of others. Many weren't especially eager to collaborate with promising young women. Yellen's first job was as an assistant professor at Harvard. The school didn't offer her tenure, and she left.

Janet and George were in their thirties in the fall of 1977 when they sat down together to listen to a speech at an empty side table in a Fed cafeteria. The head table was filled with dignitaries.

Janet was the model student who made sure she got all of her facts straight and sweated the details. George didn't always fit in; when his father tried to turn him into a chemist as a boy, he'd burned his hands on glass jars. Janet dressed in dark suits. George showed up to formal meetings in hiking boots. She wanted to write a textbook. He wanted to prove that the textbooks were fundamentally wrong.

Janet and George fell in love at the Fed. She was drawn to his inventive mind; he was drawn to her calm and grounded nature and the devotion she brought to her work. They felt a common sense of purpose in their research. They were playful together and laughed. Life was odd, and they were a little odd, too, and they found the oddities amusing. They decided just a few weeks after meeting to marry, setting out on a journey through an era of upheaval together.

When they traveled, they took along suitcases full of books. Janet also packed her own pillow, because hotel pillows were often too fluffy and hurt her neck. On vacation they made time to read and study. In Washington, a town where powerful people relished being chauffeured in black limousines with police escorts, Janet and George puttered around in an old brown Toyota, Janet often driving, their heads barely visible above the back of their headrests. Eventually the limousines were thrust upon them.

They spent the 1980s in Berkeley together studying a common interest—work and jobs. As a twelve-year-old boy, George had seen his own father switch from job to job and started worrying about the bad things that he reasoned could happen to society when people lost work. Janet, as a girl in Brooklyn, sat at the dinner table with her father, a doctor, hearing about the misfortunes of his patients who lost paychecks and the dignity of employment. No issue in economics mattered more than work, both believed from an unusually early age, so they set out to understand it better. Before they even met, they had the same audacious goal: to fix the problem of unemployment.

In their own lives, Janet and George forged an equal partnership. They started a family in a time when a woman's role in the workplace and home was changing. Husbands and wives were adjusting as women went to work in growing numbers. Janet and George split their own household duties evenly. Their research on wages informed how they paid babysitters. Rearing their son, Robby, was a joint effort. George often picked up young Robby from school, confusing young mothers who thought perhaps he was unemployed. Why else would a young man be out with his son in the middle of a workday? On hikes after school, father and young son discussed history and George's experiences from his travels in India. When Janet landed jobs in Washington at the Fed and then the White House, George became Janet's traveling spouse, following where she led. As she rose, he enjoyed the fact that friends called him "Mr. Janet Yellen."

The two came on the scene after the death of the leading economist of the Great Depression era, John Maynard Keynes. Janet and George played leading roles in the weighty intellectual battles that trailed Keynes, long-running battles about the messy interplay of government and the market economy. Then in her next act Janet became the economist with her hands on the lever, guiding the nation through successive epochs of prosperity, chaos, and reformation, the elegant equilibriums of markets and good governance elusive as ever.

By December 2009 a new postcrisis era had begun. A shaken nation was struggling to forge a path, uncertain about its direction. Economics, it turned out, was not the exact or predictable science that many economists once confidently thought it could be. Nor did it adhere faithfully to the ideologies of any group, person, or textbook.

Economics, it turned out, was an endeavor.

Most good love stories are too.

Part I

Love Stories

1

Yellen's Youth

"I'm Gonna Tell Your Mother"
1946–1967

When Janet Yellen was an infant, her father, Julius, fell down a flight of stairs and fractured his skull, losing sight in one eye. Janet's mother, Ruth, then set about making everything right.[1]

Julius was a physician in a working-class Brooklyn neighborhood, during an era when patients paid their medical bills in cash and doctors made house calls. Ruth didn't wake Janet or her older brother, John, the night their father fell. First she got Julius to the hospital and stabilized.

Julius returned to his medical practice after he recovered, but he wasn't all well. Janet and John later noticed he had trouble lining up the house key at the front door of their brownstone stoop because of vision problems. He also couldn't drive to visit patients in their homes. Ruth, who had been a schoolteacher before having children, became her husband's driver. She sat in the car at the curb, waiting patiently outside while he made his daily rounds.

Ruth was all about keeping order in the Yellen household. Julius kept the cash he received from patients in a wad held together by a rubber band and handed it over to Ruth at the end of every week. She paid the bills and stashed what was left in savings, mostly stocks and certificates of deposit. When she discovered that Julius wasn't keeping careful track of his profits, she took over the accounting too. His office was in the basement of the family's three-story home. Once a week, Ruth took out a floor buffer and waxed the linoleum floors in his waiting room herself.

This was Brooklyn in the late 1940s and 1950s.

Janet Yellen was born in 1946. Her father, Jewish and of Polish descent, had grown up on Manhattan's Lower East Side. He studied medicine in Scotland; US medical schools limited the number of Jewish people they admitted.

"When he graduated from medical school, during the Great Depression, he looked for a home in a place to hang his shingle near the Brooklyn docks," Yellen recalled later. "Back then, Bush Terminal on the upper New York Bay was a thriving hub for manufacturing and transportation and for the union workers whose livelihoods depended on them. Knowing they didn't have cars, my father found a home near a bus line."[2]

Julius and Ruth chose Bay Ridge, a few blocks from New York Bay, with views of Staten Island and the Statue of Liberty. One neighbor, Mr. Rasmussen, was a ship captain who disappeared for months at a time making transatlantic trips. Another was a welder. Jimmy Gallagher became a cop. The neighborhood was safe. Some neighbors suspected it was because of the Mafia's presence there; people knew not to step out of line.

The Yellen family wasn't rich, but they lived well. They took the occasional half-hour trip by bus or train to Ebbets Field in Flatbush, where the Brooklyn Dodgers played and Jackie Robinson, Pee Wee Reese, and Duke Snider ruled the day. On Sundays they dressed nicely and had a fancy meal out in Brooklyn or Manhattan. Ruth made Janet wear white gloves that matched her white shoes when visiting nicer restaurants. They took boat cruises for vacation and hired a housekeeper, Elsie Johnson, a short, stout Black woman, to maintain the home and keep an eye on the children while Ruth drove Julius on his rounds.

Anna Ruth Blumenthal, who grew up in Brooklyn, was Jewish and of German descent. It caused a stir in her family when she married a Polish Jew. The Poles were seen as a little rough around the edges, but Ruth and Julius were in love. They married secretly and spent a lifetime together, devoted to each other and their children.

Julius was consumed by his practice. He visited patients in their homes and hospitals in the morning, then returned for office hours in the afternoon. Dinner was served promptly every day at 4:45 p.m. The children had a little more than an hour to play or study after school, then Julius ascended the stairs and the family sat and listened to the radio or listened to Julius's stories about his patients.

"He would talk to me, my brother, and my mom about what work meant to his patients, our friends and neighbors, especially if they lost a job," Janet recalled. "The financial problems, the family problems, the health problems, the loss of dignity and self-worth. The value of work always stuck with me." In some families, Janet heard, loss of a job descended into bouts of alcohol abuse or mental illness for husbands and wives. It destroyed marriages. That impression was drilled in even more deeply by dinner-table stories about the Great Depression and the suffering it had imposed on people Ruth and Julius knew when they were young.

Ruth was a do-gooder. She learned to read braille and translated books for the blind. When John's friend Frank struggled with Latin in school, Ruth tutored him. When Elsie fell ill, Ruth took the children to visit her in a high-rise building near the Brooklyn Navy Yard.

More than anything, Ruth made sure the household functioned like clockwork. The Yellen family had two sets of window curtains and covers for the couches. Ruth arranged to have them changed in summer and winter. A local handyman neatly folded the out-of-season curtains and couch covers and stored them away. When the family took transatlantic boat cruises departing from Manhattan, a short cab ride away, Ruth ensured early arrival at the terminal by arranging to stay at a hotel near the dock the night before.

Mischief in the Yellen household amounted to young Janet and John, who was four years older, dropping pillows on Elsie's head from the stairs.

"I'm gonna tell your mother," Elsie would respond, and that was the end of that.

Elsie was one of the few Black people Janet encountered in her childhood, and she kept her business mostly to herself. "It was an entirely white world," John said.

Ruth was always properly dressed, and kept her hair in a neat bun. In the evening, she often sent John down the street to Mintz's, a newspaper stand and candy store, where he fetched the *New York World-Telegram & Sun*, an afternoon newspaper, for a nickel. Still in her dress, Ruth put her feet up on the couch and recorded stock price movements on the backs of envelopes.

Ruth meant well, but she could be a pest. She sometimes nagged the keepers at the newspaper stand about the untidiness of the shop. John once had a Boy Scout meeting, and a boy in his troop showed up with improper socks. Ruth, the troop leader, wouldn't let him participate in the event. The boy's parents never talked to her again. During family vacations Janet was expected to keep a log of events and reflections, then write about them for family scrapbooks when they returned. Ruth checked the grammar before filing the written reflections away.

Ruth had no tolerance for apathy when it came to her children's schoolwork. In her mind, if the children were going to do something, they were expected to do it well. All homework had to be completed, and it had to be completed correctly. She reviewed the children's work every night. Writing, grammar, and John's Latin studies received the most attention. Janet looked on aghast as Ruth badgered her brother over Latin long into the night. When John was kicked off the Fort Hamilton High School newspaper, the *Pilot*, for refusing to complete an assignment, Ruth was furious.

John went back to writing for the school newspaper when he went off to Hobart College in 1960. When he proudly sent articles home, Ruth returned them with corrections of grammatical errors that had made it into print and asked why the articles hadn't been edited properly. She also caught him on errors in his personal correspondence. "Johnny, please try to be careful of your spelling when you do written work," she wrote to him during his first month away from home. "'<u>Their</u>' is possessive, and should not be used when you say 'There are.' Also, the word is <u>prescription</u>, not perscription."

Other letters instructed him on how much underwear to pack for visits home and detailed how he should spend every dollar he received from his parents while away.

Julius softened Ruth's harder edges, slipping Janet and Johnny money to buy ice cream around the corner. When Ruth wasn't around, he showed young Janet how to make prank phone calls, dialing random phone numbers and asking the recipients of his calls if their refrigerators were running. When they said yes, he said, "You better go catch it," and then hung up. When battles with Ruth became especially contentious, Janet and John went to their father, and he reassured them that it would settle down. When they were older and heading back to school, he slipped them a few extra dollars when Ruth wasn't looking so they'd have money to spend for fun.

Janet Yellen grew and thrived in this crucible, where intense discipline mixed with general tranquility. Among other things, her mother's hounding made her an exceptional writer, but also an anxious one, paranoid about being reprimanded for mistakes. She wrote clearly but didn't much enjoy it.

As a child she befriended Barbara Schwartz, a small girl pushed ahead in her grade, also Jewish, whose family had relocated from Mississippi to Brooklyn. Janet called her "Schwartzie" and made her feel at home with sweet notes. One was a poem Janet wrote:

The stork was flying north by south
With Little Barbara in his mouth
When he came to Barbara's little hut
There he dropped a little nut

In another she signed off, "OUQTINVU"—"Oh you cutie, I envy you."

By the time she entered William McKinley Intermediate School, Janet already stood out, one of about two dozen boys and girls selected among hundreds of classmates for an accelerated program called "Special Progress" that allowed them to finish three years of schooling in two years. The girls wore matching Pandora skirts and sweaters and attended courtyard dances at lunchtime.

Top boys were selected to attend the prestigious Stuyvesant High School in Manhattan. Stuyvesant didn't take girls. Smart young ladies could go to Hunter High in Manhattan, but Janet didn't want to make the long trip from home every day, so she chose to stay local at Fort Hamilton High School, like her brother. Janet's ninth-grade English teacher was so impressed with her writing that he assigned her to the school newspaper as a cub reporter during her first month of high school. Soon after that he asked her to help correct class writing assignments submitted by her schoolmates.

Ruth came to see that Janet could be a bit of a worrywart when it came to school, though perhaps she didn't realize she was the reason. "Janet is going to have to write a composition in English class tomorrow on some aspect of the Odyssey," Ruth wrote to Johnny while he was away. "She's scared stiff at the thought of it because she likes everything to be just perfect and that isn't easy to do in a 40 minute period."

Janet was a little competitive with her big brother. By her senior year she had become the top editor of her high school newspaper, the same paper that booted John for failing to complete an assignment. John, who would go on to earn a PhD in anthropology from Harvard University, started a rock collection as a child. Janet followed his lead and for good measure took weekend geology classes at the Museum of Natural History in Manhattan.

"I've been collecting rocks since I was 8 and have over 200 different specimens," she said in the *Pilot* when she was also its editor, boasting about her samples of fluorite and wulfenite. The newspaper had a tradition of interviewing the class valedictorian every year. Because Janet was valedictorian and also the newspaper editor, she interviewed herself in the piece. It was her idea of a joke, but also spoke to a competitive appetite that drove her to excel and take pride in good grades.

Like her mother, Janet would come to revel in study, preparation, and order. One English literature teacher who liked to drop pop quizzes on her students was one of Janet's few school frustrations. "It drove Janet nuts, because she couldn't figure out ahead of time what you had to know and study," her childhood friend Susan Grosart said later. Janet got an A in the class anyway.

While Janet was tightly wound about schoolwork, she was easygoing with friends and curious about life. She had a big laugh that started down in her belly and rose up into a round toothy smile and squinty eyes. She seemed to want to soak everything in. She studied piano and bridge and explored Manhattan theaters and music at Lincoln Center. She read the *New York Times* regularly, and in one day of high school mischief she and Susan skipped school to ride Coney Island's Cyclone roller coaster. A few days later Janet graduated from Fort Hamilton High School at the top of her class.

"Janet always seemed to come out on top," said her childhood friend, Barbara Schwartz.

Yellen decided to attend Pembroke College, Brown University's sister school, in part by a process of elimination. She didn't want to go to a girls-only school, where she thought the social life wouldn't be much fun. That ruled out places like Wellesley College. Princeton and Yale didn't accept women. Harvard required a record of studying Latin, which Janet decided not to do when she saw her brother battle Ruth over his homework in the subject. That left Pembroke, an elite school, and Janet had liked the campus when she visited with John some years earlier. John was rejected by Brown, but Janet got in.

When Janet Yellen went off to college in 1963, three big lessons seemed to stick with her: do your homework, maintain order, and do some good in the world.

Talented students were flocking to mathematics and economics back then. The disciplines seemed central to managing a cold war with America's confounding adversary, the Soviet Union. Between 1951 and 1970, the number of students seeking bachelor or graduate degrees in economics at US universities more than doubled, to nearly twenty thousand. By 1980 it was a more popular major than history. [3]

Many of the great minds of the time were anchored in mathematical thinking. Alan Turing, the British mathematician and Princeton PhD, used computational skills to crack German communications during World War II, making math and computers central to modern spycraft. Einstein's mathematical work unleashed the power and perils of nuclear technology and was put to work in part by another math savant, John von Neumann, a Princeton professor, in the Manhattan Project, which led to the bombing of Hiroshima and Nagasaki.

A new branch of mathematics, game theory, emerged as a tool to manage negotiations with Soviet adversaries, and *Fortune* magazine profiled a young game theorist named John Nash in 1958 as proof of its importance. [4] Von Neumann, considered a founder of game theory, helped devise the theory of mutual assured destruction, the notion that neither the United States nor the Soviet Union could attack each other because an attack by either would lead to the total destruction of both.

For all of the fear that circulated around this high-tech new cold war, economists saw in mathematics the potential to tame the ills that had ruined so many lives a generation earlier during the Great Depression. When John F. Kennedy became president in 1961, he brought with him a collection of brilliant young economists full of ambition to tame the beast of recession and broaden prosperity.

Janet Yellen fell in love in the first semester of her freshman year at Pembroke, not with a person but with the discipline. Like her friends, she dated, but unlike her friends she was in no rush to marry. Yellen didn't want to chase men just for the sake of getting married. In her mind it was too big a decision to rush. Her dating life became a new source of mild frustration with Ruth, who wanted her to marry and quizzed her regularly about whom she was seeing.

The disconnect with friends about marriage contributed to feelings of loneliness at Pembroke. Yellen's only enduring college connection was with Carol Greenwald, another economics student, two years older. Instead, she steeped herself in study. Economics seemed to mesh with her aptitudes in math and science, and also the desire to do some social good that she had picked up at the dinner table from her father and mother. There was a precision and order to economics that appealed to her.

"She took her first economics course and came home and gave me the one-hour lecture on why economics was the greatest thing going," Susan Grosart said.[5] "It was pretty obvious from then on that that was her passion." As they walked, Yellen tutored her old friend on the differences between government and household debt.

"After my first economics course, that was kind of love at first sight and I stuck with it," Yellen said later.[6]

Her one act of rebellion in college came in a course in German. Foreign language was a requirement, but she had little interest in the subject. She didn't see much reason to invest her time in a subject that wasn't going to matter to her in the long run, which was also a bit how she felt about some of the boys she dated. Perhaps she was also rebelling against her mother, who hounded John about his Latin studies. Yellen shirked in her German studies and got a B in the course, the only B in her life. Ruth was not happy.

A course on central banking exposed Yellen to the important role that the Federal Reserve played in managing the ups and downs of the economy. That left a much bigger impression on her than her German studies. Economists were coming to realize at the time that the Fed had worsened and prolonged the Great Depression by failing to keep bank loans expanding. One of the main proponents of that theory was an economist named Milton Friedman at Chicago. "I remember sitting in class and thinking, 'Gee, I didn't realize how much influence the Federal Reserve has on the health of the economy. If I ever have a chance at public service, a Fed post would be a worthwhile thing to do,'" Yellen said later.[7]

Economics was dominated at the time by men with big ideas and even bigger egos. Three men stood at the top. The first was Friedman, a University of Chicago professor who had worked for the government during World War II, devising wartime tax policy and using statistics to test weapon designs. By the time Yellen fell for economics, Friedman had established himself as the era's most prominent advocate for free markets. Another giant was Paul Samuelson, at the Massachusetts Institute of Technology, who drove the field to formalize its theories into precise and rigorous mathematics. Samuelson, who advised President Kennedy and believed the government should have a hand in helping the economy, was a rival of Friedman and the leader of a movement to introduce mathematics to economics.

But it was the third of the giants of that era, James Tobin, another Kennedy adviser, who would have the most enduring effect on Janet

Yellen's future. When she graduated from Pembroke summa cum laude, with plans to earn a doctoral degree in economics, her grades and math chops earned her many choices. Harvard accepted her, as did Chicago, Stanford University, the University of California at Berkeley, the University of Michigan, and Yale University. She chose Yale after hearing a talk by Tobin during her senior year.

Tobin came to Brown to deliver a seminar on a complicated subject: how individual choices about saving and retirement affected the wealth of the nation as a whole. The talk was for graduate students, but as a star undergraduate, Yellen was invited too. Tobin broke down the issue with such command and coherence that she decided she wanted to study with him and learn his way of thinking. She left the seminar without introducing herself, but when the acceptance letter came, she chose Yale. It would be another two years before the school admitted women as undergraduates.

Something else drew Yellen to Tobin: his abiding sense of idealism about what economics was actually meant to do. "He had a passion for social justice and a moral compass that pointed straight north," she said.[8] She saw in Tobin a belief that math was merely a tool toward something bigger: "Economics was important because it had the potential to make the lives of people better."

Ruth gave young Yellen discipline. Julius gave her heart and laughter. Tobin gave her purpose.

She arrived at Yale in 1967. From a youth built upon order, Janet Yellen entered into an age of chaos.

2

Akerlof's Youth

Exotic Furry Creatures
1940–1967

George Akerlof was born in 1940 in New Haven, Connecticut, as war made its way toward America and the nation was harnessing science to meet its gruesome potential.

His father, Gosta, was a taciturn chemist from Sweden who received an appointment at Yale University and worked on the Manhattan Project, the government's effort to build a nuclear bomb. His mother, Rosalie (née Hirschfelder), was an extroverted graduate student who met Gosta at Yale and married him. George's uncle and Rosalie's brother, Joseph Hirschfelder, was an acclaimed chemist and physicist who researched fireballs and shock waves from nuclear explosions during and after the bombing of Japan. George's grandfather and Rosalie's father, Arthur Hirschfelder, was a chemist and doctor who pioneered the use of electrocardiograms and pharmacology to treat heart disease. Arthur, who enrolled at the University of California at the age of thirteen, built a chemistry lab for his children in the family basement.[1]

George recognized at a young age that chemistry was the family business. He also learned he had little interest in the subject, nor much aptitude for it.[2]

Gosta, known to some colleagues as Gus, moved the family frequently for jobs. Failing to advance at Yale, he took the family to Dayton, Ohio, during the war to work on the Manhattan Project. From Dayton, they moved to the Mellon Institute of Industrial Research in Pittsburgh, where businesses contracted scientists to bring research to the marketplace. When Mellon terminated Gosta's contract, he was off to the Naval Powder Factory, which designed ship propellants and explosives at Indian Head, Maryland, near Washington, DC.

Along the way, Gosta developed an innovation in the use of titanium rings that aroused the interest of Princeton University, which was opening its Forrestal Campus, aimed at researching aerospace, mechanical physics, plasma physics, and other hard sciences. Princeton hired him; the family moved again; he made no progress with the rings; Princeton let him go. The family moved one more time, staying near the university but in a less stately home than Princeton provided. Gosta set up his own lab with help from colleagues and a government research grant.

By the time George was twelve, he had moved a half dozen times. Amid all of that moving, he got to thinking: "If my father lost his job, and my family stopped spending its money, then another father would lose his job, and so on. The economy would spiral downward." Thus the problem of unemployment became a lifelong obsession for young George.

For Gosta, science was a way of life, and he wanted his children to follow it. When they lived in Pittsburgh, Gosta took George and his brother, Carl, who was two years older, to his lab at the Mellon Institute on Saturday mornings. George burned his hands trying to handle hot glass. "I did not want to confess my foolishness," he said later, "but I also did not want to return."

George was a bit of a misfit who remembered himself as a somewhat sickly child. "I was dismissed from kindergarten, not for misbehavior, or for academic failure, but rather for throwing up in school," he recalled. "My brother was an exceptional student, and I think that this may have caused the school to take some pity on me, since they allowed me to return to first grade, only with a special place at lunch away from the other students."

His older brother's IQ, he learned later, was four points higher than his. Carl became an astrophysicist.

George had a vivid imagination. At five he gave his stuffed bear the name Oscar and concocted stories that he shared with his grandmother about what life was like in bear world. He also had a propensity to say out loud what he thought was true, which sometimes made others uncomfortable. Early in grade school one December, his teacher told the kids she hoped Santa would be nice to them over the holidays. George, whose father was Christian, blurted out that there was no Santa. His teacher pulled him aside after class to tell him that he might know that, and she might know that, but it was up to the parents of the other children to tell them. George meant no harm. He didn't say it again.

George loved books and history and goofing around with nerdy friends on bicycles. The Akerlof family settled in a Princeton home not far from that of Albert Einstein and Princeton's Institute for Advanced Study (IAS), made famous by Einstein and von Neumann. An academy of some of the world's great mathematicians and theoretical physicists, the institute's faculty changed not only the field of physics, but also space travel, computing, and Cold War strategy.

George didn't pick up the affection for chemistry, but he did pick up the family's value system. What mattered most was to find the truth, and to find answers to meaningful questions. "You were supposed to be questioning what is right and what is not right," George said. "You were supposed to *learn* what everybody else thinks, but you weren't necessarily supposed to *think* what everybody else thinks."

George came to realize that his father's failure to land a secure job as a chemist was because he was a step behind in mathematics; his methods were based on trial and error. His titanium rings worked once, but never again. Improving at math became another of George's obsessions.

For all of the moving and insecurity about his father's work, George's early years were also comfortable and happy. Once the family was settled in Princeton, he and his friends rode bicycles to the IAS Building, a grand brick structure with a clock tower and steeple at its top. They sat at its footsteps and played Go, a board game of strategy that was the rage among Princeton mathematicians. George was often on the lookout for Einstein, but never saw him.

Rosalie took the children to New Hampshire in the summer, where George played at Squam Lake, trailed along with his mother and grandmother while they searched markets for nice tomatoes, or tried to help Carl when he was ensconced in some building project. Gosta liked to move large rocks around on building projects, including the construction of an outdoor sitting area. Moving big rocks didn't much interest George. Instead, as a young boy, he sat and devoured the stories of Thornton Burgess, an American conservationist whose books featured lovable animals named Paddy the Beaver, Reddy Fox, Buster Bear, and Peter Cottontail.

At the Lawrenceville School George became a star student, excelling in English, history, math, Latin, and French—but not in the sciences that mattered so much to his father, nor in athletics, as he was scrawny and unexceptional. Among George's gifts—and also an occasional nuisance—was an ability to focus intensely on subjects for long stretches of time. He could play solitaire for hours on end, work school assignments over and over in his head, and page through books in single sittings.

In 1958 George followed his brother to Yale. Since he lacked aptitude in science, his parents hoped he might become a lawyer. Economics interested him, in part because of his childhood worries about the problem of unemployment. He also took an early interest in the *Yale Daily News*, the student newspaper.

The newspaper dominated his life at first. George thought the paper toed the university line too often, and wanted it to develop its own bolder voice. He also wanted to cover big events, not just mundane affairs on campus. When John F. Kennedy toured the area for the 1960 presidential campaign, George got himself onto the campaign bus.

During spring break of his freshman year, he traveled to the South with his pal Monroe Price, and they covered sit-ins and growing racial strife. From Macon, Georgia, he made his way into a Ku Klux Klan meeting and reported on twenty-five hooded men burning a cross at the Bibb-Jones county line. From Montgomery, Alabama, they reported, "The hibiscus is blooming and the sun is warmly shining here today. But the city is edgily quiet. Only two weeks ago 4,000 whites faced 1,000 negroes in what was potentially the most violent clash in the current Southern racial crisis."[3]

His journalistic endeavors weren't all so deadly serious. George also brought a puckish sense of humor to the undertaking.[4] As a gag, during an intense exam period in April 1961, his newspaper friends wrote about a one-mile race in which they claimed George beat a standout Yale basketball player, Parks Odenweller, despite conceding thirteen inches in height to the varsity athlete. The race did happen, but George lost. As their punch line, his friends used George's byline as author of the story, claiming his own false victory.

Three days later he wrote a letter to the editor of the paper, disputing the article purportedly written by him about a victory that never happened. "I would like to express doubts as to the winner of that race, as reported by your paper," he wrote sardonically. "In view of these doubts, I hereby challenge Mr. Odenweller to a rematch."

Akerlof won a university award for his coverage of racial conflict in the South. Nevertheless, he failed to advance to the upper ranks of the newspaper because he had a habit of making careless errors in his stories.

Stumbling in journalism, he decided to focus on math and economics. He slipped up there at first too. As a freshman, he was asked by an economics professor to go to the board to draw a demand curve. It was meant to slope down—as the price of a good increased, demand for it goes down. Having spent so much time at the newspaper, he was confused and behind in his studies. George went to the board and pointed the curve up. The teacher sent him back to his seat, thinking he was a dunce.

Math also presented early challenges. "I found myself failing to understand, and literally flunking, my course in modern algebra," he said. "It was only through the intervention of my family that I survived. My mother's best friend's husband was a leading mathematician at Princeton. He gave me an hour's tutoring; he diagnosed my problem and showed me where my thinking was lacking. After that I was able to make headway in the course, and later got a perfect score on the final."

The family friend was Salomon Bochner, one of the great Princeton mathematicians, who had von Neumann as the best man at his wedding. Bochner took George for a walk in a garden over the Christmas holiday during his freshman year and realized the young man had never been taught how to do simple algebraic proofs. George learned the skill, aced his final, and escaped his introduction to mathematics at Yale with a B. He also aced that freshman year economics course, despite his early stumbles in drawing supply-and-demand curves.

Math was all the rage in the study of economics. To really excel in his chosen subject, George decided he needed to know more math than anyone else. More than a decade earlier, as a Harvard doctoral student, Paul Samuelson had written a dissertation that, published as a book, became a must-read for any determined economist. *Foundations of Economic Analysis* sought to use math to formalize the economic thinking of Keynes. Without it, as Samuelson saw it, economics was just words and ideas without order or proof. The opening page of *Foundations* borrowed a quote from the late engineer Josiah Willard Gibbs: "Mathematics is a language."[5]

While George turned his attention to economics and math, he got a job as a clerk at a Yale library where the school's economics doctoral students spent much of their time. He befriended the students, and they

told him about a promising young economist named Robert Solow, who
was formalizing new studies on what made economies grow and companies invest. The work intrigued George. He thought he'd like to know
how people figure things like that out.

In 1962, having overcome his early stumbles and become an accomplished student, George Akerlof was admitted into the hottest economics program in the country, Paul Samuelson's department at MIT.
Samuelson's protégé was Solow.

Akerlof showed up at MIT's campus in a ten-year-old blue Ford se-
dan, a family clunker. At a gathering for new students in the common
room of a boxy concrete slab known to some as E52, the first person he
met was Solow.

Solow was tall and lean, with an angular face, and had just finished
a stint in Washington on President Kennedy's Council of Economic
Advisers. He had also been honored with the prestigious Clark Medal,
given to the top economists in the nation under the age of forty. The
medal came to be called the "Baby Nobel," because recipients tended to
go on to win the Nobel Prize, the highest honor in scientific research.

Solow's growth studies broke the economy down into component
parts, including workers, machines, and, most importantly, the technology and know-how that made workers and machines more productive. The economy was booming, and Solow's growth models helped
explain why, and how to keep it that way.

Meeting in the common room for the first time, Solow asked Akerlof
what he wanted to study. The new economics student told his MIT elder
that he wanted to learn topology, which was a little odd. Topology is the
study of shapes and how the properties of these shapes adapt when they
are stretched or bent or twisted; say, when a circle is stretched into an
ellipse, or a square squeezed into a rectangle. Economists didn't typically study topology, but Akerlof thought the class would help him to
look at problems differently, which would make him a better economist.

He also thought Harvard taught the subject better than MIT. So the first thing George did when he got to MIT to study economics was go to Harvard to study math.

Solow supported the new student, intrigued by the young man's interest in looking at things differently. There was something else about studying topology that attracted George. In addition to his gift for storytelling from his days as a journalist, he was a visual thinker who tended to put images to his ideas. The math of shapes was a natural draw.

"There was always something original about George," Solow said.[6]

Akerlof became so good at math that he once marched to the blackboard during one of Samuelson's microeconomics classes and stumped his elder with a proof Samuelson didn't think could be shown. George's audacity delighted his classmates.

The MIT economics department in the 1960s buzzed with some of the field's most exciting economists and young geniuses drawn to study with them. Franco Modigliani, an Italian-born American, arrived as a professor from the Carnegie Institute of Technology in Pittsburgh. Slight, gregarious, and athletic, Modigliani was breaking new ground studying corporate finance and also analyzing how people made decisions about how much money to save and how much to spend. Solow, Modigliani, and Samuelson would all go on to win Nobel Prizes.

The students often lined up outside Solow's office, seeking out the advice of their generous elder. They also formed lines in the basement, where a giant IBM mainframe computer ran programs they filled out on paper punch cards. Samuelson tended to keep to himself.

One of George's classmates was an absentminded young man from Gary, Indiana, named Joseph Stiglitz who'd been entranced by the social justice movements of the 1960s. Stiglitz rented a country house far from MIT's buildings and ended up sleeping in his office many nights. A free spirit, he liked to take off his shoes when he entered the building and tended to forget where he left them. Late at night, George and his friend Bob Hall routinely found themselves searching E52, muttering "Find Stiggy's shoes," to save their pal from being forced to venture out in the Cambridge cold in his socks. In the summer George took his MIT friends up to his family house on Squam Lake. They wandered around barefoot and unwound at the lake, a bunch of useless young hippies in the minds of many locals.[7]

Despite the genius around him, it occurred to George during his studies that something wasn't quite right with what he was learning about economics in the 1960s. He got to thinking about his favorite cartoonist in the *New Yorker*, Edward Koren, whose characters included exotic furry creatures, alive in a complex, surprising, and often ironic world. In one cartoon, a dentist with a long, furry doglike snout would admonish a hairy monster with sharp pointy teeth that he needs to spend more time flossing.

The topology of Koren's cartoons was different, Akerlof thought. Many other cartoon characters were boxy stick figures. Koren's were more dimensional and complex, and in that way more human, even though many didn't look human at all.

The economic world, as Akerlof saw it, was more like Koren's than the boxy conventions he was learning at MIT. Many of the economic theories he was taught were based on mathematics that failed to fully capture the complexity of what actually happened in the economy. To write down a model of the economy in mathematical terms, you had to make assumptions that certain relationships would always hold constant. Moreover, these models tended to rest on the idea of an economy that settled into finely calibrated states of equilibrium. Economics was more nuanced than many of these simple mathematical formulas could hold, and also more fragile, he thought.

By 1967, as Janet Yellen was preparing to enroll at Yale, entranced by the order, precision, and possibility for social progress in economics, George Akerlof decided that he was going to take it all apart.

3

Yellen at Yale and Harvard

Rowing Upstream
1968–1976

One event and one man loomed large over the education of Janet Yellen. The event was the Great Depression. The man was John Maynard Keynes.

The United States emerged from World War I in 1918 as a rising industrial superpower, while European empires crumbled. Economic booms and busts—often tied to speculation in railroads, canals, gold mining, or some other new investment flavor—ebbed and flowed in the 1800s, but prosperity kept marching forward. A middle class grew, and prosperous cities with large towers sprouted up—Chicago, Detroit, Pittsburgh, Cleveland, San Francisco—all tied together by the very railroads and canals at the center of the booms and busts that had earlier disrupted economic activity.

The nation seemed to solve a problem in 1913 when it created the Federal Reserve, a central bank modeled after the big national banks of Europe, like the Bank of England. During the 1800s, American banks were prone to financial panics. Depositors rushed to withdraw their funds all at once after some period of wild speculation, leaving the banks drained of money and forced to shutter. When banks failed, businesses were starved of funds. They laid off workers and unemployment rose. The purpose of the Fed was to lend funds to banks until the panics subsided, and thus to help tame the boom-and-bust cycles that had become so common.

Yet nothing tamed the Great Depression of the 1930s, and nothing measured up to its scale. In a bank panic in 1873 tied to railroad speculation, 101 banks failed. In an 1893 panic, 503 banks failed. In the 1907 panic that led to the creation of the Fed, 73 banks failed. During the Great Depression, around ten thousand banks failed. That was fifteen times as many failures as happened in the three preceding panics combined.[1]

The depth of the downturn was tragic and confounding, and so was the duration. Between 1929 and 1933, average annual individual income fell 46 percent, equivalent to a drop from today's average of $55,000 a year to $29,700.[2] Imagine going from the middle class to the lower fifth of the economic ladder in four years. That's what happened to the average family during the Great Depression. Household incomes rebounded, but then fell again and didn't return to 1929 levels until 1941.

Behind it all, the great American job machine stopped. From 1929, when the stock market crashed, to 1931, the unemployment rate climbed from 3.2 percent to 15.9 percent.[3] That's worse than what happened when the Covid-19 pandemic that began in 2020 temporarily shut down the US economy. In the 1930s, however, it kept getting worse: the jobless rate climbed to 25 percent by 1933 and didn't return to less than 10 percent until 1941, a dozen years of consistent double-digit unemployment. Nothing like that had happened before, or has happened since.

America's indomitable optimism took a beating. In 1926, during an economic boom, the Manhattan musical *Americana* became a hit, with upbeat songs like George Gershwin's "Sunny Disposish," which promised that "life can be delish / with a sunny disposish" and encouraged a listener not to be "a gloomy pill." When *Americana* was revived in 1932, the centerpiece was the haunting melody of "Brother, Can You Spare a Dime." The lyricist, Yip Harburg, whose own appliance business had gone bankrupt, was inspired by the entreaties of an unemployed man he met in Manhattan's Central Park during the Depression.[4]

The generation that lived through the Great Depression carried forth stories of breadlines and soup kitchens, joblessness, shantytowns, and a learned devotion to thrift, shared over dinner tables with future generations.

During the Depression, Yale was home to one of the more prominent economists of the time, Irving Fisher. He made a fortune starting an index card filing business that later became Remington Rand, then Sperry Rand, then Unisys Corp. Fisher speculated in the stock market himself, often with borrowed money.

Fisher drew important conclusions about the causes of the Depression, perhaps drawn from his own experience. Debt was at its root, he said. As profits and incomes fell, debt became harder for households and businesses to pay off. They sold assets—like their homes or cars—to make their payments, pushing down the prices of those assets even more and squeezing profits and incomes, setting off a self-feeding downward spiral he called debt deflation.[5]

Fisher's academic insights were overshadowed by bad prognostications and his own personal misfortune. Caught up in the boom of the 1920s, he declared just before the 1929 crash that stock prices had reached a "permanently high plateau." The prediction haunted him. His son estimated he lost a fortune of about $10 million, which amounted to more than $150 million in 2020 when adjusted for inflation. Yale bought his house and rented it back to him to keep him from being evicted. In other words, he got himself caught in the debt deflation he described.[6]

John Maynard Keynes, on the other hand, always seemed to win.[7]

Tall and stooped, with full lips and a bushy mustache, he wore all of the confidence—some might say arrogance—of England's Cambridge elites. In 1918, as Germans bombarded Paris, young Keynes traveled to the French capital by boat and train to secure a treasure trove of French Impressionist paintings as collateral for British loans. Better to collect priceless paintings than "dubious French bonds," he argued.[8] The thirty-five-year-old economist, an art aficionado who socialized with British painters and writers including Virginia Woolf and E. M. Forster, made out with a Cézanne piece for himself. Of the Bloomsbury group in which he socialized, the writer Dorothy Parker said, "They lived in squares, painted in circles and loved in triangles."

When the war ended, Keynes presciently blasted the 1919 Treaty of Versailles as a disaster that would spark inflation and tear the continent apart. The treaty focused on German reparations rather than unity and rebuilding. It forced Germany to relinquish land, disarm, hand over foreign financial holdings, and give up its merchant shipping fleet. Keynes resigned from the British government in disgust and wrote a book, *The Economic Consequences of the Peace*, arguing that Germany's impoverishment would lead to a dangerous demand for vengeance.[9]

To regain advantage in a competitive postwar world beset by enlarged burdens of debt, European nations erected trade barriers that slowed the wheels of global commerce. Germany's banks failed,[10] its currency tumbled, and its central bank, the Reichsbank, pumped money into the economy, sparking inflation. As Keynes predicted, the peace after World War I led directly to economic disaster and World War II.

Keynes also happened to be prone to private expressions of noxious anti-Semitism. Evidence can be found in his personal reflections upon meeting Einstein in Berlin in 1926, more than a decade after the brilliant physicist published his seminal works on the relationship of time, space, and gravity. "He is a naughty Jew boy covered with ink—that kind of Jew—the kind which has its head above water, the sweet, tender imps who have not sublimated immortality into compound interest," Keynes recorded in his personal notes of the Einstein meeting.[11]

In his time this kind of comment might be dismissed as ordinary British snark, perhaps considered impolite or snooty, or, depending on the audience, witty or clever. But reflected in a twenty-first century light, it's hard to see it as anything other than hostile toward Jewish people, especially considering what Keynes wrote next. Einstein was nice and talented, he averred, but other Jews, the bankers and politicians in what was then Prussia, were "serving devils, with small horns, pitch forks, and oily tails. It is not agreeable to see a civilisation so under the ugly thumbs of its impure Jews who have all the money and the power and the brains." The reference to ugly thumbs was especially poisonous coming from Keynes; he had a strange compulsion about hands, seeing them as a window into a person's character. He routinely sized up the digits of his counterparts, inferring from them whether a person had sensitivity, finesse, intelligence, or strength.

Hitler's atrocities seemed to mellow Keynes's apparent malice toward Jewish people later in life. During the mid-1930s he helped Jewish refugees from Germany in Cambridge. However, even that was against a backdrop of private derision. "I had some nice refujews to lunch," he wrote to his wife, the ballerina Lydia Lopokova, in 1934.

Keynes's worldview is notable in part because many of the men and women who followed him in economics—some strongly supportive of his ideas and some strongly against—were Jewish, including Yellen. It says something about their devotion to their work that most of those intellectual descendants cared more about his ideas than they did about his reflections on their religious identity or motives.

What cemented Keynes's place in history was his 1936 diagnosis of the economic malaise that gripped the Western world in the 1930s. His book *The General Theory of Employment, Interest and Money*,[12] was an immodest echo of Einstein's general theory of relativity, the 1915 framework for the workings of the entire universe. Keynes believed he had developed a unified theory of the workings of the global economy, and he was certain of his book's success at the very outset. His *General Theory*, he told his friend George Bernard Shaw, the playwright, "will largely revolutionize—not I suppose at once but in the course of the next ten years—the way the world thinks about economic problems."[13]

Keynes was correct in that too. Classic theory saw the modern capitalist economy as something like a self-correcting engine. During a boom, prices for goods and services shot up, and companies over-invested in new buildings and equipment. Then there was too much supply. Prices fell, drawing new demand for cheaper goods and creating a new equilibrium that restarted the economic engine. Interest rates worked the same way. During a bust, interest rates fell, inducing businesses and households to borrow, invest, and spend, recharging the economy. Interest rates then rose as the economy gathered momentum, acting as a brake when activity overheated.

Keynes argued that the economy could get stuck in depressed equilibriums. For example, individuals might decide it was best for them to save, but when they all did that at the same time, there was a paradox of thrift—nobody spent and the economy halted, further reducing the incentive to invest and hire. On those occasions it was the government's job to recharge economic activity, he argued. It could borrow money at low interest rates to invest and spend, restarting the engine when the private sector wouldn't. Keynes's theory served as an intellectual underpinning of Franklin Delano Roosevelt's New Deal spending programs. It also established, in Keynes's mind, a middle ground between the freewheeling capitalism that led up to the Great Depression and Karl Marx's socialist ideas, which placed the government at the center of all activity and had already taken hold of Russia.

Keynes helped shape the world economy following the end of World War II, arguing with allies in July 1944 at a Bretton Woods resort in the White Mountains of New Hampshire that the winners must not repeat the mistakes of the disastrous peace attained after World War I. They had to focus on rebuilding rather than forcing the losers to repay, and tighten the bonds of global trade through cooperation rather than tearing trading partners apart with tariffs and currency manipulation. The Bretton Woods Agreement that he helped design marked the beginning of the modern era of globalization.

Keynes's main intellectual adversaries were two exiled economists from Austria, Joseph Schumpeter and Friedrich Hayek, who saw encroaching socialism up close after World War I and didn't like it. The Austro-Hungarian Empire had been shattered by World War I, and Vienna was a postwar mess, but Schumpeter and Hayek didn't lose faith in the market economy's self-correcting properties. Hayek's 1944 *The Road to Serfdom* declared, "A policy of freedom for the individual is the only true progressive policy."[14] Keynes agreed with Hayek, but said he found a middle way.

Economic arguments over the next fifty years largely boiled down to whether markets should be left to their own devices—as Hayek and Schumpeter favored—or the government should be involved, as Keynes advocated. One group tried to build up the foundations of Keynes's thinking through mathematical analysis. The other group sought to tear Keynes's ideas down. For half a century Keynes's analysis was in vogue, out of vogue, and then back in vogue again in mainstream economics. Classical thinking, personified by Hayek's devotion to the market's self-correcting properties and Schumpeter's belief in economic rejuvenation through the "creative destruction" of the marketplace, traveled a similar topsy-turvy path, ruling the day at one time and at other times running into its own limitations.

These debates were passed to Janet Yellen through her mentor at Yale, James Tobin, who was one of Keynes's most devoted followers. Tobin was a child of the Depression, born in Champaign, Illinois, in

1918. His mother was a social worker who directed government relief programs during the 1930s. "From her first-hand accounts I learned of the human suffering of unemployment and poverty," he said.[15]

In 1935, Harvard was looking to expand its reach to the Midwest. Tobin's father suggested he take an entrance exam to see if he qualified. Without preparation, Tobin aced it and won a full scholarship. One of his advisers was Schumpeter, whose ideas didn't win over Tobin. Instead, during his sophomore year Tobin read Keynes's new book and chose his side.

"I was hooked," he said. "The miserable failures of capitalist economies in the Great Depression were root causes of worldwide social and political disasters. The depression also spelled crisis for an economic orthodoxy unable either to explain events or prescribe remedies. The crisis triggered a fertile period of scientific ferment and revolution in economic theory." Like Yellen, Tobin wanted to put his math skills to work. Also like Yellen, he wanted to do some good in the world.[16]

Tobin was earnest and deeply serious and scared many of his students. One of the few hints of emotion that he ever gave off was that his ears sometimes turned red when people annoyed him. He taught some seminars in the manner of Socrates, the ancient Greek philosopher, who probed students with questions about their reading and then steered them toward his ideas based on their answers. Thoughts came out of Tobin's head fully formed. His sense of humor was ironic, and often too subtle for others to grasp.

After Japan's Pearl Harbor invasion, Tobin enlisted and spent nearly four years on the destroyer USS *Kearny*, serving as gunnery officer and then navigator. A colleague from his naval reserve training, Herman Wouk, would later base his novel *The Caine Mutiny* on Tobin's war experiences. Wouk described Tobit, a character modeled after Tobin in the book, as having "measured quiet speech, and a mind like a sponge."[17]

After the war, Tobin landed a teaching job at Yale and became part of John F. Kennedy's brain trust in the Council of Economic Advisers. The council's 1962 *Economic Report of the President* was an embodiment of Keynesian thinking at work: the strong hand of government would bring down unemployment and stabilize the economy through tax cuts and spending programs. The unemployment rate had risen to more than 7 percent in 1961, and Keynes taught his disciples not to stand idly by, a lesson Tobin later passed on to Yellen.

"In our free enterprise economy, fluctuations in business and consumer spending will, of course, always occur," Kennedy's *Economic Report* said. "But this need not doom us to an alternation of lean years and fat. The business cycle does not have the inevitability of the calendar. The Government can time its fiscal transactions to offset and to dampen fluctuations in the private economy. Our fiscal system and budget policy already contribute to economic stability, to a much greater degree than before the war. But the time is ripe, and the need apparent, to equip the Government to act more promptly, more flexibly, and more forcefully to stabilize the economy."[18]

When Yellen arrived at Yale in September 1967, Tobin had returned to campus. Kennedy had been assassinated, but the economy was booming. Kennedy had set out a goal of 4 percent unemployment, and it was by then down to 3.8 percent and heading toward 3.5. Economists had begun to recognize that there was a tradeoff intrinsic in low unemployment: when it got very low, inflation seemed to rise, a signal that the economy's resources were becoming strained from booming demand. In 1967, though inflation was inching up, it was still below 3 percent. War was building in Vietnam, protests were coming to American campuses, but the economy still seemed to be doing pretty well.

Yellen didn't leave Brooklyn a full-blown Democrat. She became one in the 1960s.

Politics hadn't been a big topic of discussion in the Yellen household. Her dad talked a lot about patients at the dinner table, and they listened to the radio, but political identification didn't much consume them. Ruth confided to Janet's brother in a letter that she voted for Nixon over Kennedy in the 1960 election. Ruth wasn't sure whom John preferred in that election, and he wasn't sure whom his father had voted for either. As for Janet, Ruth seemed more interested in whom she was dating.

Janet Yellen came to identify with Tobin's worldview, however, translating her family's do-gooder ethos into Tobin's sense of economic purpose. She and Tobin described their interest in economics almost identically. They both had similar methodical personalities, were both drawn to math, and both saw economics as a way to put those interests to work for a greater social good.

Tobin's intense personality intimidated Yellen at first, as it did so many others. He had a way of sitting, silent and unresponsive, as a person spoke, perhaps an artifact of his quiet midwestern upbringing, or perhaps because he was thinking through his response. Whatever the reason, the silences left an awkward void in conversations that Yellen and many others tended to try to fill by rambling on. Students came up with a term for what happened to them in oral exams with the illustrious professor: "the Tobin spiral," when his simple questions sent them talking in incoherent circles.

At the same time, there was a doggedness about Tobin that stuck with Yellen and his other students. Once during the late 1960s he came to class with a broken right arm. The class involved writing long equations and graphs on the blackboard. Tobin was right-handed. "We expected that he would ask someone to take over the chalk duty," recalled one student, Robert Goldfarb. Instead, Tobin picked up the chalk and wrote lefty, with a precision that surprised his class. "We found out later that he had never written with his left hand and that this was his first try at being ambidextrous, which he mastered quite quickly. Whenever I see a reference to Harry Truman's quip about one-handed economists, I'm always reminded of this."[19]

Yellen was the only woman in her graduate school class. She took her introductory macroeconomics course with Tobin's friend and collaborator William Brainard, and didn't form a bond with Tobin until her third year. The Vietnam War was raging then. Many of her male colleagues were consumed with the fear of being drafted; some dropped out to become full-time schoolteachers, which positioned them for deferments.

Yellen was the star student of the class, and likely would have been even if the men hadn't been so preoccupied with getting shipped off to war. Tobin made her his teacher's assistant. Her task was to work with younger students, helping them to decipher his lectures.

Like her mother, Yellen was a careful notetaker. Also like her mother, she was almost compulsively intent on getting her answers right. In a first-floor classroom that opened up to an airy back porch, she listened intently to Tobin's lectures, taking notes as he roamed the room imposingly. The classroom was in a three-story home on Hillhouse Avenue in New Haven that housed the Cowles Foundation, famous at the time for morning coffees where luminary professors gathered to discuss events of the day—at that time, often the war. After class, Yellen would go home and rewrite her notes late into the night, transforming them into a formal presentation, handwritten, in careful square lettering with key points and phrases underlined. She also hand-drew charts to illustrate Tobin's points, so precisely that they looked like architectural renderings drawn with scale ruler and drafting board.

Every page had the same heading at the upper left side: "Econ 100 (Mr. Tobin)." On the upper right side she noted the date of the lecture and numbered the page. The first few sentences were always a summary of what had been learned in the previous lesson. She reproduced these reports for students on copy machines that were starting to replace the old mimeographs, gadgets with cranks that spat out copies in messy blue ink.

By the end of the semester Yellen's notes made a stack nearly two inches thick, hundreds of pages giving a detailed road map into Tobin's intimidating brain. If a classmate accidentally dropped the notes on the floor and they scattered everywhere, her page numbering system ensured that they could be quickly reassembled. Known simply as "The Yellen Notes," they would be reproduced for years after she left for succeeding PhD students at Yale. Some students bound them or tucked them away in boxes, keeping them for decades as both a reference and a keepsake. Willem Buiter, who would become chief economist for Citigroup, compared Yellen's notes to the Old and New Testament for Yale PhD students. Rick Levin, who went on to become president of Yale, said they got him through Tobin's class.[20]

Yellen's dissertation advisers were Tobin and a young professor recently minted by MIT—Joseph Stiglitz, George Akerlof's brilliant, absentminded activist friend. Stiglitz helped Yellen work out her thesis on labor markets. One of the central papers she referenced in her work was a study by Stiglitz and his old pal George.

A new women's movement was coming to life when Yellen started working on her dissertation three years into her studies. One of the movement's targets was a tradition-bound private men's club near campus called Mory's, founded in 1849, where a cappella singing groups known as the Whiffenpoofs and Spizzwinks held regular performances. Faculty members held their staff meetings at Mory's. Women weren't allowed in the front door.

One of Tobin's students, a protester named Heidi Hartmann, stood outside Mory's one day and caught Tobin going in. She asked him if he was a sexist for using the restaurant, the obvious implication being that he was. Flustered, he wrote her a long note several weeks later, explaining why he was not. The economics department eventually canceled its faculty meetings at Mory's. In 1974, after the state threatened to strip its liquor license, the club began accepting women. Yellen signed on to a petition calling for its opening to women, but she wasn't involved in the movement. Instead, she was off to Harvard, where she landed a job as an assistant professor.

These were not easy years for Yellen. She was single, and Harvard wasn't a welcoming place. Assistant professors were rarely promoted to tenured jobs at Harvard, and as at Yale and many other places, women were often treated as second-class citizens, forced to take a back stair-case to the university's faculty club. On all three floors of the august Littauer Building, which the economics department called home, there was only one women's bathroom, shared by professors and students.

Yellen's office was in another building. She sometimes joked with friends that if she died at her desk, nobody would notice for days.

The economics profession was starting to recognize that it had a problem. More women were studying the discipline, but very few were teaching it.[21] Among 440 universities surveyed by the American Economic Association in 1972, more than half had no women on faculty. Among the forty-three largest and most elite schools, eighteen had no women. When women were on faculty, they were typically in junior po-sitions. Of the seventy-three women at the major universities, fifty-one were assistant professors or lecturers, and just fourteen were tenured professors. The American Economic Association set up a committee to study the imbalances.

Claudia Goldin, a young economics professor who trained at Chi-cago, remembered being mistaken for a secretary on her first day on the job at Princeton in those days. Francine Blau, an economics professor at Cornell University who trained at Harvard, recalled a male student re-ferring to her class as "sex ed." Stanford University's Myra Strober, who trained at MIT, said she tried on clothes at department stores just for a chance to talk to other women.[22]

By the time Yellen got to Harvard she had picked up an unhealthy habit. She was a chain smoker, her tendency to prepare for everything having backfired on her badly. While studying at Yale, a classmate had invited her to a party where she was told people would be smoking marijuana. Yellen had never done such a thing before and decided she should practice smoking before the party. She bought a pack of cigarettes to try inhaling and was quickly hooked on the nicotine. The marijuana left no impression on her, but by the time she got to Harvard she was plowing through three packs of cigarettes a day. Her ashtrays filled up within hours.

There was one other woman on the faculty in the economics department when Yellen arrived. Gail Pierson was a national champion trapshooter from Louisiana and an avid swimmer. Pierson took up rowing at Harvard after she learned she couldn't use the university's main campus pool.[23] It was only for men, and they often swam naked. Instead, she took to rowing the Charles River, which snaked along Cambridge, Massachusetts, connecting Harvard and MIT, which sat just one and a half miles apart.

Pierson was always in motion and often dressed in athletic warmup clothes. In one of their first encounters she asked Yellen if she wanted to run up and down the steps in the football stadium, which sat like a Roman coliseum near the Charles River. Pierson called it "running stairs." No chance, Yellen thought, and politely declined. Their relationship never went much beyond that.

Pierson went on to compete in the 1976 Olympics; it was the first time women had been allowed to compete in the sport at that level. *Sports Illustrated* described her as "rowing's answer to Wonder Woman." Janet Yellen didn't quit smoking until a trip years later with her mother to Europe. Her father had recently passed away and Ruth demanded she toss her cigarettes before getting on the plane. Janet complied and never smoked again.

After Pierson left, another woman, Rachel McCulloch, joined the faculty. She and Yellen became friends and collaborators on research.

Few other professors showed interest in working on papers with Yellen. One source of her isolation was the fact that her office was a few blocks away from the Littauer Building. Another may have been the fact that she was a woman, though that was never stated explicitly.

Instead of connecting with other professors, Yellen formed bonds with her students. One was William Adams, who was interested in how firms used monopoly power in marketing and pricing their products. Yellen helped him think through and formalize his ideas. After he graduated and landed a job at the University of Michigan, she sometimes flew to Ann Arbor to work on research with him. She stayed with him and his wife, Barbara, a doctor and budding pediatrics professor. Janet and Barbara enjoyed cooking together when she and William weren't working out the math of their research.

Yellen and Adams produced a paper that was initially rejected by the *American Economic Review*, a leading academic journal. Its editor, George Borts, found Yellen's thinking about the ills of monopoly power too expansive. They got the paper published elsewhere, and it became one of her most often cited papers, though it was still not on the subject she really cared about, which was jobs.

Yellen's lectures had a slow, steady cadence. Her answers to student questions were always detailed, thought-out, and sometimes exhausting. She had a tendency to analyze questions from every possible angle. She differed from Tobin in one respect: where he was uniformly serious, she had a light side, one that included a disarming belly laugh that rose inside her and could stream out in tears and howls over drinks with the graduate students she was teaching.

One of her students in macroeconomics was a rising star in the field, a young man named Lawrence Summers, who had two uncles who had recently won Nobel prizes. One was Kenneth Arrow, a Harvard professor. The other was Paul Samuelson. Summers was sloppy, supremely confident, and very good at math. He had done his undergraduate studies at MIT, where he led the school's competitive debate team. He didn't stand out in Yellen's class, perhaps because he already knew the material so well and didn't see much to challenge or question in her carefully prepared presentations. The talks were clear and compelling, he remembered later. "She was an extremely nice and considerate person," he said.[24] "If you came up and asked her a question, she gave you a thoughtful answer and then she asked if she fully answered your question. She really wanted to be a helpful and devoted teacher."

Summers aced the class in what was an unremarkable start to a complex, lifelong relationship. Everyone seemed to know Summers was going places, including Yellen. It turned out that she was going places too.

Yellen became involved in another project in her later Harvard years: Tobin wanted her to help him turn her lecture notes into a textbook on economics. It would be a joint collaboration with her and two other colleagues. They had a problem, though: economic developments were outrunning Tobin's views about how the economy actually worked.

The inflation that had started creeping up during the mid-1960s was running rampant by the 1970s, and the government didn't seem to know how to stop it. By 1974 it had hit 12 percent. The idea of government intervention in the economy was falling out of fashion. Part of the problem was that the government had pumped so much money into the system in the booming 1960s, a function of war and Lyndon Johnson's Great Society programs. All of that money spurred demand for goods and services, driving the price of those goods and services higher: in a nutshell, creating inflation.

At the University of Chicago, the profession was buzzing about a new way of thinking. People were rational and tended to look forward, the thinking went, which nullified many government efforts to interfere in the business cycle. For example, if the government tried to stimulate economic growth with more spending, people wouldn't respond by spending more money. Foreseeing that their taxes would need to go up to tame rising budget deficits, they would store money away instead of spending, offsetting the government's intervention. In the same way, if people expected that inflation was going to rise, they would demand higher pay themselves, setting off a self-feeding cycle of upward inflation.

In academia, economists called this the rational expectations theory. Its chief proponent was a University of Chicago economist named Robert Lucas. The skepticism about government intervention in the economy that it promoted jibed with the times, and it became the University of Chicago's answer to Keynes. It was soon followed by another idea, the real business cycle theory, which argued that economic booms and busts were driven by changes in technology, and that government had no business intervening in these cycles. With the idea of rational expectations in vogue, Yellen and Tobin got nowhere with their book. The ideas of Keynes were going out of style.

Harvard assistant professors typically were given a few years to teach and produce research before they were considered for tenure. Harvard turned Yellen down, as it did most assistant professors. As her time there was running down, the Federal Reserve came calling.

It was 1977. The economy was a mess, and the Fed was at the center of it. A former Yale professor wanted Yellen to come work at the Fed's international division. Unattached and eager to be in a more social place, with a book that couldn't be written and no prospect of tenure at Harvard, she jumped at the chance.

4

Akerlof's Early Voyages

Lemons and the Hills of Olympus
1968–1976

The 1960s were in full bloom when George Akerlof showed up on campus at the University of California, Berkeley, to become an assistant professor.

Akerlof had gotten a taste of the protest era at MIT. Once, he and his friends Stephen Marglin and Giorgio La Malfa were returning from participating in an anti–Vietnam War protest when some local kids picked a fight with them on a Boston train. Marglin, a Brooklyn boy, and La Malfa, from Italy, fought them off. It became a local legend that a small group of geeky MIT economists took on local ruffians and escaped in a draw. Akerlof was on the train but shielded himself from the mayhem. "It wouldn't have occurred to me to get into a punching fight," the wiry pacifist said later.

Berkeley in the late 1960s was inflamed by campus protests.[1] Prior to Akerlof's arrival, students launched the Free Speech Movement, demanding the right to engage in political activities on campus. They often congregated at a park near campus they dubbed the "People's Park."

In 1966 Huey Newton and Bobby Seale formed the Black Panther Party for Self-Defense, a militant group that divided the public, describing police as "pigs" and supporting Communist government while also providing meals for the poor and pressing for more representation in government by Black people.

When Akerlof joined the faculty that year, Ronald Reagan was campaigning for governor with a promise to "clean up the mess at Berkeley." He called the campus "a haven for communist sympathizers, protesters, and sex deviants." Reagan won, and in May 1969 he ordered People's Park cleared. Confrontations grew, and protesters threw bottles, rocks, and bricks at police officers. Officers fired back with tear gas canisters and buckshot. Within a few days, Reagan ordered National Guard helicopters to fly over campus, spraying tear gas even more widely. People started calling the town the "People's Republic of Berkeley" and "Berzerkeley." Akerlof joined antiwar protesters on occasion, though it was economic research that dominated his time and attention.

The academic buildings on campus sat serenely on a hill overlooking the mayhem in the town below, like sanctuaries for the Greek gods on Mount Olympus. For all of its madness, Berkeley was also home to a growing crop of top scientists.

There was a pecking order in the placement of Berkeley's buildings, with the most revered spots sitting highest in the Berkeley Hills. At the top of it all was Lawrence Berkeley National Laboratory, the physics lab that by 1968 had produced eight Nobel Prizes. It was home to a machine called the cyclotron, which whirled charged particles around and then hurled them toward targets to smash open atomic nuclei, unlocking the mysteries of the universe.

The football stadium, with vivid views of San Francisco across the bay and men smashing into each other within, wasn't far below the Lawrence lab in the Berkeley Hills. In 1968 the team had its best record in a decade—seven wins, three losses, and a tie. A defensive juggernaut known as the "Bear Minimum," coached by a Canadian named Ray Willsey, landed four players in the National Football League. "With all that turmoil, parents wouldn't send their kids to Cal. I don't know how Willsey did it," Ken Wiedemann, a safety on that team, recalled later.[2]

The economics department had a pecking order too. The whole department was growing when Akerlof arrived, enjoying the fruits of a booming 1960s economy with an influx of bright young professors from top economics PhD programs from around the country. But the department was split in two. Mathematical theoreticians, the most brilliant and esoteric in their work, stayed with the math department in Evans Hall, midway up the Berkeley Hills. Among them was Gerard Debreu, whose treatise *Theory of Value: An Axiomatic Analysis of Economic Equilibrium* used elaborate equations to prove Adam Smith's eighteenth-century premise that an "invisible hand" in markets led to an efficient and balanced economy. It won Debreu a Nobel Prize in 1983. The rest of the economics department was stationed closer to town in Barrows Hall, which sometimes reeked of tear gas during protests and riots.

Akerlof worked out an odd arrangement for himself. He kept his math books and an office in Evans, with the esteemed mathematicians, but spent most of his time in Barrows, with everyone else. Graduate math students took up space in his Evans office, and he showed up on occasion, sheepishly introducing himself as he sought to retrieve a book from his own shelves or to join a math seminar.

Akerlof's childhood concerns about unemployment had led him to the ideas of Keynes, and a belief in Keynes's prescriptions. Under the circumstances, his attention also was drawn to the automobile market.

This was the era of the muscular Ford Mustang, the Chevy Corvette, and the curvy VW Beetle. Car manufacturing and retailing was a source of many jobs in the country and also a great deal of economic fluctuation. More than two million Americans—about 3 percent of the entire workforce—worked in auto plants, auto retailers, wholesalers, repair shops, and gasoline stations.[3] It was an era of drive-in movies and diners.

Detroit, the mecca of auto production, was one of only five cities in the nation with more than one million residents.

The auto manufacturers tended to shut down plants temporarily and lay off workers when they overproduced and stocked up too much inventory. The shutdowns, in turns, drove the economy down, and then reopenings livened it up. If he could better understand this volatility in the auto industry, Akerlof figured, he could help to solve job problems. But in looking at the industry, he discovered a more abstract problem: the economics of the industry simply didn't work the way conventional models said they should. Standard economics was premised on an idea that there was an equilibrium in markets where the supply of products was balanced against demand for those products. The key was finding the price where that equilibrium could be established, a process driven by the market. As demand rose, the price went up; as supply rose, the price went down; and vice versa.

For simplicity's sake, think of a market for oranges. If people want more oranges, they'll bid up the prices. That gives growers an incentive to produce more oranges. If they produce too many, prices will then fall. Consumers and producers found equilibriums in demand and production in a continuous and dynamic bidding process that uncovered the needs, desires, and capabilities of buyers and sellers through the simple prism of a market price. It was elegant and the essence of Adam Smith's "invisible hand" concept, laid out in his book *Wealth of Nations*.

Akerlof came to think the market for cars wasn't that simple. If the prospective buyer of a used car didn't trust the seller to disclose problems under the car's hood, the buyer wouldn't be willing to pay good money for it. A buyer might even infer that a used car had problems simply because the seller was trying to get rid of it. Because of a fear of clunkers, used cars would be constantly underpriced, and new cars constantly overproduced. The market was plagued by an asymmetry in the information possessed by buyers and sellers: sellers knew something that buyers didn't, which made buyers suspicious. Because of this information problem, and the related problem of distrust, Akerlof believed that the natural equilibrium for used cars was a collapsing market.

Shortly out of MIT, Akerlof produced a paper on his new theory. A direct shot at his colleague Debreu and the broader presumptions of economists, the paper was spare in its use of mathematics; George had learned in his Harvard topology course to boil problems down to their essentials and dispense with distracting extras. Papers that relied on too many equations, he thought, often danced around the core of a problem, masking some oversight or unrealistic assumption with a pretense of precision. His topology professor, Raoul Bott, had taught him that lesson.

With a few neat mathematical formulas Akerlof showed how the problem of asymmetric information lurked in the car market and other places, such as the market for health insurance. A prospective patient might know that she has a condition that her insurer does not see, creating a problem of distrust and a challenge for pricing insurance. This is especially a problem as people age and accumulate health problems. The market succumbs to a related problem called "adverse selection"; that is, those most in need of insurance bid up the price, driving healthy people out of the markets, which drives up the price even more and makes the market dysfunctional without intervention.

After setting out to address the practical issue of unemployment, Akerlof walked away with something far more theoretical: the single disruptive idea that sometimes a marketplace just doesn't work, proven with a boiled-down version of the advanced mathematics that had become the language of his field. With a headline writer's flair he titled his paper "The Market for 'Lemons,'" and sent it off to top academic journals. Then he did something he would do over and over again for the next decade: he picked up and left.

His buddy from MIT, Stephen Marglin, was a development economist working on a dam project in India. Akerlof wasn't a development economist himself, but he did enjoy hanging out with them. He also thought he could learn a thing or two in India, and so he took a leave from Berkeley a year after his arrival there and joined his friends in a nice Delhi neighborhood where poinsettias grew in gardens and friends stayed up late into the night.

Akerlof befriended a bright young economist named Amartya Sen at the Delhi School of Economics on the other side of town. In the evenings they gathered with Marglin and others, drank whiskey and wine, told stories, and talked about economic ideas. Sen was the erudite son of a university chemistry teacher, raised when the people of India were searching for national identity and struggling with sectarian violence. India broke from British rule in 1947 but found peace and unity elusive. When Sen was a boy, a man once came screaming through the gate of his family's home near campus, bleeding after being knifed in the back. He was a Muslim day laborer, stabbed while looking for work in a Hindu part of Dhaka. Sen's father took the man to the hospital for care, but the man died.

"Some of my own disturbing memories as I was entering my teenage years in India in the mid-1940s relate to the massive identity shift that followed divisive politics," Sen later remembered.[4] "People's identities as Indians, as Asians, or as members of the human race, seemed to give way—quite suddenly—to sectarian identification with Hindu, Muslim, or Sikh communities. The broadly Indian of January was rapidly and unquestioningly transformed into the narrowly Hindu or finely Muslim of March. The carnage that followed had much to do with unreasoned herd behavior by which people, as it were, 'discovered' their new divisive and belligerent identities, and failed to take note of the diversity that makes Indian culture so powerfully mixed. The same people were suddenly different."

Sen was brilliant, skilled in math, physics, and the study of Sanskrit. He was sent off to study at Cambridge, where the legacy of John Maynard

Keynes loomed large. While faculty there battled about the role of government and markets, Sen found himself drawn to another question, one that shadowed his youth: How are a diverse people to rule themselves?

A long line of academic research found that democratic rule was not just hard in practice, it was also hard in theory. This research traced back to a French mathematician named Nicolas de Condorcet, who wrote at around the same time that Adam Smith was formulating his Enlightenment-era ideas about an invisible hand in markets.

Condorcet came up with an abstract version of the following proposition: Say you have three children and give each child a chance to rank and vote for one of three choices for dinner—chicken, steak, or fish. If one ranks chicken above steak and then fish, another ranks steak above fish and then chicken, and the third ranks fish above chicken and then steak, then no matter which one is selected as the winner, a majority will prefer some other choice, and discord will break out.

Condorcet was a champion of the French Revolution, which broke the shackles of monarchal rule. As if to prove his own theory about self-rule true, he was arrested in the violent aftermath of the revolution and died in jail, either by suicide or murder.

The American scholar Kenneth Arrow, who was the uncle of Lawrence Summers, in 1950 extended Condorcet's analysis to show that under certain conditions it was theoretically impossible to build an effective system to aggregate individual choices into large group decisions. This had disturbing implications for democracy at a time when totalitarian single-party rule was sweeping Eastern Europe and China under the guise of communism.

Sen believed in the virtues of freedom and democratic government, having been raised under the thumb of British rule, longing for independence. However, he also saw its flaws. In his own country, poor minorities were underrepresented, and thus often left to starve and die. How do you protect a minority when majority rules?

While Akerlof formulated ideas that showed that Adam Smith's invisible hand didn't always work, Sen sought to show that the conundrums of democracy posed by Condorcet and Arrow could be resolved. In Delhi in the late 1960s, in other words, these two young men were trying to rewrite the biggest ideas of the Enlightenment for a threatening new age.

Sen and Akerlof were fast friends. Sen prodded Akerlof to join him at local cinemas, and invited him to present the early versions of his "Lemons" paper to classes at the Delhi School. All the while, Sen was working on his book, *Collective Choice and Social Welfare*.

"He was a likable, friendly guy," Sen said of his new friend, "and we shared a skepticism of standard, mainstream economics."[5] His students were spellbound by Akerlof's lectures. "He always had something intelligent to tell you, and he was very funny," Sen said.

But for Akerlof, the news from back home wasn't encouraging. He received his first rejection letter for "Lemons" while working as a visiting professor at the Indian Statistical Institute. John Gurley, editor of the *American Economic Review*, wrote tersely, "I do not believe that your paper quite meets the stiff competition of the manuscripts under consideration: I simply feel that I have somewhat better papers."[6] Rejections typically came with detailed comments from peer economists on how to improve the work, but Gurley offered no such suggestions. The next rejection came from *The Review of Economic Studies*, which also found that Akerlof's work didn't measure up.[7]

Akerlof had mishaps in Delhi. Once he decided to ride a local bus, which presented two problems. One was that the buses were packed with people and hard to board. The other was that the buses didn't come to complete stops on their routes, which also made them hard to get off. Akerlof tried to dismount from a bus that was still in motion and was thrown off it and scuffed up in the process. He decided not to ride the local buses again.

The dam project didn't go much better. Marglin wanted to help authorities better manage the release of waters from the Bhakra-Nangal dam in northern Punjab. Akerlof's job was to predict winter inflow of water into the dam, but he quickly realized that he couldn't do this reliably; the weather was too unpredictable. Instead he wrote a paper on fiscal policy in India and beefed up "Lemons" with new examples of the information problem in poor countries. How was a bank in India to distinguish creditworthy poor people from those bound to default on their loans? (The solution: just don't lend to any, or lend to them all at extraordinarily high rates.) He also started working on his next paper— another shot at the idea of efficient markets that used India's caste system to show how culture and social customs blew up optimal economic outcomes for large groups of people.

A third journal—the *Journal of Political Economy*, the centerpiece publication of Friedman's University of Chicago—rejected George's "Lemons" paper. Its editors took his argument seriously, at least; they went to lengths to demonstrate how he was wrong, pointing to other markets, like the market for eggs, that worked perfectly well despite the problem of quality differences that also occurred in cars. If George's paper was correct, the journal's editors argued, then no goods could be traded, and economics itself was all wrong.

George's fallback plan, if US journals kept rejecting the paper, was to take up Sen's offer to publish it in the *Indian Economic Review*. But finally, after three years, it was accepted by the *Quarterly Journal of Economics*. The paper finally appeared in the journal's August 1970 issue, the same year Sen published his book on social choice. (Twenty-eight years later Sen would win a Nobel Prize for turning the attention of the economics profession to problems experienced by underrepresented minorities in democratic societies, such as famine and discrimination.)

By 1970 Akerlof was back at Berkeley, recovering from ailments he'd picked up during his travels in India. He had a sensitive digestive system and hired a private cook in India to prepare him simple meals, but came down with something anyway. His digestive ailment led to colitis, and the medication he took to cure the colitis induced depression.

Once he had recovered, he didn't stay very long in Berkeley. In 1973 George Akerlof, the antiwar activist, next decided to go work in Richard Nixon's Council of Economic Advisers. His friends were shocked, but Akerlof saw his peripatetic habits, odd and out of place as they might look to others, as useful excursions and learning experiences. A person could learn simply by wandering, forming mental maps of the world during the process of exploration.

One evening in Washington he went to visit his friend Judy Graves, a former Berkeley student who was having a few friends over. When George arrived with a bottle of wine in each hand for his host, Kay Leong, one of those friends, was immediately smitten. The gesture seemed so thoughtful and generous to the young architect, who had just returned from traveling in Latin America. The two started dating, and Kay discovered that the young gentleman also seemed to burst with original stories and thoughts from his travels in India or his explorations in economics. A walk or a bike ride with George Akerlof was never dull.

In Washington Akerlof put his forecasting skills to the test and found himself somewhat wanting. The Organization of Petroleum Exporting Countries (OPEC) had imposed an embargo on US oil supplies, sending energy markets into a frenzy. Akerlof produced a paper predicting shortages in home heating oil and prescribed a rationing system in response. Heating oil ended up in surplus, gasoline for auto fuel in shortage, and his idea went nowhere.

The Council of Economic Advisers job didn't last long, nor did it alter his Keynesian economic perspective, but it did change Akerlof's life in one important respect. After a few months of dating, he proposed to Leong. In 1974 they agreed to go back to Berkeley, her hometown, together.

George's "Lemons" paper was by then causing a stir among academics, who came to see it as a breakthrough in thinking about the workings of markets and the problem of asymmetric information. It was a technical problem with a broader point that would over time usher in a new perspective on economics. Markets were more complex than many mathematical models in modern economics allowed. Lurking beneath the models were the complexities of the human animal itself, bent toward unpredictable behavior by emotions and tendencies—suspicion, deceit, greed, myopia—that didn't fit neatly with the math. Previous models had made the simple assumption that people did what was in their best interest, but self-interest turned out to be a complex world unto itself, like the odd cartoons of Edward Koren.

Years later Akerlof would say that the early rejections didn't bother him much; he just kept trying. Thirteen pages in length, a challenge to his peers, repeatedly rejected by many of them, "Lemons" would go on to become one of the most cited economics papers of all time, and helped open the door for a new branch of research called behavioral economics.

Akerlof's new paper on the economics of the Indian caste system was on course to be published in 1976, along with other work that he would eventually gather into his first book, *An Economic Theorist's Book of Tales*, published in 1984.[8] He was becoming a student of "animal spirits," a phrase used by Keynes to describe how emotion affected economic activity. "These essays represent an alternative approach to the advance of economic theory," he wrote in his *Book of Tales*. "That alternative approach is to explore the consequences of new behavioral assumptions." All economic problems, he came to think, were ultimately grounded in the idiosyncrasies of human behavior. Economists ignored those idiosyncrasies at their peril.

His days at the *Yale Daily News* had imprinted Akerlof with a flair for fun headlines, offbeat analogies, and counterintuitive ideas. One research paper likened human behavior to that of beetles; the tendency of these little creatures to eat the eggs of other beetle species was like in-group favoritism and out-group antagonism among humans, he argued.[9] Another paper, titled "Irving Fisher on His Head," used the Yale academic as a way to examine the role of money in the economy. Another tried to make economic sense of the counterproductive human tendency to procrastinate.

Akerlof's path didn't go in straight lines. Some of his projects ran into dead ends, including a book he tried to write about the interplay between jobs and inflation. He ran into the same problem Yellen encountered at Harvard around the same time. He didn't incorporate the rational expectations theories being popularized at the University of Chicago at the time and thus his work looked outdated. He put the book aside and it was never published.

Berkeley had granted Akerlof tenure thanks to his "Lemons" paper, but his advancement there stalled. Department elders concluded that he hadn't produced enough to warrant promotion to full professor, which would have meant more pay and status. Easygoing George was upset by Berkeley's decision not to promote him from associate professor, and became consumed in trying to right the wrong.

Leong noted that for all of his interest in caste and the sociology of life in India, George had been raised in a kind of caste system himself. His mother, who moved to the San Francisco Bay area after Gosta died, traveled in a world of elite academics and pedigreed scientists. When his family settled, it was in Princeton, near Einstein. When he struggled with elementary math as an undergraduate, his mother had him tutored by one of von Neumann's best friends, Salomon Bochner. Some mothers wished for their children to become presidents or captains of industry. In the Akerlof family, a Nobel Prize was the highest honor.

Kay Leong was coming toward a conclusion that she and George weren't right for each other. She fell for another professor—an architect like herself—and split up with her new husband. Akerlof decided to leave again, this time accepting a teaching job at the London School of Economics. Amartya Sen had put in a good word for him. However, first he would spend a year back in Washington, this time at the Federal Reserve.

It was 1977. Janet Yellen was on her way there, too.

5

Yellen and Akerlof Meet

In the Grips of a Long Inflation and a Fast Romance
1977–1978

When Janet Yellen and George Akerlof arrived at the Fed in the fall of 1977, the place was a mess, and its leader, Arthur Burns, was on his way out the door.

The Fed's original mission when it was created in 1913 was to prevent financial panics by providing funds to banks during emergencies. It played a second critical role in the economy, though: it also managed how much money circulated in the financial system, a role that affected interest rates, inflation, and the cycles of expansions and recessions that drove unemployment up and down.

To understand why the Fed mattered so much in the 1970s, it helps to take a moment to explore how money works in the economy.

If you pick up a US dollar bill of any denomination, you will notice that on its face side it bears the words "Federal Reserve Note" near the top. The Fed is responsible for deciding how much money flows through the financial system, including paper notes as well as electronic accounts credited to banks.

While managing the supply of money, the Fed also affects the cost of that money. The cost of money is the interest rate. If a household wants to borrow money to buy a home, it has to pay interest, which is the extra money it owes as it pays off the loan. If a business wants to borrow money to put up a factory, it has to pay interest like the household, extra money in the future to get its hands on cash today. The interest rate, expressed as a percentage, tells you how much extra a household or business has to pay back for every dollar it borrows.

The interest rate—like the price of anything—is in part a function of the demand for money, meaning how much people want to spend and invest right away. It is also a function of the supply of it. When demand for money sinks, because people don't want to spend or invest, interest rates fall; when demand is stronger, they rise. On the other side of this equation is the Fed, with its hand on the lever that drives the supply of money. Other factors, such as how much money banks want to lend, shape that supply—but still, it all starts with the Fed, which means it has an enormous role in determining interest rates. And interest rates, in turn, impact how much people and businesses want to borrow, spend, and invest, making the Fed perhaps the most powerful single institution in the economic system. Every dollar borrowed, not only in the United States but also around the globe, has the Fed's fingerprints on it somehow. Credit cards. Car loans. Mortgages. Business loans. Student loans.

Why do stock investors obsess about the Fed every day? This is why.

Inflation is also affected by the supply of money. Imagine a make-believe economy where people do nothing but produce and consume oranges. Each person, on average, makes one dollar a day and purchases one orange a day. On a typical day, the orange will cost around one dollar. If orange production and consumption hold steady at one per day, but you put extra dollars in every person's bank account, the only thing that will change is that people will bid up the price of oranges with those extra dollars. In other words, as the supply of dollars increases, the price of goods and services rises and the purchasing power of the dollar drops. That's an example of inflation.

The problem in the 1970s was that inflation was running rampant. The problem for Arthur Burns in particular was that he ran the money machine that helped to make it happen.

Inflation didn't occur overnight. During the late 1960s and 1970s it gathered force, building through a cascade of policy missteps and misfortunes until it became so embedded in the psychology of nearly every American that few thought it would ever end.

While Akerlof was participating in antiwar protests, another kind of protest was happening on American streets: protests against inflation.[1] The foot soldiers of these protests were often middle-class women with children. In 1966 one group of women picketed in Denver to protest rising grocery prices. The protest swept through other cities in what the popular press dubbed a "housewife revolt," prompting *Time* magazine to report that supermarket boycotts were spreading "like butter on a sizzling griddle."[2] Fed up with the increasing cost of living, women marched outside supermarkets with placards demanding lower prices, sometimes printed in lipstick. Marches and boycotts over the prices of coffee, meat, and other everyday products cropped up time and again over the next decade.

Presidents Lyndon Johnson and Richard Nixon fell into a pattern of badgering the Fed to keep pumping money into the economy to keep interest rates low. Johnson and Nixon thought low interest rates would boost growth and drive unemployment down, which they hoped would help their economic programs and their electoral prospects. The Fed often complied, which instead helped to drive prices higher and made the White House less popular.

A display of this unhealthy loop showed up just before the 1972 election. In 1971 the annual inflation rate was over 4 percent. Though it showed signs of slowing, the supply of money in household bank accounts and bank lending was still growing rapidly, which suggested that the Fed still wasn't doing enough to stop inflation from building.

The Fed raised interest rates early in the year to tamp down inflation, but then abruptly reversed course and started cutting rates late in the summer, meaning more money flowing through the financial system. Why the move? Political pressure appeared to be at play.

Reelection was on President Nixon's mind, and he was close to Burns, whom he had appointed to the office. Nixon made his expectations for economic growth clear. "I would never bring this beyond this room: My view is that I would rather have it move a little bit slower now, so that it can go up and get a real big verve later," the president told Burns in one taped conversation in March 1971.[3] After the meeting, Burns wrote in his diary that his friendship with Nixon was one of the three most important in his life, and he wanted to keep it that way.[4]

Before Burns cut rates later that year, Nixon's lieutenants sought to squeeze him, threatening the Fed chairman by planting stories in newspapers that the president was considering stacking the central bank with White House supporters, as well as falsely accusing Burns of seeking a pay raise while the rest of the country suffered.

"We got his attention," Nixon told his advisers after the smear. "Don't let up on him."[5] Then they tried to win him over with gifts, like sunglasses and a jacket from Camp David.

Much else went wrong for the economy in the 1970s. Arab nations, protesting American policy toward Israel, cut off supplies of oil, sending the cost of gasoline soaring. Associated with soaring oil prices was an upheaval in currency markets. After World War II the value of a dollar relative to other global currencies was fixed to the price of gold, an artifact of Keynes's negotiations in Bretton Woods. This fixture of the post–World War II economy meant that other central banks could come to the Fed and exchange their holdings of dollars for gold bars at a fixed price. But US gold reserves were dwindling as countries like Germany and Japan rebuilt their economies and cashed in their newfound dollars for gold. Fearing that the United States would run out of gold, Nixon severed the link in August 1971,[6] sending the dollar's exchange rate tumbling. The falling dollar sent the cost of imported goods soaring. Inflation increased.

President Nixon tried to manage the problem by fiat. When meat prices soared in 1973, some likened the ensuing consumer boycott to the Boston Tea Party. In response the administration imposed price caps on meat. "Meat prices must not go higher,"[7] Nixon said in a televised address to the nation. "With the help of the housewife and the farmer, they can and should go down." But the price caps didn't work. Over the course of the decade, meat prices more than doubled.[8]

The Keynesians were in retreat. The government was proving inept and some of their theories flimsy. For many years they had believed that there was a tradeoff between inflation and unemployment. If they ran the economy a little hot, they thought, there would be some inflation, but the reward would be lower unemployment.

That idea was in part tied to a New Zealand–born economist named A. William Phillips, who saw an inverse relationship between wage inflation and unemployment in UK data during the late 1800s and early 1900s. But the relationship proved unreliable. In the 1960s, the US unemployment rate averaged 4.8 percent, and its inflation rate averaged 2.3 percent. In the 1970s the unemployment rate averaged 6.2 percent, and inflation 7.1 percent—worse on both counts.

. . .

Janet and George met briefly at the going-away party of a colleague in the fall of 1977, while the Fed was in this state of upheaval. The event was on the eighth floor of the Watergate complex, where the Fed had a satellite office, a few blocks from its main building and two floors up from the Democratic National Committee headquarters that Nixon's operatives fatefully raided before his 1972 reelection.

Fed economists at the Watergate had a pet theory about the break-in. A back door in the Watergate complex led to a bakeshop at its base. Some Fed researchers had rigged the door to remain unlocked so they could get to the bakeshop quickly, without taking the longer route through the main entrance. Some jokingly theorized their unlocked door was the point of entry for Nixon's burglars.

George was preoccupied the evening he met Janet—but not with Watergate history, or his research, or the inflation problem consuming the nation, or even with Janet. He was spellbound by a cake set out for the affair, with delicious vanilla frosting that he was enjoying licking off his fingers. He and Janet didn't talk much, and quickly went their separate ways.

A few days later, however, they found themselves sitting together at a side table during a lecture by a visiting researcher in the cafeteria of one of the Fed's two main buildings, the Martin Building. It was a large room, with floor-to-ceiling windows that looked out on the Lincoln Memorial and the vast expanse of walkways around it. The cafeteria food was ordinary, but it served as a hub of activity in the central bank's daily affairs.

This time Janet, petite with a bob of dark hair and a broad, friendly smile, had George's complete attention. They realized they had friends in common. One of Janet's thesis advisers, Joe Stiglitz, was George's friend from his days at MIT. She knew George's name as Stiglitz's coauthor on one of the papers she'd referenced in her thesis. She also knew his "Lemons" paper. The two quickly discovered that they had a common devotion to Keynes's ideas, and were both driven by lifelong preoccupations with the problem of unemployment. They agreed to go on a date.

Janet was a student of chef and pop culture personality Julia Child; she owned Child's bestselling book *Mastering the Art of French Cooking* and watched her television show *The French Chef*. She invited George over and spent hours preparing an elaborate chicken dish with a rich cherry sauce for him, but they got their signals crossed. George, who thought Janet had forgotten about the date, called her at the last minute and invited her to his place. Janet didn't want to make a fuss about the miscommunication, so she put her fancy meal in the refrigerator and went. She was greeted at George's unkempt town house by a bland and messy boiled rice dish and a rescue dog George had taken in. Half pit bull terrier and half Dalmatian, the dog had torn up papers everywhere. George had named his mischievous pup "Sweetie."

It was October, and Janet and George were quickly smitten. A second date ensued the following day at Janet's neat and orderly place. George marveled that she had whipped up such a nice chicken and cherry dish for him so quickly, and with seemingly so little effort.

George had already suffered through one hasty marriage that ended in failure, but he had no hesitation when he met Janet. He felt he had found his match in her, a woman whose worldview and temperament meshed perfectly with his. In George, Janet felt she had found a good soul with a value system just like hers and an uncommonly inventive and unconventional mind that she found attractive. Besides, he made her laugh.

"I learned as a child that you're supposed to do what's right," Akerlof remembered. "Maybe that's what she liked about me."

In many ways Janet and George were opposites. Janet was disciplined, grounded, sensible, orderly; George was creative, contrarian, and unorthodox. His mind went fast and in different directions; she thought through problems slowly and linearly. To each, this was all a natural fit.

They had only known each other a few weeks when George told Janet he had a theory about decision-making and marriage. When a person isn't sure about a decision, he said, that person will analyze the choice carefully, at length and from different angles, taking the time needed to understand the issues and the tradeoffs possibly involved. But when a person is really sure of something, time isn't needed to make a decision. A decision can come fast.

Janet saw his point. Then she did the most impetuous thing Janet Yellen had ever done in her life: she agreed to marry the man.

She was thirty-one years old. He was thirty-seven.

Janet had planned a trip to Norway in November, to deliver talks on the economy with James Tobin. She arranged to stop in London along the way to seek a job the following year, when George would be teaching at the London School of Economics. Then they started planning a wedding.

The new couple shared laughs in the months that followed, sometimes involving the dog. George liked to bring Sweetie to his office at the Fed. One time the mutt urinated on a brand-new blue carpet near the elevator as George and Janet waited to board. The doors opened to a crowded elevator as Sweetie relieved herself, to the shock and dismay of its occupants. When the Fed's new chairman, G. William Miller, who valued order in the office, arrived to visit staff at the Watergate, George locked Sweetie inside his messy office, hoping his new boss wouldn't notice.

It also was a stressful time for Janet, though. Her father, Julius, had passed away, and Ruth had suffered a stroke and heart attack. Janet and her brother, John, arranged for her mother to sell their childhood home in Brooklyn, box everything up, and move to a nursing home in Maryland.

Janet and George married that July at the Cosmos Club, a fancy men's club for Washington elites. Fifty friends and relatives were there, including their friend Stiglitz. The club didn't allow women to enter through the front door during normal business hours; nor were they allowed to enter a wing where single men had housing. Neither Janet nor George was happy about that, but they proceeded anyway, making an informal and hesitant entry into Washington society.

The following fall, they moved to London. Amartya Sen, who was also teaching at the London School, was already there. Sen admired George Akerlof's new wife. "She was very likable, very intelligent," he said. "Pleasant sounds too weak. She was enchanting company."

Janet and George rented a home in the city's Clapham neighborhood south of the Thames River, a short walk to the London School. The place had a piano in the living room, a throwback for Janet, who had practiced as a child. She dug up the sheet music for Mozart's Sonata in C Major, a light, fast-moving piece for piano that Mozart said he wrote for beginners. "I'll bet you can play this," she told George. He took it as a challenge and started practicing the piece. When he messed up, the newlywed politely asked his new wife if she minded if he started again. She politely said she didn't mind at all.

George practiced for hours on end, and then for days. Then days spilled into weeks. By December, before they headed home for the holidays to visit family, he was still trying to learn the piece. Janet threw her hands in the air. "I can't take it anymore," she shrieked, exasperated by her new husband's obsessive new habit.

In fact, she could.

. . .

Many years later Janet, George, and their son, Robby, watched a Japanese movie called *Big Joys, Small Sorrows*, by director Keisuke Kinoshita. Set during the 1970s and 1980s, as Japan's economy reemerged from the ravages of war, the movie traced the often lonely life of a family of Japanese lighthouse keepers as they shifted from place to place along the island-nation's rugged coast. Husband and wife come to realize in the movie that their union is bound together by the duty they feel to a cause bigger than themselves, that of protecting ships along the nation's coastline. The joys and sorrows they experience in life, and the relationships they develop with family and friends, grow out of the path they have chosen together to serve as lighthouse keepers.

Watching the movie, George and Janet came to think of the movie as a metaphor for the marriage they started together in the late 1970s. Their purpose, as they saw it, was a larger journey as stewards for the economy. Their own joys and sorrows, their own family and friends, all grew out of that. They saw themselves as lighthouse keepers.

Back in those early days, Janet and George developed a pet name for each other. They started calling each other Sweetie. George sometimes shortened that to 'Weetie, just for kicks.

Part II

Battlegrounds

6

Redefining Keynes

Inside the Ideological Battles
That Shaped Yellen's Generation
1940s–1980s

When Yellen was still studying at Yale, Milton Friedman once came to campus to give a talk to a packed room on money and the economy. At the end, James Tobin rose and challenged Friedman's logic. Yellen was at her mentor's side in the audience.

What transpired filled Yellen with a feeling she hadn't experienced much in life before: a sense of righteous anger. She disagreed with Friedman's view that government spending couldn't help an economy in recession. That was normal; economists often disagreed. What really outraged her was Friedman's responses to Tobin's challenge, which she found to be glib and evasive. Friedman seemed to want to score points for style with the audience without engaging with Tobin in a deeper debate about the facts and logic of his thinking. Every time Tobin seemed to corner him on some point, Friedman moved the discussion somewhere else.

"Friedman gave a spell-binding talk on monetarism," Yellen said after Tobin's death in 2002. "The audience, which was hushed, waited for the lecture to end. After a brief pause, as we all hoped and expected, Jim responded to the bait. It was a duel, which seemed to last a lifetime between these two giants. Jim gave not a single inch to Friedman, and as

Jim attacked, argument after argument, Friedman's ground kept shifting. But Jim's argument remained steadfastly the same."[1] Yellen saw in Tobin something she called "moral passion," which became a part of her own temperament. It was what she drew on, she said, to keep her own bearings during the turns she would take in Washington in years to come.

The Friedman visit placed Yellen right in the middle of a debate about the role of government in the economy. Friedman defined that debate, and Yellen and Akerlof became central players in a counterattack against the Chicago view that Friedman represented.

Milton Friedman, just around five feet tall, with a round face and round glasses, was raised twenty miles from New York City in Rahway, New Jersey, the youngest of four children. His parents, Sarah and Jeno, immigrated to America in their teens and scraped to get by, living above a small dry goods store. Their son had a spirited immigrant ethos. "The family income was small and highly uncertain; financial crisis was a constant companion," Milton reflected.[2]

Friedman's father died when he was a teenager, and he financed his college education with scholarships and odd jobs like waiting tables. He thought he would work toward a stable life as an insurance actuary, but at Rutgers College he met a young Arthur Burns, then an assistant professor, who convinced him to pursue economics. Burns and economist Homer Jones then helped send him off to Chicago to study. Friedman said his choice of economics over an actuarial life was driven in part by the experience of the Great Depression, which seemed to him more relevant to the burning issues of the day than insurance. In other words, he was drawn to the field by the same event that attracted Tobin, and for the same purpose, but he would come away with far different conclusions.

Following his studies, Friedman landed a job in Washington and then a teaching position at the University of Wisconsin, which he later called "the most traumatic event"[3] of his early professional life. As Friedman saw it, Wisconsin department feuds over whether he deserved tenure were laced with antipathy toward Jewish people. Negative stories about him appeared in local newspapers and he was denied a secure position on staff. Friedman left after a year and landed a job in the Treasury Department, where he worked on wartime tax policy.

It was there that Milton Friedman—future apostle of small government and the countermovement against Keynes—came up with a plan to help fund the war effort. The government would withhold taxes from household paychecks. Federal tax withholding became the spring through which trillions of dollars in future tax raising would flow, to Friedman's later chagrin. He also put his statistical skills to work in the war effort, analyzing the effectiveness of antiaircraft equipment and the use of metal alloys in aircraft turbines.

Friedman's turn toward free markets came later, after the war and upon his return to Chicago. In 1946 he wrote a paper with his friend George Stigler, arguing against government-imposed urban rent controls.[4] Capping the price of rent, he believed, impeded the actual solution to the problem of high rental costs—the construction of more housing. To Friedman it was an obvious example of the perverse consequences of the government's seemingly altruistic interference in a market.

In the spring of 1947 Friedman traveled outside the United States for the first time in his life, to a gathering organized by Friedrich Hayek. The University of Chicago had published Hayek's popular book *The Road to Serfdom*, and he was organizing a ten-day conference in Mont Pelerin, Switzerland, a resort overlooking Lake Geneva. Aiming to advance the cause of individual freedom as Soviet power rose and socialist ideas expanded into Europe, Hayek gathered thirty-eight historians and scholars to debate and discuss the endeavor. Friedman was among a small group of Chicago economists invited. Another economist in attendance, Walter Eucken of Germany, hadn't seen an orange in more than half a decade of postwar Europe.

The discussions were intense and members of the group often

disagreed, evidence that economic liberty wasn't easily defined, even among those who believed most in free markets.[5] At one point, during a debate about the government's role in addressing income inequality, Ludwig von Mises, an Austrian economist who had perhaps the strongest laissez-faire views in the group, stormed out of the room, declaring that all the rest were themselves a bunch of socialists. Friedman, for his part, saw inequality as a problem. He wanted elevated taxes for the wealthy and a negative tax for the poorest, meaning government payments to those with the lowest incomes.

After days of disagreement, the group finally concurred on a mission statement. "The central values of civilization are in danger," they concluded.[6] "Over large stretches of the Earth's surface the essential conditions of human dignity and freedom have already disappeared. In others they are under constant menace from the development of current tendencies of policy. The position of the individual and the voluntary group are progressively undermined by extensions of arbitrary power. Even that most precious possession of Western Man, freedom of thought and expression, is threatened by the spread of creeds which, claiming the privilege of tolerance when in the position of a minority, seek only to establish a position of power in which they can suppress and obliterate all views but their own."

They called themselves the Mont Pelerin Society, and Friedman became the group's most successful champion.

Two women played central roles in Friedman's development. One was Anna Schwartz, a bookish economic historian from New York, introduced to Friedman by his Rutgers mentor, Arthur Burns. Schwartz was a maverick in a field dominated by men. A mother of four who earned her master's degree from Columbia University by her nineteenth birthday, and much later received her PhD there, she joined the National Bureau of Economic Research in 1941 and kept writing professionally into her nineties. Schwartz had an encyclopedic knowledge of financial statistics. For many years she and Friedman communicated mostly by mail. In 1963 they produced an exhaustive history of money in the United States, tracking over nearly a century how the circulation of dollar bills and bank deposits rose and fell, and how the economy's fortunes rose and fell with these ebbs and flows of money.

One might think of the economy and finance as two separate systems, intertwined. The economy is the actual goods and services that workers and companies produce and exchange—the cars and oranges produced and consumed, the restaurant meals and doctor visits purchased and served. Money is a parallel system that lets the engines of commerce run efficiently, an accounting system that keeps track of who gets what, an essential alternative to medieval barter. The economist Narayana Kocherlakota once described money as an elaborate form of memory.

Friedman and Schwartz drew a conclusion that rocked the economics profession. The Great Depression was mostly the fault of the Fed, they said, which had botched the management of the money supply and thus the financial part of this interconnected system. The central bank had been too restrained in how much money it allowed to circulate in the 1930s, starving banks and businesses of funds needed to keep the wheels of commerce running, and leading to bank and business failures and relentless unemployment.

The book Friedman and Schwartz wrote together, *A Monetary History of the United States, 1867–1960*, was an absorbing statistical analysis, but also a very human drama. They traced the economic calamity that was the Great Depression to the untimely death of a single man, Benjamin Strong. He was the leader of the powerful Federal Reserve Bank of New York and a veteran of the 1907 crisis that led to the Fed's creation in 1913. Strong had suffered from tuberculosis, and in 1928, at fifty-five, a year before the infamous stock market crash of 1929, he died of complications from the disease. His death left the central bank rudderless during the 1930s as the Fed cascaded from one bad decision to another.[7]

"Strong, more than any other individual, had the confidence and backing of other financial leaders inside and outside the system, the personal force to make his own views prevail, and also the courage to act upon them," Friedman and Schwartz concluded.[8] (Ben Bernanke inadvertently echoed those words decades later, after a new depression threatened, titling his memoir *The Courage to Act*.) The subversive theme lurking in their book was that Keynes's prescriptions of activist government were largely unnecessary; much of what was needed was a competent central bank.

The other woman at the center of Friedman's work was his wife, Rose. Like Schwartz, Rose Director pursued an education beyond college, and also like Schwartz, Friedman found in her a strong and equal intellect. Milton and Rose met while sitting next to each other in class in Chicago because their names—Friedman and Director—put their assigned seats next to each other.

Unlike Schwartz, Director chose not to complete her PhD or pursue scholarly work after starting a family with Friedman, but the Friedmans said later that Rose was involved in all of Milton's work in economics.[9] "Milton never did a piece of work without my reading it and criticizing it," Rose said in a 1996 interview.[10] She cowrote Friedman's popular bestseller *Free to Choose* with him. His other bestseller, *Capitalism and Freedom*, published a year before his work with Schwartz on the Great Depression, was assembled in part by Rose.

Before Janet and George, Milton and Rose were the power couple of economics, though their ideas about how to improve the human condition were starkly different from those of the couple that emerged after them, and so were their styles. The Friedmans were boisterous. Yellen and Akerlof were unassuming.

The University of Chicago took on Friedman's combative persona. At workshops on central banks or business regulation, young researchers and visiting scholars gathered with professors around large oak tables to hash out their theories, hoping to refine the research papers they were trying to publish. The meetings became fierce and often intimidating intellectual battlegrounds. At Friedman's banking workshops, presenters were given little time to present or explain their findings. The papers were expected to be read thoroughly beforehand. Instead, the aim of the workshops was criticism. Friedman proceeded page by page to tear apart the work of presenters, poking holes in their methods, logic, conclusions, and even grammar.

Elite visitors sometimes got the toughest treatment. Fischer Black, a mathematician whose theories about asset prices and stock options sparked waves of Wall Street innovation, visited in the early 1970s to challenge Friedman's ideas about money and inflation. Friedman introduced Black by saying, "We all know that the paper is wrong. We have two hours to work out why it is wrong."[11]

Friedman's colleague George Stigler was even tougher. Legend had it that one visitor from Cornell excused himself from a session to cry in the hallway; another was asked to leave at a lunch in the university's Quadrangle Club before his presentation even started. Stigler had found an error in his paper and deemed it pointless to proceed.

"They weren't polite," Deirdre McCloskey, an economic historian at Chicago in the 1970s, said years later in a moment of pointed understatement.[12] It was survival of the fittest at Chicago. The department took in dozens of graduate students every year. Most were expected to fail or quit.

In the Chicago view of the world, individual liberty was both a virtue in its own right and the central mechanism for economic good. Chicago scholars saw individuals making personal choices in markets everywhere: stocks, cars, oranges, cigarettes, even spouses. This led to the most efficient outcomes for society, they believed; government's best role was to stay out of the way. Individuals were largely rational in their choices, the thinking went, and markets were largely efficient in how they turned those choices into the goods and services demanded by society. Socialism was no answer, nor was Keynes a middle ground to it.

By the 1970s Friedman had become a household name. He appeared on the cover of *Time* magazine in 1969 and won a Nobel Prize in 1976. A succession of Chicago colleagues received the award, too. Robert Lucas, with his work on the implications of the rational expectations theory, was one of Friedman's most influential allies. Another was Eugene Fama, who extended the idea of the rational actor to financial markets, seeing in stock prices and other financial instruments an efficient distillation of all of the information available to an ocean of individual investors. You can't beat the market, Fama said. Indexed mutual funds grew out of his ideas.

As inflation soared during the 1970s, Chicago theories about the futility of government interference in the economy seemed to prove all too true. Even before Ronald Reagan and Margaret Thatcher turned to Friedman's ideas as the centerpiece of their small-government economic agendas of the 1980s, Gerald Ford in the 1970s moved to deregulate railroads, and Jimmy Carter deregulated airlines and trucking. After the failures of Burns and Miller at the Fed, Carter named Paul Volcker Fed chief to tame inflation and runaway money supply, tacitly concluding that Washington's price control systems had failed badly. Friedman's call for an end to the military draft and the creation of an all-volunteer army became the law of the land. His call for personal choice in schooling led to voucher programs and charter schools. Economic disciples took his ideas to Chile and elsewhere in Latin America. Even China's Communist Party leaders, recovering from decades of devastating state-run economic mismanagement by Mao Zedong, invited Friedman to tour the country in 1980 and give lectures on money and markets.

"The great achievements of civilization have not come from government bureaus," Friedman told Phil Donahue, a daytime television talk show host, in 1979. "Einstein didn't construct his theory under order from a bureaucrat. Henry Ford didn't revolutionize the automobile industry that way. In the only cases in which the masses have escaped from the kind of grinding poverty you're talking about, the only cases in recorded history are where they have had capitalism and largely free trade. If you want to know where the masses are worse off, it's exactly in the kinds of societies that depart from that."

Yet behind the scenes, as Friedman's prominence reached its apex, the world of economic thought was subtly changing under everyone's feet.

Tobin debated Friedman for decades, believing that Friedman's views about money and central banks were oversimplified, as were his views on government spending and unemployment. "In a Vermont ski line," the Yale professor reflected in 1986, "a young attendant checking season passes read mine and said in a French-Canadian accent, 'Tobeen, James Tobeen, not ze economiste! Not ze enemy of Professeur Friedman!' He was an economics student in Quebec; it made his day. He let me pass to the lift."[13]

Akerlof's alma mater, MIT, was another center of the countermovement against Friedman. In the 1960s and 1970s MIT attracted many of the brightest young researchers entering the field. The leader there was Paul Samuelson, and his partner was Akerlof's mentor Robert Solow.

Samuelson, a bit taller than Friedman, with a sharp, straight jawline and a fondness for cutting verbal barbs, was born in Gary, Indiana. Like Friedman, his father died at an early age, a fate Samuelson was convinced he would share. That made him a young man in a hurry, though he actually ended up living to ninety-four.[14] Also like Friedman, Samuelson studied during the depths of the Great Depression at the University of Chicago. One of his first teachers was a Russian immigrant named Aaron Director, Rose Friedman's brother.

Samuelson was later off to Harvard, where his writing flourished. At the age of thirty-two, he was awarded the American Economic Association's Clark Medal, given to top economists under forty. That same year he published *Foundations of Economic Analysis*, formalizing the ideas of Keynes with mathematical precision. He also worked on an economics textbook that became a long-running bestseller. Economics in literary form, without math, Samuelson said, was just "mental gymnastics of a peculiarly depraved type."[15]

Despite his accomplishments, Samuelson couldn't land a good job in Harvard's economics department. He clashed with its chairman, Harold Hitchings Burbank, who seemed unfriendly to the ideas of Keynes and to the Jewish people. "I used to say that there were three things that would exclude you from the economics department at Harvard in those days: you couldn't be Jewish, you couldn't be a Keynesian, and you couldn't be smart. So what chance did a smart, Jewish Keynesian have," Solow said years later.[16] Of Burbank, Samuelson said the man "suffered fools gladly, but not Jews."[17]

By 1940 Samuelson had decamped for MIT, which then had little impact in the economics profession. Solow later followed him. They saw themselves as scrappy underdogs. Samuelson came to quote an Avis car rental commercial slogan to sum up the department ethos at MIT: "We Try Harder."

Samuelson wasn't much of a teacher. His lectures rambled. Once some of his class materials went through a mimeograph machine backward. When a student alerted him to the problem, he told the class to hold the pages up to a mirror to read. Samuelson had a quirky, at times immodest personality. When asked to contribute an autobiographical note to a book on Nobel-winning economists, he covered his career in the third person, referring to himself by his initials, PAS.[18] "Every honor he aspired to came his way, and came early," he wrote of himself. Having achieved fame for formalizing the ideas of Keynes, he then achieved fortune through the sales of his textbook, he added about himself.

Samuelson and a succession of protégés developed a reputation for finding and training the best PhD talent. MIT was an engineering school, and Samuelson—with Solow's leadership—turned it into a place that constructed the world's most respected economic engineers. A long succession of people who emerged in the coming decades as top policy makers or researchers came through Samuelson's department in the 1960s, 1970s, and 1980s, often as classmates or returning teachers: Ben Bernanke, Lawrence Summers, Paul Krugman, Mario Draghi, Gregory Mankiw, Christina Romer, Stanley Fischer, Alan Blinder, Joseph Stiglitz, Laura Tyson—the list went on and on. They tended to be sympathetic to Keynes, though more bound to observation and data than rigid devotion to any single ideology. Krugman, who veered into political commentary later in his career, was perhaps an outlier in his regular outspoken political commentary.

Samuelson's rivalry with Friedman was different from Tobin's. In *Newsweek* columns Samuelson and Friedman publicly jousted over the government's proper role in the economy, but they also carried on long-running personal correspondence that was mostly warm. In private notes, Samuelson described Friedman as having been a "God-like" figure in their days as Chicago students in the 1930s.[19] For decades the two corresponded by mail, politely checking in on each other with postcards and inquiries about health, family, and summer travel plans, while also occasionally quibbling about each other's work.

Samuelson sometimes sounded awestruck by Friedman but wasn't always so deferential toward his rival when he was communicating with others. After Friedman's death, Samuelson expressed modest disdain for the man he had publicly admired for many years. When Samuelson's nephew Lawrence Summers praised Friedman in a *New York Times* column as "the most influential economist" of the second half of the twentieth century, Samuelson privately chided Summers: "For your eyes only, I had to grade [Friedman] low as a macro economist" and "stubbornly old fashioned."[20]

The task taken up by many in the new generation of young economists

who studied under Tobin, Samuelson, and Solow—Yellen and Akerlof among them, as well as Bernanke, Summers, and the rest—was to
redefine the ideas of Keynes in an era when Friedman's philosophies
prevailed. Many of these young economists were convinced the government had some role to play in the economy, but they had to acknowledge
that the government also was an imperfect actor. The 1970s had made
that all too clear, and the Chicago economists had a point that couldn't
be totally dismissed: humans take the future into account when they
make decisions about spending, saving, hiring, and other economic actions. These expectations can shape or distort the impact of government
actions, and had to be included in the formulas economists wrote down.

Some in Yellen's new generation of economists would come to be
known as New Keynesians, guardians of a new economic order rising
behind the scenes in an era ruled by Chicago's market-oriented school
of thought. Yellen, the protégé of Tobin, and Akerlof, the protégé of
Samuelson and Solow, were groomed to become leaders of this movement. Many of the New Keynesians built up their ideas by making small
observations about how the economy really seemed to work, something
Akerlof had pioneered with his look at the used-car market. And from
their ranks rose the people who would manage the levers of the world
economy in a new millennium.

In 1980 Ronald Reagan was on his way to Washington. Carter had
already shaken up the Fed with a new leader, Paul Volcker—tall as a basketball player, with giant hands and a gravelly voice—who was intent on
beating down inflation with high interest rates that crippled economic activity. After a short stint in London, Yellen and Akerlof were on their
way back to America as the Reagan era dawned with recession and rising
unemployment.

7

Yellen and Akerlof
at Berkeley

Labor of Love
1978–1990

Yellen and Akerlof's early experiences in London were a window into their different personalities. One morning Akerlof quietly wandered into a large lecture hall filled with hundreds of students at the London School of Economics. Then he meandered erratically and silently around the classroom for several minutes among a cast of bewildered young men and women. He turned right, then left, then backed up, then right again, up the lecture hall steps, down, left, backward, all without any apparent pattern or reason. It seemed a little nuts until Akerlof explained that he was demonstrating an economic concept called the random walk theory, which premised that the behavior of stocks on any given day was unpredictable.

In the afternoon, Yellen lectured. She delivered clear, concise explanations of textbook economics with precise graphs on the blackboard, sometimes clearing up abstractions that Akerlof had left behind.

Their grading styles were different, too. When they disagreed about a student's grade—for instance, one of them wanting to give a student a C, and the other an A—George wanted to split the difference, give the student a B, and move on to the next student's grade. That was efficient.

Janet wanted to discuss why they had come up with different grades and try to determine which argument won out. That was fair. She got so frustrated with George about the grading issue that she once kicked him out of their car and made him walk the London streets for a little while alone.

The newlyweds also debated how to find a house. Akerlof wanted to buy a run-down place in the Hampstead neighborhood, known for the long list of intellectuals and artists who had settled there, including T. S. Eliot, George Orwell, and Sigmund Freud. It reminded him of the airy Princeton neighborhood where he'd been raised near Einstein. Yellen favored a nicer home in a blue-collar neighborhood, Cricklewood, which felt a little more like Brooklyn. As they debated about where to live, home values soared and priced them out of both markets.

They had a bigger problem living in London; Yellen didn't feel much at home across the Atlantic. Almost as soon as she stepped off the plane, she felt like an outsider. During their first summer as Londoners, Akerlof took Yellen to visit Berkeley, where they stayed in the apartment of a friend. By then Berkeley's 1960s mayhem had settled down, and Yellen fell in love with the place on her first day there. All the way back to her family's Sunday meals at New York City restaurants, Yellen had loved eating and cooking well-prepared food. Berkeley was at the center of a food movement emphasizing fresh, creative, locally grown food, which started at a Berkeley restaurant called Chez Panisse, the creation of a 1960s activist named Alice Waters. It was also less than an hour from Napa Valley's wine country. And the weather beat Brooklyn or Boston or London. "Does anybody do any work here?" she asked Akerlof when they arrived.

After less than a year in dreary London, they decided they wanted to move back across the Atlantic. One challenge was dealing with Akerlof's books, forty boxes of them, which in the space of one year had traveled from Berkeley to Washington, DC—where the boxes fell off a forklift and were strewn over the ground—and then to London. Now they would need to be shipped off once again. By the time the books got back to Berkeley in 1980, they had traveled more than ten thousand miles in three years and never been unpacked.

The other challenge would be getting satisfying jobs in the same place. George Akerlof was born into a long line of strong women. His mother came from an academic family of German Jews. Like so many others in his family, she studied chemistry in graduate school, in her case at Yale, where she met his father. Her own strong-willed mother spent time with the family during summers on Squam Lake. "My mother and grandmother would have considered themselves equal to anybody," Akerlof reflected later.

He was comfortable being married to a strong woman. As far as he was concerned, Yellen's career stood on equal ground with his own. "It was automatic that we wouldn't go anyplace where she didn't have a job she was happy with," Akerlof said. "It was always expected that everything was equal."

Yellen landed an offer from Berkeley's business school, and the university economics department was eager to have Akerlof back. She was told she would be reviewed for tenure soon after their return, though it wasn't guaranteed. The main stipulation was that she had to teach a class on international business, a subject about which there was little formal literature and in which she had no background. They had competing offers from Cornell University, but the scene at Berkeley won out. In August 1980 they were back in the United States, and Yellen started studying up on international business.

Women were finding their way into the workforce in large and growing numbers then, and American society was straining to adapt to the influx. Between 1963, when Yellen went off to Brown, and 1980, when Yellen and Akerlof went together to Berkeley, an additional twenty-two million women entered the American workforce, nearly doubling the number of working women to forty-six million.[1] The percentage of women who had a job or wanted one increased from 38 percent to 52 percent in that time. By the end of the decade another eleven million had joined their ranks, and their labor force participation rate marched toward 60 percent.

Many women delayed marriage and childbearing and looked toward lasting careers, as Yellen had before them. "In 1972 women wondered hard about the possibility of having a family and a career, and being able to manage both," *Time* magazine wrote in a 1982 cover story.[2] "In 1982 more women—including some of the daughters of the past generation—take all this as a birthright."

Contraception gave women more control over work and family decisions, as did access to legal abortion.[3] As roles changed, these decisions became politically and culturally complex and a new source of social division for many Americans. *Kramer vs. Kramer*, the highest-grossing film of 1979, traced the work and family traumas of a husband, wife, and son navigating divorce. John Irving's bestselling book of 1978, *The World According to Garp*, told the story of the son of an outspoken feminist icon and single mother as he learned to become a devoted father in his own home.

Time pointed toward social exhaustion with the women's movement in 1982. "They were the politics of long frustration and new anger," the magazine said of feminism, "and it was men who took the heat: as repressive husbands, lackadaisical fathers, selfish sex partners, exclusionary businessmen, blind-sided artists and perpetrators of a patriarchy that had to be overthrown. Even Shakespeare was a sexist for a little while." The backlash of the women's movement spurred a backlash of its own. A constitutional amendment encoding equal rights for men and women was quashed in Reagan's Washington, and Hollywood twisted the plot on feminism. In *Kramer vs. Kramer*, Meryl Streep played the role of antagonist in leaving her husband. Garp, a sensitive wrestling coach, was the victim of his wife's infidelity. In another hit, *Fatal Attraction*, Glenn Close was a single businesswoman who became a crazed adulteress.

Amid all of this social upheaval, Yellen and Akerlof organized their lives as equals both at work and at home. At the center of their new life was their first and only child, Robert, born in June 1981, ten months after their return to the United States, and named after Akerlof's MIT mentor, Robert Solow.

A few months after Robby's birth, Yellen went back to teaching her international business class. The next spring she taught two classes and was on course to have two papers about technology published with her Harvard colleague, Rachel McCulloch.[4] It helped that Yellen and Akerlof were both academics with flexible schedules. It also helped that Akerlof was eager to take on his duties as a father.

Yellen and Akerlof doted on Robby. Lawrence Katz, a labor market researcher and colleague at the time, recalled that the only time he ever saw Akerlof wear a suit was for an interview the couple had to get Robby into an elite Berkeley preschool. Both were very nervous about the affair. On campus, Akerlof's typical uniform was khaki pants, wrinkled blue button-down shirts, and ragged sweaters. His casual style rubbed off just a little on Yellen; sometimes she dressed the same.

When Robby was a boy, Janet's hair started going gray early, in her thirties, as had her mother's. She thought about coloring it, but Robby protested, telling her that wouldn't be her. She thought he had a point and didn't want to upset him, so she let it go gray. The more silver it became over the years, the more she liked it.

As Janet's career advanced, George and Robby became constant companions. On trails behind Berkeley's campus they hiked to places like Inspiration Point in Tilden Park, with its expansive views of San Francisco Bay. Robby liked to wander along and listen to George's stories about his days in far-off India and its colonial history, when the British ruled its vast population. George's stories often came with a mutinous flare. A favorite story was that of a garrison town called Meerut north of Delhi in 1857, where Indian soldiers called sepoys rebelled against British rule in an uprising that spread east and north before the British brutally put it down, killing hundreds of thousands.

In class with PhD students, Akerlof used characters from Robby's bedtime stories as teaching tools. He used the names Mr. and Mrs. Buckett, from *Charlie and the Chocolate Factory*, for the hypothetical actors in one of his economic equations. He often picked Robby up at school and took him to a popular cheese and pizza shop called the Cheese Board Collective. Along the way, they came up with theories about the quirks of everyday life. What strange and silent signaling between people makes them hesitate and lurch when they drive at stop signs? When Akerlof met with famous scholars, Robby often tagged along. At one Chez Panisse meal with Akerlof's friend Robert Shiller, the two professors turned to the boy for input on the menu. A duck dish with figs and honey also came with frisée. The dish interested Shiller, but what was frisée?

"It's sort of a frilly lettuce," young Robby explained to his elders.

"Robby impressed me," Shiller wrote in his diary that night.

Father and son spent so much time together, some mothers wondered aloud whether Akerlof had a job. How could he be showing up for the boy in the middle of a workday? Their confusion delighted Akerlof. Why did people think he should conform to a traditional role as a father? He relished that he was breaking old parenting conventions and carving out his own approach. Along the way, Robby took on Akerlof's intonations and the sound of his laugh as well as his theoretical and subversive way of thinking.

Robby took on Yellen's meticulous approach to life and a love of cooking, craftsmanship, and order. How else could he have known the definition of frisée? They watched cooking shows together. Robby was at her side preparing meals for the family in the kitchen, and for dinner parties when they entertained Berkeley academics. Akerlof mostly stayed out of the way when they were at work there and then did the dishes when they were done.

Yellen was one of Robby's Boy Scout leaders, as her mother had been for John. One of her jobs was to fetch medals and trophies from a small shop in downtown San Francisco. It seemed like she was always running from campus to pick up a new batch.

When Robby entered the Boy Scout pinewood derby—a race of brick-size wooden vehicles hand-sculpted by the scouts—Yellen stepped in and Akerlof stepped aside. Robby wanted to craft a replica of a Batmobile from the Batman cartoon. Robby had a friend whose father was an engineer, and Yellen was determined not to be shown up by the more skilled and practiced rival. She bought a Dremel and studied woodworking. When she messed up during their work, she grumbled and started over.

Robby was awarded a prize for design and the next year he wanted to step up their game. He asked to make a replica of an antique Bugatti, the European luxury and race car manufacturer founded in 1909. Their pint-size Bugatti had a spare tire on the back with a latticed silver hubcap, big round exterior headlights, intricate silver door handles, and a sunroof atop a boxy passenger compartment. They beat the engineer's son for top design prize, but somehow saw their own victory as an injustice. Believing that the engineer's car was even better, they insisted he get a trophy too.

Yellen had certain rules and rituals in the household. When a visitor came, the place would be neat and clean, in fact spotless, something she often attended to herself. For dinner there were two sets of dishes, one for preparation and one for serving. Akerlof and Robby found it odd that the dirty prep dishes were often family heirlooms, including fine dishes passed down from Brooklyn or keepsakes made by Robby in art class. When Akerlof and Robby needled Janet about the logic of using the most precious dishes for making meals, she tried to explain her thinking. She liked to keep Robby's handiwork close to her. When pressed further with complaints that the cooking was discoloring Robby's childhood keepsakes, she shrugged and dismissed the matter.

"Sometimes it just is what it is," she said.

Though Yellen was demanding of herself and echoed her mother's habit of keeping a tidy household, she was careful not to smother Robby over schoolwork as Ruth had done to her. Robby was smart and motivated enough to do well on his own, and Akerlof was always filling their boy's imagination with new ideas. When he did his schoolwork near the kitchen, she made a point not to bother him.

In the kitchen Robby and Yellen were mostly allied. They had similar tastes for spicy and exotic food. Akerlof, who couldn't bear the smell of garlic and suffered from an upset stomach, stuck to bland chicken dishes. When Yellen and Akerlof went to the supermarket together, each got their own cart and went separate ways.

At the dinner table, conversation turned to ethics, economics, history, and other high-minded subjects. Robby and Akerlof liked to challenge Yellen with unconventional ideas. She usually found the holes in their arguments. Akerlof delighted in saying he never won an argument against his brilliant wife. When she could only find a few weaknesses in his arguments, he knew he was on to something. When they played Scrabble together, she usually won. When they played bridge with their friends David and Christina Romer, who were also economics professors, Akerlof got a little too competitive for her taste.

As Yellen's family had done in her own childhood, the family went on trips together. Yellen insisted on arriving at airports hours before departure. They typically packed four suitcases, one for each person and a fourth for the books they brought along. Each family member got a third of the fourth suitcase for books. They liked to sit at resorts—Hawaii, Bora Bora, Bali—look out at the ocean, and read.

The family's favorite spot was a luxury resort on the Hawaiian island of Lanai called the Manele Bay Hotel, where they sat on the balconies and read most days, took in the ocean views, and pored through books and research papers. Sometimes they walked in a nearby garden. Lanai had for many years been the home of the Dole family's pineapple business. Yellen's mother had bought a small share of Dole stock years earlier, and Yellen inherited half of the stock when her mother passed away. When Dole offered a discount at the Manele Bay resort to its shareholders, Yellen and Akerlof decided to give it a try. They took to the lovely scenes and relaxed feel of the place.

Akerlof had his own resort uniform: khaki pants, worn and collared short-sleeve shirts, long white tube socks, and old sneakers. He had clip-on shades that fit over his reading glasses, so he could read in the sun. When he lost the clip-ons, he bought oversize sunglasses at a pharmacy. At dinner, the conversation turned back to economics.

"They're both kind of nuts in different ways," Robby would say later of his parents. "The staff at the resort thought we were just these very odd people."

Robby became a part of the family business. It would remain a family of three. Akerlof once joked to a friend that with one child you could have democracy, with more it must be dictatorship.

That Akerlof and Yellen family business in the 1980s centered on two issues. One was a broadening counterattack against the Chicago school's unthrottled faith in markets, a faith that now ruled Wall Street and Reagan's Washington. The other was the study of the issue that had drawn their interest since childhood: jobs.

In her early academic work, Yellen dabbled in a range of other issues, including research into how firms used monopoly power, how they managed new technology, and international trade. One of her challenges was finding compatible research partners with common interests. With Akerlof she homed in on the issue that mattered most to her and produced the best work of her academic career.

The problem of unemployment was at the forefront again. By late 1982 the unemployment rate jumped to more than 10 percent, its highest level since the Great Depression. It stayed there for nearly a year. But why? How did this market work? Did the government have any business trying to fix it?

The Chicago crowd saw in markets an exquisite signaling mechanism in which prices were like the songbirds of the economy. When the price of a car or a Twinkie was rising, it was a signal to producers that demand was strong and that the item was in short supply. Producers responded by increasing supply to take advantage of the higher price, or consumers felt the increased cost and pulled back, so there was a reduction in demand. Then some new equilibrium was reached. The reverse happened when a price was falling. There was an excess of supplies—perhaps because business built too much capacity in anticipation of more demand than it got, or perhaps because some shock made consumers less willing to spend. The falling price drew consumers back in and spurred producers to curtail production and the market cleared at a new equilibrium.

Hayek argued that the pricing mechanism in a market economy was a marvel that distilled information and coordinated action with a precision and elegance that no single human mind—and certainly no government bureaucrat—could design or manage. It was a miraculous accident of human interaction, a way to surface and coordinate the wisdom hidden in crowds through free individual choice.[5]

In the view of New Keynesians, however, the pricing mechanism sometimes failed, and this was part of the riddle of unemployment.

Think again about a market for oranges. If an orange producer sees a downturn in demand for oranges, the producer will cut the price of the oranges to clear the shelves of excess inventory. The producer doesn't just throw away the oranges. But that's not how the job market works. When companies need to cut their costs, they don't cut worker wages;

they fire the workers. It's like throwing away good oranges, and leads to all kinds of collateral damage to both workers and society.

For Yellen and Akerlof, the starting point was that the labor market simply didn't work like other markets, something that became evident when they studied the market's pricing signal, which was worker wages.

One simple reason that the labor market is different from the orange market is that humans respond to the wages they are paid. An orange doesn't respond to the price at which it is sold. Yellen and Akerlof theorized that if individuals felt they were being unfairly paid, they would shirk on their work, hurting a company's productivity and profits. If workers felt they were paid well, they would be more productive and reliable. Human feelings thus meant that wages didn't find a market-clearing equilibrium in the same ways you would expect of oranges. To accommodate these feelings, according to Yellen and Akerlof, employers tended to pay wages above the level that on paper would have cleared simpler markets. That wage dynamic in turn left some fraction of workers routinely on the sidelines, even in good times unable to secure work and thus unemployed. Companies tended to hoard the best workers with higher wages and leave others out. Complex sociology helped to explain persistent joblessness.[6]

When Yellen and Akerlof advertised for a babysitter in the local newspaper, twenty to forty hours a week, they were sure to include the words "good pay" to entice the most reliable people. They were putting their theories to work. Other people might have been available at lower pay, but the couple didn't want to hire babysitters who might not show up when needed. If other parents behaved the same way, then some group of babysitters would not find work.

Babysitters were one example of the complex dynamics of worker pay. Yellen was another. Because she worked at a public university, it was easy to find out what professors on the faculty made. It was well known that she was among the lower-paid of Berkeley's economics staff. Was this sexism? It was hard to know. It might also have been because she was unwilling to move; it was also well known at universities that the best way to get a nice pay raise was to threaten to leave for a competing department. Yellen liked Berkeley and didn't have any intention of going anywhere. Still, she felt the potentially demoralizing effects of not being rewarded more.

Yellen and Akerlof's work became part of a literature known in the 1980s as efficiency wage theory. There was sometimes an above-market clearing wage that left less productive people routinely out of jobs. Stiglitz worked on the same subject, as did Lawrence Summers.

A related question was why unemployment rose so much in recessions, as happened in the 1980s. Classic theory suggested that in a recession companies would reduce wages rather than fire workers—but in reality it didn't work that way.

One theory was that wages had another unique characteristic: they were unusually inflexible, or "sticky," and didn't adjust quickly. This was in part because companies and workers had long-term contracts, so instead of cutting wages in a downturn, companies fired the workers, effectively killing the contracts that bound the wages in the first place. The companies might fill open positions with people at much lower wages, but then they risked being stuck with inefficient workers when the economy turned up. It was better to keep the position open and wait out the downturn.

Akerlof loved attaching metaphors to his ideas. To illustrate this point, he conjured up an unusual image from his visit to Punjab, India, for his work on a dam project in the 1960s. Suppose a firm has an open space on which it might build a large dam to direct water to village farming, he proposed. Suppose also that economic or weather conditions are such that the dam will be underutilized for some extended period if it is built. Better not to build the dam at all and wait for conditions to improve than to tie up the space unproductively, he wrote in a paper called "Jobs as Dam Sites."[7]

Behind the work was a broader point. In the Chicago school's view of the world, all unemployment was voluntary. There was a job out there for anyone, provided that person was willing to accept a low enough wage. If that were true, however, why had unemployment risen so much again in the 1980s? Labor markets didn't operate efficiently, the New Keynesians countered. And in light of that, they asked, then might not the government have some role to play helping workers left out in the cold? If unemployment could rise and get stuck at some high level because wages didn't respond fluidly, could the government help to unstick it with programs—like spending or tax cuts—to boost demand, or help for the unemployed? Could the Fed help by lowering interest rates to restart borrowing, spending, and investing during a downturn?

Over a decade Yellen and Akerlof coauthored more than a dozen research articles, published in top academic journals. He pushed her creatively. She gave structure and rigor to his ideas. He got a second wind in an already accomplished career. She went from being a promising mind who struggled to find steady research partners to being a force in the area of economics that mattered most to her. Together, they became central figures in the New Keynesian movement.

They had a long, uphill battle to fight in the 1980s. Other theories from the Keynes crowd had proven flawed. One glaring case was their belief in an inverse relationship between unemployment and inflation. If they let inflation run just a little high, they believed, they could bring unemployment down. Why? Higher prices meant there was more demand in the economy, which would call for more workers. After Friedman argued in 1967 that this was a false hope, the 1970s seemed to prove him right. By the 1980s the word *discredited* had become attached to the word *Keynesian* as the word *damned* was attached to the word *Yankee*, Tobin joked grimly to his students at Yale.

The Fed was discredited too. In 1979 Burns had shocked an audience of leading bankers in Belgrade with a speech called "The Anguish of Central Banking," in which he effectively declared defeat. "It is illusory to expect central banks to put an end to the inflation that now afflicts the industrial democracies," he said. The problem wasn't that the central banks were incapable of doing it. The problem, he said, was that politics made it impossible to achieve the goal.[8]

Why did unemployment rise so much in the 1980s? Once again, the Fed was at the center of it. Volcker was intent on stamping out inflation and reestablishing the central bank's credibility. He was at the Burns speech in Belgrade and returned to Washington intent on proving his predecessor wrong. To fight inflation, Volcker focused on restraining the supply of money stampeding through the financial system. Restraining that supply meant pushing up interest rates, starving businesses and households of funds used to spend and invest. That meant recession. Interest rates for conventional home mortgages rose to more than 18 percent in 1981. Home builders sent Volcker blocks of unused wood to voice their displeasure.

Volcker won in the end. His policies drove down inflation, and after he loosened the noose on interest rates the economy roared back to life. The stock market soared, as did Reagan's popularity and the apparent efficacy of the tax cuts that Reagan also championed. The primacy of markets seemed to have won out, but the countermovement to the Chicago school was still gaining ground in the ivory towers.

8

Behavioral Economists

Remarkable Errors in the
History of Economic Thought
1980s and 1990s

Another bedrock assumption of the Chicago economics crowd was that people are rational and act in their own best interests, carefully taking account of their present and future prospects before making decisions. Markets are efficient because the individual—*Homo economicus*—behaves in logical and predictable ways. The math formulas of economics don't work so well if that basic assumption about rational and predictable humans doesn't hold. To a small crowd in and around the economics profession, including Yellen and Akerlof, that assumption was fantastical. Their work in the 1980s helped to fuel a countermovement against that idea, too.

Economists at the time didn't like to involve themselves much with social sciences like psychology or sociology—those disciplines were simply seen as soft. Samuelson glorified the math that underlay physics. In 1969 the Royal Swedish Academy of Sciences had begun handing out Nobel Prizes for what it called "economic sciences," paired to the fields deemed most rigorous, including physics, chemistry, and medicine. Robert Hall, one of Akerlof's former MIT classmates, told the *Wall Street Journal* in 1985 that he stopped reading research papers when he saw the word *sociological* in them. In the same story, Yellen acknowledged that bringing psychology and sociology into economic research was a bit like "wearing a loud shirt" in a room full of serious men and women.[1]

To Akerlof, who never fussed much about his clothes, psychology and sociology were entirely logical fields to explore. The profession's resistance only gave him more motivation to delve deeper. If you want to understand the nature of markets, he thought, you need to understand the nature of the central actors. Feelings, like a sense of fairness, as he and Yellen saw it in the 1980s, shaped how the labor market worked. In other papers they used mathematical models to show that even with a smattering of "near-rational" people in a marketplace—people who don't always make the most sensible choices—the whole economy could be thrown off course, upending old ideas about how markets behaved.[2]

As Akerlof and Yellen explored notions of near-rationality and fairness in labor markets, two other professors, one a psychologist and one an economist, were pushing the examination of quirky human behavior even further.

Daniel Kahneman, Jewish and of Lithuanian descent, was raised in France in the 1930s. Life became progressively harder for his family as Nazi Germany encroached, invaded, and occupied his country. The Kahneman family fled to the south of France for safety. Young Kahneman seemed to live in a world of true good and evil, yet even as a boy he took note of the surprising wrinkles of human nature that defied his expectations of behavior. Once, with his country occupied by menacing Nazis, a scary-looking SS soldier in black uniform called out to him when he was out after curfew. Terrified, Danny approached the German soldier as ordered, thinking he was doomed. Then the soldier picked him up, hugged him, showed him a picture of his own son, gave him some cash, and sent him on his way.

Kahneman became the psychology professor.

Richard Thaler was raised in Chatham, New Jersey, in the late 1940s and 1950s, halcyon days for America. His father was an actuary, his mother a retired schoolteacher. He saw himself as an undistinguished student, hampered by a mild case of dyslexia and the habits of day-dreaming and laziness. Finding the board game Monopoly boring, he insisted on changing the rules to speed it up so that the players got their properties faster.[3] His father once tried to discipline young Dick when he was a boy by getting him to copy, verbatim, the first two pages of Mark Twain's book *Tom Sawyer*. After several days of trying, Thaler still couldn't do it. His father gave up, but somehow Twain's irreverence sunk in with Thaler.

He became the economics professor.

Though they were from vastly different worlds, Kahneman and Thaler shared unconventional mindsets and an interest in exploring the judgments people commonly made that seemed to defy logic, common sense, or rigid mathematical analysis.

Kahneman posed this question among others: Given a choice between a sure gain of $240 versus a 25 percent chance of a $1,000 gain, why was it that most people he surveyed would take the sure gain even though the other choice was mathematically superior? Thaler posed his own question about a friend with a lawn mower: Why is it that the friend insisted on mowing his own lawn, even though he could hire a kid to do it for $8, yet he wouldn't go to the trouble of mowing his neighbor's lawn if offered $20? In each case, the choices weren't purely about the dollars at stake.

The two professors drew broad conclusions from these and other observations: People viewed gains and losses differently; their decisions were shaped by how choices were framed; and they also valued goods they owned—like a lawn mower, or a lawn—differently from other goods in a marketplace.

Kahneman and Thaler worked with other people and sometimes they worked with each other. One time, along with the economics professor Jack Knetsch, they came up with a novel way to measure how perceptions of fairness affected the economy: they simply asked people what they thought. To many economists, this was sacrilege. Asking people to talk about their feelings and drawing conclusions about economic behavior from what they said wasn't science; it was pop psychology. The two professors did it anyway. They conducted telephone surveys of households in Toronto and Vancouver over the course of fifteen months.

Suppose a hardware store sells snow shovels for $15, they proposed in one question to their Canadian participants. Would it be okay to raise the price of the shovels to $20 the morning after a big storm? More than 80 percent of the Canadian respondents said that would be unfair. Suppose a landlord learns that a tenant has taken a new job nearby and thus has no intention of moving, they proposed in another question. If he knows the tenant is staying, would it be fair for the landlord to raise the rent by more than usual when the tenant's lease comes up for renewal? More than 90 percent said no, unfair.[4]

The underlying lesson from the study was that community norms can affect the buying and selling behavior of individuals and firms, leading them away from outcomes that standard economic models would have predicted to be most efficient. The hardware store can increase profits by jacking up prices for its shovels on a snowy day, but it generally doesn't. People didn't appreciate it, Kahneman and Thaler's research showed, when firms took advantage of customers or workers after some unexpected event; it was okay to maximize profits, but not when a person was down or unusually exposed.

Akerlof loved the paper and championed its publication in 1986 in the *American Economic Review*, a journal at which he was an editor. "It was the only time in my life when the referee liked the paper more than I did," Thaler said later of Akerlof's reception of his work. "It was like he gave us a standing ovation."[5]

The paper was one of Thaler's first breakthroughs. Soon after that he was offered a column in a new economic journal called the *Journal of Economic Perspectives* that raised his profile among peers. He called the column "Anomalies."

Kahneman earned his doctoral degree in psychology at Berkeley in the 1960s and returned the year the fairness paper was published. He taught a class there with Akerlof on psychology and economics. Akerlof tried to recruit Thaler to Berkeley too, but the economics department didn't want him. Thaler instead decamped to the University of Chicago's business school, where he taught the idiosyncrasies of markets in the citadel of free-market thought. He spent more than two decades there battling Eugene Fama, father of the Chicago school's efficient market hypothesis.[6] Thaler and Fama were friends and played tennis together at the faculty club, but not everyone at Chicago was so welcoming to the new campus heretic. When Thaler showed up in the 1990s, an older finance professor there, Merton Miller, quipped to a reporter that every generation had to make its own mistakes. His not-so-subtle implication: Thaler was Chicago's mistake. Thaler never forgot the slight and slapped a sign on his new office door as a reminder to all who entered. It read: "This Generation's Mistake."

Thaler and Kahneman developed stories and theories about how humans deviated from a traditional economist's view of rational, self-maximizing behavior. At the time many other economists responded, "Why did it matter?" These were just stories, clever anomalies. Markets as a whole still functioned properly.

Another economist and a friend of Akerlof and Yellen—Robert Shiller—found his way to the heart of that critique by zooming in on financial markets. These were the most ruthless, fast-moving, and perhaps consequential markets of all, with trillions of dollars sloshing around the world every day at lightning speed in stocks and bonds. Investors had only one point in mind—economic gain—and they weren't rational or orderly at all, Shiller thought.

Shiller had a mild, shy, hesitant demeanor, with a midwesterner's polite sensibility. A pen in his hand, however, was like a match to kindling. The idea that stock markets were efficient, Shiller wrote in 1984, was "one of the most remarkable errors in the history of economic thought."[7] Stocks were in fact far more volatile than could possibly be explained by the fundamentals that were meant to drive their valuations, namely profits or dividends, he asserted in another explosive paper published in the *American Economic Review.*[8] For many people, investing in stocks was a social activity, prone to gossip, hype, and fads just like politics or fashion, he said.

As a grade schooler, young Bobby, as his parents called him, couldn't sit still. He had a habit of getting up from his chair, wandering to the seats of other children, and interrupting their work. "My second-grade teacher, Mrs. Ashdown, would say to me, 'Bobby, if you get up from your seat one more time I am going to tie you down,'" he said. She gave him low marks in "citizenship," making his parents worry their little genius might have to repeat the grade.[9]

Sunday school was even worse. Shiller did not at all like being manipulated as a child. He often had a feeling in hearing stories about parting seas, burning bushes, and other unexplainable miracles of the New and Old Testament that his teacher was doing just that. He thought that was morally wrong and pressed for proof and clearer answers. Complaints from his Sunday school teachers found their way home, too.

As a Yale professor many years later, Shiller doubted pet food makers when they marketed the idea that they were selling "gourmet" pet food. What is gourmet to an animal? To test the proposition, he tasted his cat's food himself and found no difference in taste between regular and gourmet brands, proving to himself that the pet food makers were lying when they marketed upscale products.

Odd? Yes. But his genius was unmistakable. As a teen he wanted to learn the workings of Euclidean geometry, the Greek system that put forth basic definitions of a point, a line, an angle, a shape, and so forth. To do so, Shiller decided he must learn ancient Greek and read the writing of Euclid in its mother tongue. He taught himself ancient Greek. To communicate with family in distant Lithuania and complete a family history, he sent his relatives handwritten letters in their own language. When he read Tolstoy's great works, he read them in the original Russian.

His parents convinced him to stay close to their Michigan home after high school and attend Kalamazoo College. After a year there, ready for larger things, he was off to the University of Michigan in Ann Arbor. He liked to wander during those college days, for hours and hours: through library stacks, fishing through books that took him to other places and times; through the university medical center, to imagine what life might be like as a medical doctor. He wandered so much in college that once he went to the doctor to complain about pain in his feet. His doctor discovered he had a stress fracture from all of the walking.

Eager to put his math skills to work and try to do some social good, Shiller decided in the 1960s to become an economist. There was one obvious place at the time for someone with his promise to do that: MIT, where, like Akerlof not long before him, he came to believe that modern economics was missing some central points.

Other researchers followed Shiller's lead in the 1980s on the psychology of financial markets. Summers and his Harvard protégé Andrei Shleifer, for example, found markets swayed by "noise traders," who made stock investments driven by beliefs and sentiments that had nothing to do with a firm's fundamental value.[10] But from much of the rest of the field the initial blowback against Shiller was fierce. At one economics conference, Shiller told a colleague he was starting to wish he had never done the work. "As a young economist it was quite uncomfortable to be attacked for work that was seen as so out of line with professional conventions," he said.[11]

Akerlof took Shiller's side. The two chatted at a Berkeley economics conference in 1986 and two years later Akerlof tried to recruit him to the Berkeley faculty. Shiller didn't come, but they became close friends.

One meeting with Yellen and Akerlof got Shiller thinking about relationships and research. "I am thinking that it is often the very best economists who involve their wives as coauthors," he recorded in his diary. "I am thinking of George Akerlof and his wife Janet Yellen." Milton and Rose Friedman also came to his mind, and got him thinking he should start collaborating with his wife, Ginny, a clinical psychologist. After visiting Yellen and Akerlof's Tudor-style home in the Berkeley Hills, he wrote, "I was impressed that the house was PERFECTLY neat." The backyard had terraced gardens, with flowers that Yellen later kept as a screen saver on her computer in Washington. The kitchen was remodeled and kept a pristine white.

In 1994 Shiller and Akerlof began a study program at the National Bureau of Economic Research to examine the effects of psychology on the broader economy. "We work well together," Shiller said in his diary, "augmenting each other's imaginations, often indulging even more in speculative thinking together than we would alone."

The new revolution to hit the field was a redefinition of how humans behaved in the marketplace, called "behavioral economics." With their work on fairness and their support for people like Kahneman, Thaler, and Shiller, Yellen and Akerlof were at its forefront too.

Homo economicus was a complicated beast. Human idiosyncrasies could steer the economic ship in unexpected and sometimes dangerous directions. The economy's engineers grasped that lesson a little bit too late.

9

Yellen, Akerlof, and Socialism's Failure

The *Richtungskoeffizient*
1989–1994

Hayek, Friedman, and the Chicago school were undoubtedly right on one issue. Socialism in its most extreme forms was a failure with disastrous consequences for hundreds of millions of people in the twentieth century. By 1989 it was coming apart everywhere. Mao Zedong's command and control policies led to famine and impoverishment during China's inaptly named Great Leap Forward in the 1950s, and then his Cultural Revolution cracked down on free thought and helped to wreck China's economy in the 1960s and 1970s. By 1989 China's Communist Party was a decade into installing market-oriented reform, with Friedman's support and blessing, but still suffered a crisis of legitimacy that led to an uprising in Tiananmen Square.

In Czechoslovakia in 1989 a democratic uprising dubbed the Velvet Revolution tore socialist orthodoxy down. As the Soviet Union decayed from the inside, Poland, East Germany, Hungary, and their Soviet bloc sisters broke free of Communist Party rule. In Romania people executed their despot, and in Germany they tore down the Berlin Wall that separated east and west, symbol of an era's end. The party collapse in

Russia was just a few years away. Even mild social democracies in Europe looked burdened by slow growth and high unemployment.

It was a transcendent time for human liberty and also for the triumph of market economics. In a talk at the University of Chicago in 1989, Francis Fukuyama, a thirty-six-year-old political scientist, declared that history itself was ending: "The twentieth century saw the developed world descend into a paroxysm of ideological violence, as liberalism contended first with the remnants of absolutism, then bolshevism and fascism, and finally an updated Marxism that threatened to lead to the ultimate apocalypse of nuclear war. But the century that began full of self-confidence in the ultimate triumph of Western liberal democracy seems at its close to be returning full circle to where it started: not an 'end of ideology' or a convergence between capitalism and socialism, as earlier predicted, but to an unabashed victory of economic and political liberalism." By liberalism, he meant liberty itself, not left-leaning ideas in American political circles.[1]

Western economists were called upon to help reconstruct failed Soviet states in America's image. It was like a gold rush for academics. How do you build a market economy from the embers of a failed authoritarian state overnight? One of the first people to jump at the task was Jeffrey Sachs, a Harvard professor and another of Yellen's 1970s students. Having advised Bolivia on reform, he was soon off to Poland, promoting radical moves to privatize business and quash inflation, a plan others called "shock therapy." It seemed to work for Poland. Economic output per person there expanded 44 percent in the 1990s, and triple-digit inflation disappeared.[2]

Russia went in a far different direction. Its economy contracted and its attempts at reform led instead to a quagmire of corruption. Along the way, Harvard and another of its economists, Andrei Shleifer, ensnared themselves in a costly embarrassment. In the early 1990s, Shleifer headed up a Harvard project that used US government funding to help the country to develop modern financial markets. A gifted Russian-born scholar, he was accused of investing in places he was advising, an alleged conflict of interest. Years later Shleifer and Harvard settled the case with a payment of $30 million to the US government, though Shleifer denied culpability. Harvard shut the development program, while Shleifer, a leading financial economist who was close to Summers, kept his place on the faculty.[3]

The rush to fix broken Iron Curtain economies landed Yellen and Akerlof in Berlin in 1990, for a project funded by the National Science Foundation. Their job was to assess the effects of a unification between capitalist West Germany and socialist East Germany—the ultimate real-world experiment involving the clash of the twentieth century's two big economic ideas.

In one year, East German output collapsed by nearly 55 percent, and the industrial sector slashed more than eight hundred thousand jobs as it opened itself to the violent gusts of market forces. To understand what integration would look like, Yellen and Akerlof realized they had to understand how East German wages and prices related to West German wages and prices, and to do that, they needed to know the exchange rate for trade between the two countries. The problem was that East Germany's official exchange rate was made up and thus meaningless, as was the case for so many of its official statistics. The real exchange rate existed in black markets, or perhaps hidden in official East German ledgers.

In all her years as a student, Janet Yellen had shirked in only one class—which happened to have been her German language course at Brown. Somehow she had learned enough, though, to wander around East Berlin libraries and statistics offices and make friends with the bureaucrats still keeping the books there. No longer beholden to corrupt bosses, many of them were inclined to help her. From them she dug up industrial statistics and also learned of the existence of a hidden number

called the *Richtungskoeffizient*, a shadow exchange rate that the government used to calculate the profitability of big state-run businesses.

Akerlof, like the sleuthing reporter he was during his days at the *Yale
Daily News*, set out to find the hidden number. Speaking no German
himself, he was led to a dreary gray building on the outskirts of the city,
where a government bureaucrat was familiar with the number. There
was something about Akerlof's blithe demeanor that seemed to disarm
the overwhelmed East Germans. The bureaucrat asked him to come
back to visit, and agreed to share the number.

Using this shadow exchange rate, Akerlof and Yellen concluded that
only 8 percent of East German workers had economically viable jobs.
"These calculations undermine prior estimates of high productivity in
socialist countries," they added, a point that had already been made all
too clear by the collapse of the Soviet empire. Hearing a presentation of
the paper at the Brookings Institution, a Washington think tank, Rudi-
ger Dornbusch, a leading economics professor at MIT, said it was "the
most thorough assessment of the collapse of East Germany's economy
to date."[4]

Yellen and Akerlof—working with coauthors Andrew K. Rose and
Helga Hessenius—described the East German experience as a depression, not a recession. They proposed not shock therapy but a massive
infrastructure spending program to cushion the blow looming over East
German workers. German chancellor Helmut Kohl had them in to discuss their work, but spent the time instead lecturing them at length
about the importance of unification. Shleifer, however, was impressed,
and asked them to take positions on his budding Russia team. They considered it seriously, and Yellen started studying Russian to prepare. In
the end they declined, deciding the language barrier would be too great.
When Shleifer's program faced government scrutiny later, it was clear
they'd dodged a bullet.

For all of the triumph achieved by the United States in winning the

Cold War decisively—after decades of conflict, armed and otherwise—
there was a sense of exhaustion back home, and a wariness about the
new global order that emerged from the ashes of conflict with socialism.
In mid-1990, the United States entered a new recession, its first in eight
years, and it didn't look like previous recessions or recoveries. The unemployment rate didn't get all that high at first, but even after business
activity picked back up, it kept rising and only retreated after a long delay. In the past, unemployment tended to surge during a recession, then
stabilize and retreat as soon as the recession ended. This felt different.

One problem was that Wall Street had become alarmed by the government debt and deficits racked up in the 1980s and early 1990s, due
in part to tax cuts and a military buildup. On trading floors, so-called
bond vigilantes pushed for Washington to tighten its belt with tax increases and government spending cuts.

When George H. W. Bush delivered what Wall Street demanded, the
conservative wing of his own party spurned him. A Republican upstart
in Congress, Newt Gingrich, led a revolt in the House of Representa-
tives, rejecting tax increases on wealthy households to finance deficit
reduction. Patrick Buchanan, a conservative commentator who worked
for Nixon, challenged Bush in the presidential primaries of 1992, weak-
ening the sitting president. Then a Texas businessman, Ross Perot,
jumped into the presidential race.

The right flank of Bush's party was in revolt not just against the tax
increases, but also against a new global order that Bush championed.
Bush wanted to build upon Reagan's market-oriented economy, but with
softer edges—a "kinder, gentler nation," as he called it, with more civic
communities that he described poetically as like a thousand points of
light. He also wanted a deal with Mexico to increase trade between the
two countries. Warning of a "sucking sound" south of the border, Perot
pointed to the threat of Mexicans taking American jobs and siphoned
off conservative support from Bush. That had the effect of clearing the

path for a young Democrat, Arkansas governor Bill Clinton, to win the presidency with his promise to focus on jobs and tough trade policy. Clinton promised to focus on economics like a laser beam. "It's the economy, stupid" became a rallying cry for his campaign. Clinton built on much of what Bush started. As part of a middle ground he sought to carve out on economic policy, the new president turned to many of the young economists who trained during the 1970s and 1980s battles between Friedman, Samuelson, and Tobin. Conscious of the power of the marketplace, but also grounded in discoveries of its real-world flaws and a belief that government still somehow mattered, these young economists also wanted a middle ground. Many of them had come to be known as the saltwater economists because they tended to study and work at universities near the ocean coasts—MIT, Yale, Harvard, Berkeley, and Princeton—as opposed to the freshwater professors of Chicago, by Lake Michigan. MIT was especially well represented in Clinton's policy-making ranks.

Paul Samuelson once said, "I don't care who writes a nation's laws if I can write its economics textbooks." He'd written the textbook, and now many of his students were shaping the laws. "It's an almost magical metamorphosis," he said of his progeny. "They withdraw from the world and dedicate themselves to technical, sometimes esoteric study. During that period they don't always have very good judgment about the world. But then they get over that acne and become leading economists. People who are slide-rule nerds turn out to be in the best position when it comes to addressing practical problems."[5]

Samuelson's students were a boisterous, ambitious, and rivalrous crowd. Larry Summers, who landed a job as the Treasury Department's top international finance adviser, developed an early reputation for stirring up public furor. Considered to run the president's Council of Economic Advisers, he was spurned by Vice President Al Gore, who didn't like his views on the environment.

Paul Krugman was in line for a job at the Council of Economic Advisers, too, but seemed to talk himself out of contention. At a meeting in Little Rock before the election, Clinton had asked a group of economists how to bring manufacturing jobs back to the United States. Krugman intemperately told the aspiring president that he wasn't asking the right question; he should focus on worker productivity. "There was this long awkward silence—I had given the wrong answer," Krugman said later.[6] When another MIT alum, Laura Tyson, got the top council job instead, Krugman sniped at her. "She's a good economist," he told a reporter somewhat dismissively, but "not one of the superstars."[7]

Tyson focused on building and leading a strong team. She recruited Stiglitz to become one of her deputies, along with MIT alum Alan Blinder. Stanley Fischer, an MIT professor, got a top job at the International Monetary Fund (IMF). Even Clinton's defense secretary, Les Aspin, had studied economics at MIT, where he was a classmate of Akerlof.

In 1994 two jobs opened at the Fed. The central bank was headed by a chairman, a vice chairman, and five other board members. Clinton offered Blinder the job of vice chairman. Stiglitz knew Yellen well, as did Tyson, who had been a professor at Berkeley's business school and helped recruit Yellen and Akerlof back from London. Clinton wanted more diversity at the Fed, an institution dominated by white males, and Tyson pushed Yellen for the job. When the White House reached out to Yellen, she was on vacation for spring break with Akerlof and Robby in Hawaii. She asked them if they were interested in moving to Washington. They urged her to say yes quickly.

Yellen got word that she'd landed the job while on a layover in Chicago on her way to a visit to Yale. The White House told her to change plans and travel to Washington immediately instead. Yellen always planned her trips carefully, but she would learn in Washington that such planning isn't always possible. She rerouted her travels, arriving April 22 to meet President Clinton in the Oval Office for the first time, her hair neatly cropped and fully gray, dressed conservatively in a long pleated skirt with a white blouse buttoned up to her throat and a black blazer.

As White House staff rushed her out to meet the press in the White House briefing room, she looked a bit bewildered. "I consider myself a non-ideological pragmatist," she told a group of White House reporters.

Seventeen years earlier, Janet Yellen had landed in Washington fresh off a disappointing stint at Harvard, thinking she might have a career as a staff economist at the central bank. Then she met Akerlof and moved on. Now she was returning as a central player.

In August 1994 Yellen took a leave from Berkeley. Akerlof took on the job of trailing spouse with glee. He accepted a job as a senior fellow at the Brookings Institution, where he and Yellen had made an impression with their work on the *Richtungskoeffizient*. Wanting the added income and not sure if Washington would work out for the family in the long run, he kept his job at Berkeley too. For the first three years that they were in Washington, he commuted back to Berkeley every spring to teach. At their new home in Chevy Chase, Maryland, teenage Robby embraced the adventure and started handling more of the cooking himself.

10

Yellen Becomes
a Central Banker

Confronting a Maestro
1994–1997

As a young man, Alan Greenspan befriended the eccentric Manhattan writer Ayn Rand, whose bestselling books The *Fountainhead* and *Atlas Shrugged* championed the indomitability of the individual human spirit and the withering effects of a controlling state. Rand initially took note of Greenspan's dour demeanor, stooped posture, and dark clothing and mocked him as "the Undertaker." Her companion, Nathaniel Branden, saw something in Greenspan and assured Rand, "I think he's a really interesting man with a very unusual brain."

Before becoming an economist, Greenspan was a jazz musician who specialized in clarinet and tenor sax and prepared taxes for fellow band members. Rand depended on his intimate knowledge of steel and railroad industry statistics to write her descriptions of American industrial power in *Atlas Shrugged*, published in 1957, and eventually came around to labeling him "Sleeping Giant." A career on Wall Street led him to Washington, where he worked for Republican administrations and then the Fed, which he led from 1987 to 2006. By the time Alan Greenspan finished his career, his nickname was "the Maestro."[1]

Greenspan didn't involve himself much in the academic debates between Friedman, Samuelson, and the others. His attention was on the use and exertion of economic power in Washington. At the center of that power was the Fed—an obscure institution that drove interest rates and could send Wall Street into paroxysms of glee and despair, yet revealed little to the public about what it actually did, how it did it, or who decided.

For many years, when the Fed shifted interest rates, it was up to a small band of highly paid Wall Street analysts to explain what it had done after scrutinizing movements in obscure money markets. Fed chairmen generally didn't seek to make the job of deciphering the central bank's actions any easier. Volcker often sat in congressional hearings and literally veiled his comments in cigar smoke, puffing away during testimony while he evaded direct statements about interest rates, to the dismay of his interrogators. Reagan's Treasury secretary, James Baker, was eager to replace him with Greenspan, whose garbled syntax made him another perfect fit as the man behind the curtain. "I spend a substantial amount of my time endeavoring to fend off questions and worry terribly I might end up being too clear," Greenspan joked in 1995.[2]

Greenspan understood that if he misspoke even slightly he could rock markets and be blamed, as seemed to happen when the stock market tumbled in October 1987, a few days after he appeared on a Sunday television talk show. He came to think that keeping investors on their toes about what the Fed would do next gave him more room to maneuver. One also had a sense that he thought the evasions and obscurity were fun. "Since I've become a central banker, I've learned to mumble with great incoherence," he once said. "If I seem unduly clear to you, you must have misunderstood what I said."[3]

The Fed had a labyrinthine operating structure, its roots closely connected to divisions present at America's very founding, when Alexander Hamilton and Thomas Jefferson squabbled about the need for a national bank. Hamilton, a New York banker, saw it as necessary to create a common currency that would help tie together, with unified finance and commerce, a new nation of disparate states. Jefferson, a Virginia land and slave owner, didn't trust New York bankers.

Hamilton won over George Washington and in 1791 created the first Bank of the United States. But forty-two years later Andrew Jackson, a populist from the Carolinas who saw a national paper currency as the seed of evil, vetoed the renewal of the national bank's charter. (Bizarrely, Jackson's face adorns the $20 bill to this day, despite his disdain for the very idea of paper money.) Through the rest of the 1800s the United States experienced regular waves of financial excess and panics that forced private banks to close and drove the economy into recession. In 1907, another of these bank panics convinced Congress that an emerging industrial power like the United States needed a central bank of its own, like the Bank of England, to help stabilize the banking system during the panics that had become endemic to its markets.

The Fed's job was to lend money to banks in a panic and to manage the circulation of dollars in the economy.

In an attempt to balance the competing interests of a nation uncomfortable with centralized power, Congress created the Federal Reserve System in 1913. Twelve different reserve banks were established across the country, in New York, Boston, Philadelphia, Richmond, Atlanta, Cleveland, Saint Louis, Kansas City, Chicago, Dallas, Minneapolis, and San Francisco. The New York bank was the most powerful of these, and a board of seven governors in Washington, DC, served at the center of the system. The Washington board gained power during the Great Depression, and its chairman became the key decision-maker, whose job was to forge consensus among the board governors and the regional bank presidents.

In the early days, money supply and interest rates were obscurely tied to the nation's holdings of gold, but that setup was quashed first by the

Depression and then by Nixon's 1971 decision to ditch the gold system entirely. As the gold system broke down, the Fed played an even more important role in guiding the level of interest rates.

Fed officials met eight times per year in the grandiose boardroom on the second floor of the Eccles Building on Washington's Constitution Avenue. On either side of the boardroom a long hallway housed the spacious offices of the chairman and six Washington-based governors. Volcker's governors were a rebellious lot, once overruling him to declare an interest-rate cut and then retreating when he threatened to resign over their insubordination.

By 1994, when Janet Yellen and Alan Blinder arrived, Greenspan had the decision-makers firmly in his grasp. Clinton's top advisers had urged the new president to leave the Fed alone to avoid the pitfalls of the 1970s. Before meetings, Greenspan would wander into governors' offices and explain to them what he wanted to do, expecting them to tell him then if they had any intention of dissenting. There was something about his approach that rubbed Yellen the wrong way. As she saw it, he was telling her his plan before asking her what she thought the plan should be. Why should she tell him whether she planned to dissent if he never bothered to ask her what she thought before formulating his strategy?

Yellen and Blinder were a new breed on the Fed board, which for years had been populated mostly by bankers, bureaucrats, and Wall Street analysts. Left-leaning academics, they had a natural affinity for the army of PhD economists that constituted much of the Fed's staff, an army trained to serve the chairman. Yellen and Blinder lavished attention on the staff, quizzing them on their research and huddling with them to discuss the economy's condition when the government released reports on inflation or employment. Moreover, Yellen and Blinder were Clinton's people—the first governors appointed to the Fed by a Democrat since the 1970s. Yellen and Blinder presented a potential front against Greenspan's decisions, and Blinder was a contender for the top Fed job when Greenspan's term expired.

In January 1995, Yellen handed Greenspan the only defeat he would ever experience on a formal vote in more than eighteen years running the institution. It wasn't over an interest-rate decision, but over regulation of banks. Regulation DD, known as the Truth in Savings rule, required that banks calculate and disclose the percentage return offered on interest-bearing savings accounts that they offered to depositors. There was one problem with the rule: it didn't account for a basic concept in finance known as the time value of money. Ten dollars earned today is worth more to an investor than ten dollars earned, say, a hundred years from now.

To properly account for the return, the formula needed to account for the timing of payments, which it didn't. The math was simply wrong. The rule was called Truth in Savings, of all things, yet it actually encouraged banks to mislead their customers. Allowing the rule to stand would be unprincipled, Yellen believed. Blinder and a Republican appointee, Lawrence Lindsey, agreed that it needed to be changed, but Greenspan didn't want to impose a new regulatory burden on banks. John LaWare, a banker, and Susan Phillips, an economist, sided with him. The decision came down to Edward Kelley, a modest Texas businessman.

Yellen doubted she could win Kelley over, but before the public vote he wandered into her office to chat, and she steered the conversation toward the Truth in Savings decision. Maybe she could convince him, she thought. It was her only chance of winning, and on a matter of principle like this, she wasn't one to back down from the powerful Fed chairman.

"This is ripping off ordinary people like my mother," Yellen blurted out. Always careful and buttoned up in public, behind the scenes her Brooklyn upbringing could surface with curses and colorful hyperbole. "It's a complete rip-off."

The discussion ended, and she had no idea how Kelley would vote. To her shock, he voted with her, Blinder, and Lindsey, defeating Greenspan 4–3. Yellen and Blinder high-fived each other after the win. A few days later, Greenspan maneuvered the board into approving a delay implementing the revisions.

For the next three years, Greenspan and a band of sometimes skeptical governors would try to find the right balance for a strengthening economy. By 1995 the unemployment rate had gradually fallen below 6 percent for the first time since the 1990 recession that derailed Bush's presidency. The question was how much further the jobless rate could fall before the economy overheated and inflation resurfaced. It had reached 5 percent in 1989 and got below 4 percent in the 1960s. Raising interest rates would guard against inflation but also risked slowing or halting the descent of the unemployment rate. If the Fed raised interest rates too much, it risked causing another recession.

Volcker had conquered the double-digit inflation rates of the 1970s and early 1980s with high interest rates. Now the inflation rate was below 3 percent. While the Fed pondered how much lower the jobless rate might go, it also explored the related question of how much lower inflation should go. If the Fed raised interest rates it could push inflation down even more; if it left interest rates too low, inflation could run wild again. The country had sacrificed so much to contain inflation in the 1980s, and the Fed had fought so hard to win back its credibility. Nobody wanted to lose that fight again.

One challenge was that after the shocks and battles of the 1970s and 1980s, there were no clear rules of the game. The old rule of thumb—that there was a predictable inverse relationship between unemployment and inflation—had fallen apart when inflation and unemployment both rose in the 1970s. So as Greenspan navigated the Fed through the 1990s, he was doing it without clear guideposts. He tended to act based on his intuitions and his personal views on data, which he liked to examine in the bathtub while nursing an achy back.[4]

Yellen sometimes challenged Greenspan on these judgments and intuitions. Four months into her term as a Fed governor, Greenspan wanted to surprise financial markets with a three-quarter percentage point increase—in central bank jargon, 75 basis points—in the federal funds rate, the short-term interest rate that the Fed controlled. Many investors were expecting a half percentage point increase, or 50 basis points. With the unemployment rate below 6 percent and economic output growing at a robust pace of greater than 3 percent a year, Fed staff projected that a hot economy would lead to a higher inflation rate.

"I think that we are behind the curve," Greenspan told the group of Fed officials gathered around the boardroom table.[5] "What bothers me about doing only 50 basis points is that even though the markets are saying that that is what we probably are going to do, I think we have to distinguish between what they are forecasting we are going to do based on our past behavior and what they think we ought to do. I suspect that while the majority think we are going to do 50, the vast majority will think that that is not enough."

Yellen countered. She thought the Fed could afford to take it slow. Among her concerns about Greenspan's proposal was that she thought investors wouldn't know how to read the Fed's intentions in this surprisingly aggressive move.

"Seventy five can backfire," she said. "A rise of this magnitude may raise market expectations both about the risks of inflation—because we are so concerned about it—and market expectations about the ultimate expected tightening that we intend here. . . . My own preference would be for 50 today."

Blinder said Yellen's assessment of the economy took his own words away. "Until about three minutes ago I thought that, even though I was speaking last, I would have some things to say that had not been said before. But that is less true now," he said after Yellen's comments.

Yellen was right. The surprise backfired.

In Orange County, California, home to Disneyland and long stretches of the state's most pristine beaches, county treasurer Robert Citron had constructed a $7.4 billion investment portfolio with Merrill Lynch, the Wall Street investment bank, for the retirement accounts of police officers and other county workers. It was filled with financial instruments highly sensitive to changes in interest rates.

Municipal funds were banned from owning stocks that might earn high returns. Instead, to charge up his portfolio, Citron arranged with Merrill to borrow extra money against the bonds it owned and invest that money in even more bonds, in what was called a reverse repurchase agreement. The Merrill Lynch portfolio was filled with these and other exotic debt instruments. The borrowing-and-investing strategy would work as long as the money Citron earned on the bonds he bought was more than the cost of all of the borrowing he was doing. But as the Fed raised interest rates in 1994, that margin for error shrank fast.

"The last straw for the Orange County fund appears to have been the Federal Reserve's three-quarter-point interest-rate increase on Nov. 15," the *Wall Street Journal* reported that December, when the county filed for bankruptcy protection.[6] "In retrospect," Citron said later, "I wish I had more education and training in complex government securities."[7]

Fallout from the Fed rate increases spread to Mexico. The dollar was the anchor of the global financial system, so when the Fed changed US interest rates, it shifted incentives for where lenders and investors wanted to park their money around the globe. US rate increases tended to draw money away from small developing countries. In this case, Mexico became the primary casualty. Greenspan's rate hikes contributed to a flood of capital away from Mexico, which turned to the United States for a financial bailout in what became known as the Tequila Crisis. Leading the US program was the Treasury's point person on international affairs, Janet Yellen's former student Lawrence Summers.

When Greenspan sought to raise rates one more time in 1995, Yellen and Blinder pressed him behind the scenes to stop. They decided not to register their dissent formally, which would have been seen as a public rebellion, because Greenspan agreed to signal that the cycle of rate increases might be over. Greenspan proceeded with the rate increase, then acknowledged a few weeks later that the time might come to reverse course. During the summer of 1995, he did just that, undoing some of the rate increases Yellen and Blinder had challenged earlier.

While these disruptions played out, Akerlof had already turned his attention to the mischief that he believed kept turning up in financial markets. In the early 1990s a wave of failed US savings and loan institutions—which offered residential and commercial mortgages—were closed at taxpayer expense after a boom-bust cycle in the market for office buildings and other commercial property.[8] A market for risky corporate bonds known as junk bonds also unraveled. In that boom Wall Street firms used the bonds to raise funds for large business takeovers. As far away as Chile, the government intervened aggressively during a banking crisis in the 1980s to prevent the collapse of its financial system.

Akerlof had a theory.

"An economic underground can come to life if firms have an incentive to go broke for profit at society's expense," he wrote in a paper with a friend, Paul Romer, then a fellow Berkeley professor and future Nobel Prize winner. They called the paper "Looting: The Economic Underworld of Bankruptcy for Profit."[9] Executives or their bankers reaped big gains when profits soared in a boom, and then the government was left to pick up the pieces in a bust. Economists sometimes called this idea "moral hazard," but Akerlof's word for it was blunter; he simply saw it as theft. Shoddy accounting rules, lax regulation, and small penalties for misconduct gave owners and executives incentives to push hard for big pay gains during a boom, even if it meant risking the failure of their own firms in a bust, he argued.

After his looting paper was published, he attended a dinner as Yellen's guest and was seated next to an executive from a large US bank who specialized in the market for derivatives. These instruments weren't plain stocks or bonds. They were investments specially tailored by the big banks to meet the specific needs of clients. For example, using one derivative known as a swap, a firm might transform a loan that had a fixed interest payment year after year into one with an interest payment that went up and down as market rates went up and down. Using interest-rate swaps to switch from fixed rates to floating rates, or vice versa, might help firms align their financial needs with the cycles of their businesses.

On Wall Street, derivatives were marketed by banks as instruments that helped their clients better manage risk. True, perhaps, Akerlof thought. But, he asked the bank executive at the dinner he was attending as Yellen's guest, couldn't they also be used by firms to hide, cheat, and steal? Wasn't that what had happened at some firms during the savings and loan crisis? Had the executive thought about how her firm's products might be abused or misused?

The executive changed the subject.

"You said what?" Yellen said to Akerlof after dinner, shaking her head. Akerlof was bemused. They seemed like reasonable questions to him. He'd thought the discussion could lead to a good follow-up to his looting paper. He was simply looking for insight and material.

Despite the ominous financial disruptions of that era, Greenspan and his Fed managed to steer the broader US economy on a steady course. The jobless rate stabilized in 1995 and then fell further after Greenspan dialed back interest-rate increases and started lowering rates again. Fed staff feared inflation would rise, but it didn't. Instead it stabilized and fell too.

Greenspan's reputation for mastery of the economy grew and Clinton reappointed him, dashing Blinder's chances for his job. The Fed, too, took on new prominence in the nation's economic affairs. According to the Chicago school's view of the world, the economy couldn't be fine-tuned by government bureaucrats, but Greenspan seemed to be doing just that by tweaking interest rates.

Yet even as the economy soared, some people inside the central bank worried that the Fed didn't actually have a road map for what it was doing. In 1977, during a decade of economic turbulence, Congress amended the Federal Reserve Act with instructions for the central bank to focus on jobs and inflation. However, the instructions were vague. The central bank's job, Congress asserted, was to "maintain long run growth of the monetary and credit aggregates commensurate with the economy's long run potential to increase production, so as to promote effectively the goals of maximum employment, stable prices, and moderate long-term interest rates."

What did all of that mean, and how was the Fed to go about achieving it? In the two decades since its enactment, the question had rarely been broached. Now, as inflation receded, officials realized they at least ought to have a discussion about how low they wanted it to go. They were prodded by the fact that several lawmakers—including Stephen Neal, a North Carolina Democrat; James Saxton, a New Jersey Republican; and Connie Mack III, a Florida Republican—wanted Congress to rewrite the law and state more clearly the Fed's economic objectives.

Greenspan set up a series of debates at Fed meetings to explore how to define the Fed's inflation mission. On one side of these debates he placed Al Broaddus, president of the Richmond regional Fed bank. A gentlemanly US army veteran and PhD economist with a southern drawl, Broaddus was widely known as an inflation "hawk" who wanted no inflation at all and thus tended to favor high interest rates to prevent the economy from heating up too much. On the other side of the debates he placed Yellen, the Berkeley "dove" who saw tradeoffs between inflation and unemployment and didn't want to push so aggressively against inflation with high rates that economic growth would slow and unemployment would rise. Hawks were seen as firmly against inflation, and doves a bit more tolerant of it. In placing Yellen at the center of the debate, Greenspan showed his respect for the professor's intellect.

At issue was whether the Fed should adopt a formal inflation target, as central banks in other nations such as New Zealand and Canada had done. A publicly stated target might make the central bank more credible in financial markets and help instill confidence among businesses and households that a repeat of the 1970s wouldn't be allowed.

In their first debate on the issue in January 1995, Yellen came out against a target, arguing that the Fed had to balance its inflation goals against the objective of keeping employment growth steady. It was better to have flexibility, and to avoid establishing a specific inflation goal that the Fed might not yet be ready to achieve, she argued. It was doing fine without one. "I would give the Greenspan Fed a grade of close to A for its performance," the professor threw in, adding some flattery for the ultimate decision-maker to buttress her point.[10]

Listening to the debate that ensued, Greenspan concluded that "we are as split down the middle as we could possibly get." Prizing his own flexibility, he tabled the conversation. In effect, the central bank dropped the idea of a public inflation target.

Eighteen months later, Yellen and Broaddus came back to the issue in another debate. The earlier debate had been over whether the Fed should publicly state an inflation target as other central banks did. This time the question was a little different. The 1977 law required the Fed to achieve "stable prices." How was it even to define price stability for its own internal purposes?

Greenspan hinted that he believed price stability meant no inflation at all. He didn't want a public target because he could be hamstrung by it. At the same time, he wanted to push inflation as close to zero as possible.

After reviewing stacks of research, Yellen argued at length that the

Fed should pursue an inflation rate of 2 percent, and no lower. A little inflation, Yellen said, greased the wheels of economic activity.[11] Citing research by her husband and others, and also the experience of Japan, where inflation was low and the economy barely growing, she said that inflation lower than 2 percent would leave firms and the Fed itself with little room to adapt when shocks hit the economy, and thus leave unemployment unnecessarily high.

Others around the table saw some reason in Yellen's argument. Robert Parry, president of the San Francisco Fed, jumped in. Why not set Yellen's 2 percent goal out as an informal yardstick? Then they could have another meeting to decide what to do next when inflation reached that mark, he said.

"I think that is a great idea," said Broaddus. Yellen's opponent was actually taking her side.

"That would mean more progress than we have made in eleven years," said Parry.

Yellen sought to steer the maestro toward the conclusion the rest of the table was approaching. "Mr. Chairman," she said courteously, "will you define price stability for me?"

He deflected. "Price stability is that state in which expected changes in the general price level do not effectively alter business or household decisions."

"Could you please put a number on that?" Yellen pressed politely, to nervous laughter in the room.

"I would say the number is zero, if inflation is properly measured."

Yellen pounced. "Improperly measured, I believe that heading toward 2 percent inflation would be a good idea, and that we should do so in a slow fashion, looking at what happens along the way."

"Could we leave it at that?" Greenspan responded. "Let us now move on." And he turned to others for their views.

Then something unusual happened. A long list of Fed officials—

governors appointed by the president and leaders of twelve regional Fed banks—agreed on Yellen's number, not Greenspan's, and the chairman acknowledged that 2 percent was the consensus.

Yellen had won the debate. Though nothing was formally stated, 2 percent inflation became the Fed's informal objective. Sixteen years later, the central bank would formally adopt a 2 percent inflation target, which by then was the standard around the world, for many of the reasons Yellen laid out in the summer of 1996.

In the realm of central banking, this was a subtle but important event. It meant that many of the Fed's decisions about interest rates and money from that point on—decisions that drove markets and shaped the borrowing and spending decisions of households and businesses—would be anchored around a more tangible goal. In time a 2 percent inflation target became the Fed's lighthouse.

Two years into her term as a Fed governor, Yellen had established her footing as a policy maker. She was pragmatic and courteous. She changed her mind when circumstances changed. She didn't back down from a fight. And she was always exhaustively prepared when confronted by disagreement.

"She does her homework and she comes to strong positions based on what she believes is correct," Broaddus said later.[12]

11

Yellen in the Clinton White House

Boom Times and Boys' Clubs
1997–1999

By 1996, Greenspan had come to the view that the economy was fundamentally changing. New technologies, powered by ever more advanced computers and computer chips, were making workers more productive in ways that hadn't yet been picked up in economic statistics, he believed. More broadly, as he saw it, an industrial age was passing and a new age, powered by information and ideas, was dawning. This called for a new central bank strategy.

"Virtually unimaginable a half century ago was the extent to which concepts and ideas would substitute for physical resources and human brawn in the production of goods and services," Greenspan said in 1996. "In 1948 radios were still being powered by vacuum tubes. Today, transistors deliver far higher quality with a mere fraction of the bulk. Fiber-optics has replaced huge tonnages of copper wire, and advances in architectural and engineering design have made possible the construction of buildings with much greater floor space but significantly less physical material than the buildings erected just after World War II."[1]

The economy, he liked to argue, was becoming physically lighter because it needed fewer big machines to function. Greenspan saw the shift to a knowledge- and information-oriented economy as a once-in-a-century development with broad implications, like the advent of railroads and telegraph machines in the 1800s, and electricity in the early 1900s. One implication was that workers were becoming at the same time both more productive and more insecure due to the risk that machines would replace their jobs. This combination, he reasoned, was likely to restrain inflation and the kind of wage spiral that had haunted investors and economists since the 1970s. The diminishing risk of inflation, in turn, meant he could keep interest rates lower than the Fed's models said they should be, which meant the economy might grow faster.

Yellen was sympathetic to Greenspan's theory, but by 1996 she came to believe he had taken it too far. She pressed him to start raising interest rates to head off inflation, advice he disregarded. The fact that Yellen pressed Greenspan to raise interest rates was odd; she tended to worry less about inflation than the Fed hawks who pushed for high interest rates. But she wasn't dogmatic about it. She believed the Fed could only push a perceived tradeoff between jobs and inflation so far before a repeat of the 1970s broke out and inflation became a serious problem. She and another Fed governor, Laurence Meyer, went to Greenspan's office before a meeting in September 1996 and urged him to raise rates to take some of the steam out of the economy. She might have been a dove, but more than that, she was a pragmatist who didn't like to take big risks.

"I would characterize the economy as operating in an inflationary danger zone," she said at the meeting, though she chose not to formally dissent when Greenspan said he wanted to hold rates steady. She didn't want to embarrass the chairman. Despite her concerns about inflation, she also agreed with Greenspan that the economy might be changing in long-lasting ways.[2]

Greenspan asked Yellen to write a paper summarizing her views. In a twelve-page document, she observed that people didn't seem to be quitting their jobs as often as they had in the past. Perhaps this was a sign that they were afraid they wouldn't find new jobs. That fear, in turn, might be restraining wages and inflation, as Greenspan predicted would happen. "The absence of any barking from this particular dog strikes me as mild evidence that something has changed," she admitted. Her research, Greenspan said later, "was very useful to me." He shared the paper with other Fed officials to back up his point.

Greenspan was right, as it turned out. An economic boom kicked in that year. Over the prior decade, economic output—all of the cars the nation produced, the restaurant meals it served, the medical visits it provided, the movies it screened, the computer chips it exported, everything—had increased at an annual rate of 3 percent a year, adjusted for inflation. Now "gross domestic product," as it is known, was revving up to an annual growth rate of 4 percent. That might sound small, but it's an immense change for an economy of the size of the United States. Annual output at the time was valued at around $8 trillion by government statisticians. An economy of that size that grew at a rate that was one percentage point faster was producing $80 billion more a year than it would produce under the slower scenario—and that much more income for businesses and households. The step-up in output from that one extra percentage point of growth was greater than the economic output of entire nations, such as Ireland, Chile, Kuwait, and New Zealand.

Worker insecurity eventually subsided when the economic liftoff was accompanied by a hiring boom. The unemployment rate slipped below 5 percent for the first time on a sustained basis since the 1960s, and inflation, as Greenspan predicted, continued to fall. He became a hero of Wall Street, and a hero in the White House. Clinton was easily re-elected, the first time a Democrat would serve two full successive terms since Franklin Delano Roosevelt.

Clinton accomplished this in part by accepting Milton Friedman's ideas about the power of markets and the limits of government involvement in the economy. "We know big government does not have all the answers," he said in his State of the Union address in January 1996. "We know there's not a program for every problem. We have worked to give the American people a smaller, less bureaucratic government in Washington. And we have to give the American people one that lives within its means. The era of big government is over."

For his second term, Clinton asked Yellen to become chair of the Council of Economic Advisers, succeeding Stiglitz. She accepted, but the job would be one of the more unpleasant experiences of her professional career.

The economy didn't trouble her. How could it? Economists started calling it a Goldilocks economy—neither so hot that it caused inflation, nor so cold that unemployment was rising. Everything, Yellen said later, "was beginning to turn up roses."[3] After one glowing jobs report, she and Clinton adviser Gene Sperling stood up and danced in the White House Roosevelt Room as part of their presentation to howling White House aides.

What was troubling was the political game. It was stressful and made her uncomfortable.

Yellen had introduced herself to Washington more than two years earlier as a pragmatic nonpartisan. She was able to pull off that persona at the Fed, an academic institution that sought to insulate itself from politics after the disastrous meddling of Johnson and Nixon in the 1960s and 1970s. But working inside the White House was a totally different game. Inside that gated compound, decisions aren't ever framed simply by mathematical equations or orderly internal debate. They are framed to win policy battles against partisans, to improve the president's public standing, to get that president reelected, to protect and win seats for the party in Congress, and to define an opposition in terms that help win the political contest. Decision-makers—from the president on down to that president's most remote assistants—are often ambitious and proud

individuals intent on advancing their own careers and building and protecting turf. Inside the Fed it felt like a quiet cathedral. Inside the White
House there are war rooms.

Yellen joined a White House already cast with big personalities. That
included Sperling, Clinton's point person on economic policy, a hyper-
active thirty-five-year-old veteran of the Clinton campaigns. He was
known for sleeping in his West Wing office, when he slept at all, and
working his cell phone while putting in time on an exercise bike. He
was made director of Clinton's National Economic Council during the
second term, and later became an adviser for the television show *West
Wing*, marrying one of its writers.

Summers rose inside the US Treasury, becoming its number-two official, making a mark with his intelligence and his unveiled ambition for
bigger Washington jobs. His boss, the Treasury secretary, was Robert
Rubin, a buttoned-down former Goldman Sachs chief executive who
worked closely with Sperling at the NEC before working closely with
Summers at Treasury.

All three had traveled in political circles for years, going back to the
failed presidential campaign of Michael Dukakis in 1988. They had been
with Clinton from the start. Clinton's 1992 campaign manifesto, "Putting People First," was written in two weeks by Sperling, a lawyer by
training who had a knack for casting economic issues in political terms.
He and Summers were tennis partners.

Sperling was demanding, blunt, and kept strange hours. Yellen sometimes found herself sitting outside his office waiting for a word while he
worked his telephones, oblivious to overdue appointments he'd scheduled with her. Sometimes he asked to have discussions well past the early
bedtime she preferred to keep. She sometimes got called into meetings
late, leaving her little time to prepare, and that made her tense. Sometimes she found herself left out altogether by a Clinton organization that
was built before she got there.

By 1997, with the economy booming, Wall Street's fears about runaway government budget deficits had disappeared. Bush and Clinton had both enacted deals with Congress that restrained government spending and raised taxes on high-income households. Shrinking budget deficits meant the government didn't have to sell as many government bonds to borrow money and raise funds for revenue shortfalls. That pushed interest rates down, as Clinton's economic team hoped would happen.

Budget restraint was aided by the end of the Cold War, which left room to cut military spending. Strong economic growth and rising stock values led to an upsurge in income and capital gains tax receipts. The federal government was on track to run budget surpluses for the first time since the 1960s. Now Republicans and Democrats fought over what to do with all the extra money.

Republicans wanted tax cuts. They also wanted to divert Social Security taxes to fund individual retirement accounts. Clinton wanted to pay down debt, arguing that would make programs like Social Security and Medicare safer in the long run. Sperling drove the process, formulating a political strategy that echoed the "Putting People First" document he'd written during Clinton's campaign. He dubbed the new plan "Save Social Security First."

Yellen knew she had walked into the job with an inherent disadvantage: she had no personal relationship with the most powerful man in the world. "People who tend to know a president best are those who were with him from the early days of his campaign. I didn't have the opportunity to develop that sort of closeness," she said later. "I wasn't even in the White House in his first term."[4]

The White House had a completely different feel than the Fed. It was tight and cramped and felt like a bunker, with grenades flying in and out between political opponents all day, every day. It elicited a bravado in people that didn't exist in the subdued and stately halls of the central bank, where she felt comfortable.

Something else bubbled under the surface in the White House. Despite his efforts to bring more women into top jobs in government, an effort that benefited Yellen, Clinton's White House still felt like a sweaty locker room where key decision-makers around the president were blunt, boisterous, and ambitious men. Women sometimes felt run over by them. One of the first people to call the White House out on the atmosphere was Clinton's first spokesperson, Dee Dee Myers, who called it a "white boys club" and a "masculine cabal" in a 1996 book by journalist Jeffrey Birnbaum, *Madhouse*.[5] During Yellen's time there, Clinton's affair with White House intern Monica Lewinsky broke into public light, which exacerbated that feeling.

Yellen managed to connect to Clinton by appealing to his wonky side. Clinton devoured her weekly reports on the economy and academic research and sometimes asked for more. Once he sent her a two-hundred-page academic book he'd read on global finance with a note: "What do you think about the comments I made in the margin?"[6] Before her weekly meetings with him, she spent hours writing out exactly what she wanted to say. When her colleague Alicia Munnell asked if she was ready, Yellen often responded that she wanted five more minutes to work something out.

Munnell, another Harvard-trained PhD economist and a member of the CEA's three-member board, viewed Yellen's compulsive preparation as an endearing window into her character. She saw Yellen as brilliant and perfectly capable of winging it if needed. She worked so hard before meetings because, like a straight-A kid at school, she didn't want to fail and made damn sure she wouldn't before the president.

Munnell at one time thought she might get the top CEA job herself, and she was a little hurt when Yellen got it instead. But Yellen quickly won over Munnell's loyalty by going out of her way to form a connection inside the office and out. Once, after a particularly long and difficult day at the White House compound, Yellen turned to Munnell and told her there was only one solution to their exhaustion: they needed to go out and down some martinis. Munnell found Yellen's laugh contagious, and she also knew how to unwind.

Yellen did have a very public role in one divisive debate: climate change. In 1997 Clinton and Gore were preparing for a meeting of world leaders in Kyoto to set out goals for reducing greenhouse gas emissions. It became Yellen's job to measure the economic costs of different scenarios and to assess how best to respond. "What really makes a difference at the Council of Economic Advisers is shooting down bad ideas," she said later.[7]

Gasoline taxes. Caps on emissions by big coal-fired plants. Investments in new technologies like solar energy or wind farms. Efficiency mandates for new cars. Planting trees that soaked up carbon. Methane-reduction mandates. There were many choices and deciphering how they would play out in the economy was a complex task. The administration couldn't just set a goal without explaining how it would reach that goal. The White House set up a task force to come up with estimates, but its efforts got bogged down by competing views from different agencies. When that process failed, Yellen took on the job to figure it out on her own.

Economists have a term, *externality*, to describe some damaging outcome of economic activity that hurts an outsider. Suppose a factory situated along a river pumps chemical waste into the water. Suppose also that the chemical waste pollutes the drinking water downstream, and kills fish that are caught to feed a community. Chicago economists and Keynesians both agreed this was a problem. In the Chicago school of thought, the victims and the polluters could work out private agreements through negotiation to compensate the victims or stop and reverse the pollution. In this view, these disagreements were about enforcing individual property rights.

But externality problems were often complicated. The polluters and the victims might not be clearly defined, their respective rights not clearly delineated, or damages not easily measured. In those cases it was often a question of whether government should step in, and if it did, which tools to employ. Chicago economists, though typically averse to taxes, agreed that in some cases a tax against a pollutant was the most efficient way to tilt behavior against activity that hurt others.

Climate change was an externality problem on a scale unlike anything the world had confronted before. Assessing and finding solutions was never going to be easy. The science on potential damages from greenhouse gas accumulation in the atmosphere was uncertain, evolving, and tended to focus on what might happen in the future. Moreover, the sources of the problem were in flux and the victims uncertain. The United States, as the world's twentieth-century industrial powerhouse, was responsible for a great deal of carbon and methane already in the atmosphere. However, emissions were rising rapidly in developing countries as they raced to escape poverty by industrializing. Thus, they were becoming a growing part of the problem. Taxes were highly unpopular in the United States and hit low-income households the hardest. Clinton proposed an energy tax in 1993 to reduce budget deficits and address climate change, but faced stiff opposition. Before Clinton, Bush's presidency had been derailed in part by his decision to go back on a promise not to raise taxes.

How much economic pain should a nation be prepared to bear to forestall a likely problem of unknown consequences in the future? Who should bear the greatest burden? How was Clinton to coordinate action on a wide and diffuse problem?

"It became a question of how it could be done without killing the economy," Yellen said.[8] She was particularly focused on China. Its industries were so inefficient that one effective way to tackle the greenhouse gas problem might be to pay Chinese businesses and households to clean up. To economists this seemed logical; to some environmentalists it seemed immoral, a cop-out on the responsibility of the United States to take its own action.

Behind the scenes, Yellen and Summers joined in a push against a team backed by Vice President Al Gore, arguing against moving too aggressively to cut carbon emissions with highly ambitious short-run goals. That could damage the economy, they said. Their advice was to focus on the long term and set flexible goals. The science behind the problem was evolving and the economics were complex; the United States would have to learn as it went.

Gore believed that technological advancement would keep the costs down. Environmentalists in the administration thought the economists were holding back an ambitious agenda with dour warnings about the costs. In internal debates they called the economists "lemon suckers," a jab at their sour pronouncements.

In addition to sizing up the costs internally, it became Yellen's job to sell the administration's agenda to Congress and the public without killing it by setting off alarms about damaging the economy. She worried to colleagues she might have to make points that she couldn't honestly defend. "It boils down to this—if we do it dumb, it could cost a lot, but if we do it smart, it will cost much less and, indeed, could produce net benefits in the long run," Yellen told a congressional committee in July 1997.[9]

But that wasn't the line from her testimony that made headlines. Instead, she was skewered publicly for saying at the same hearing that building a precise model of the economic tradeoffs had proven futile because the complexity of the problem was so great. Opponents of action seized on her words to argue that the administration had no idea what it was getting the United States into. Those who supported climate action were enraged that Yellen had undermined their argument. The truth was it was hard to say with precision in part because the administration itself hadn't set out the policies it intended to enact to get there.

That July, the Senate passed a resolution urging the president not to sign any agreement to lower emissions unless developing countries agreed as well. Why cut America's own emissions, only for China and India to increase theirs? Nobody wanted to derail the strong economy for nothing. The resolution—introduced by Robert Byrd, a Democrat from the coal-producing state of West Virginia, and Chuck Hagel, a Republican from Nebraska—passed by a vote of 95–0, handcuffing the administration before it agreed to anything in Japan.

Yellen and Summers made their case to the president and vice president together, arguing for a flexible, market-oriented, go-slow approach. They lost the argument.

When Gore went to Kyoto in December and signed on to a rollback of emissions to 1990 levels by 2010, Yellen was left in a bind. She had to defend a policy she thought was too aggressive and hadn't been fleshed out. Opponents were demanding to know what it would cost to live up to the agreement, and she had already said it was hard to know. She wanted to support Clinton's agenda, but she also didn't want to shade the truth for political advantage. She agonized over the issue and contemplated resigning if she felt she had to lie about the economics behind her thinking.

In March 1998, Yellen released estimates that said the costs could be modest if the United States employed market-friendly policies. Lawmakers ripped her from right and left, the right saying her estimates weren't credible, the left angry that she said there would be any cost at all.

She insisted that the Kyoto goals could be met with little cost, but only under conditions that rivals in the administration opposed, including the imposition of a carbon tax and involving countries like China in a global trading system that gave poor countries credit and the potential for economic gain in return for restraining their emissions.

Yellen saw that many Chinese families heated their homes with coal-burning stoves. By helping them convert to more efficient energy sources, she believed, the United States could start bringing down global emissions at little cost. In addition, a gasoline tax at home was economically appealing because it was much more efficient than government mandates, though it was politically perilous because it hit households in the pocketbook.

Before a hearing that March, Yellen practiced her responses with CEA staff members, who took turns lacing into her to ready her for the inevitable blowback. The hearing went on for four hours and Yellen found herself in a hail of criticism she'd never experienced before.

One of her fiercest interrogators was John Dingell, a powerful congressman from Michigan and a Democrat, who was determined to protect the auto industry from regulation. She had testified before his committee the previous summer. Now she was back.

"Dr. Yellen, you testified that—and I quote now—the analysis and assessment had proved futile and would be abandoned," he said. "You did that before this committee. Now how is it then that you are going to persuade the public that your new analysis is more than a post-hoc rationalization of a previously negotiated policy?"[10]

Yellen danced around the issue. "I testified before this committee and used the word futile but I never said that all economic analysis, or all modeling, is futile," she said. "I have not tried to offer a definitive analysis today. Indeed my testimony is quite clear in indicating the kinds of numbers looking at typical household impacts are merely illustrative numbers that show that modeled results are consistent with what is my real conclusion, namely: that given successful implementation of the flexibility conditions—where, what and when flexibility—that the cost will be modest."

"Your testimony includes some rather heroic assumptions," he pushed back.

Yellen tried to make a case to Zhu Rongji, China's top economics minister. She wanted China to sign on to an agreement to reduce global carbon emissions. The United States could help, but it was a tough sell. China was still a poor country, and the carbon already in the air was the result of emissions from rich countries, not poor countries. Why should China bear the burden of reducing what rich countries like the United States started when China was still impoverished?

Dingell was with Yellen for one of her visits to China, part of a large entourage traveling with Clinton for a state visit. When the group visited the Great Wall outside of Beijing, Dingell befriended Yellen. He told her he liked her and not to take the attacks too personally. It was just politics. A couple of years later, a former CEA staff economist, Joseph Aldy, approached Dingell at a luncheon. The tall congressman put his arm around Aldy's shoulder and told him, "They asked her to make chicken salad out of chicken shit with this Kyoto thing." He said he appreciated the great job she did on the economy and went on his way.

Clinton never submitted the Kyoto agreement for Senate ratification, knowing it would fail. President George W. Bush later declared it dead.

The debate left lasting impressions on Yellen about the rough-and-tumble world of Washington politics and about her discomfort being asked to say things she couldn't back up with honest analysis.

US carbon emissions would in fact rise and then fall substantially over the next two decades, to below the 1990 levels as set out in Kyoto, but not because the United States had enacted any policy to make it happen. It happened because shocks were looming to the economy that in 1997 nobody saw coming, shocks that drove the country into recession and reduced its output of carbon. Another large and unpredicted economic change drove down US emissions: a fracking boom in Texas gave drillers access to cheap natural gas, making coal a less profitable source of energy at US power plants.

China, at the same time, became an industrial powerhouse and its emissions soared far above anyone's projections in the 1990s. By 2020 its share of global greenhouse gas emissions exceeded that of all developed economies combined. It did not come around to agreeing to reduce its emissions until after its astonishing economic boom, which few saw coming either.

"When Janet was at the Fed, I supported her as much as possible by taking over household duties," Akerlof said. "When she was at the White House my role in providing psychological support in the daily political storms was yet more important."[11]

They lived in a redbrick house in the affluent Chevy Chase neighborhood, near Washington's border with Maryland. When they traveled, they flew in the coach sections of airplanes. Akerlof was perfectly comfortable with Yellen's desire to arrive at the gate two or three hours before takeoff. Like her, he was risk-averse. After flights, they stood in line inconspicuously like everybody else for taxis. Yellen's professional wardrobe came from Talbots, an off-the-rack women's clothing retailer; she dressed her suits up with silk Hermès scarves. Akerlof's uniform remained khaki pants and hiking shoes, which kept his achy feet comfortable.

One area where they never skimped was in Robby's education. High school was a prep school called St. Albans, an all-boys school near a towering cathedral in Washington's affluent Northwest area. St. Albans was home to Washington's elites and their children, spanning the political spectrum. Vice President Al Gore had studied there, as had Bill Oakley and Josh Weinstein, whose high school friendship led to collaborations as writers for the television show *The Simpsons*. Neil and Marvin Bush, sons of President George H. W. and Barbara Bush, and Jesse Jackson Jr., the eldest son of Jesse Jackson, also made it their home.

Akerlof and Yellen took turns dropping Robby off at school in the morning. Yellen was always up early, before 6:00 a.m., to have her coffee and quietly prepare for the day. She liked to be back in bed by 8:30 p.m., though working in the White House put an end to that. In the evening Robby took a taxi home. Sometimes he prepared dinner for his parents. Sometimes he and George went out for sushi dinners, stopping off to pick Yellen up a roast chicken for dinner when she worked late.

Robby spent one summer as an intern at the CEA, near his mom. By 1999 he had become a straight-A student like his parents. He was off to

Yale, which his parents attended, and majored in math and economics, also like his parents.

Akerlof's own theories branched in new directions during the family's Washington years. From the issue of looting, he moved on to a far more abstract subject tied to sociology.

One of Akerlof's former PhD students from Berkeley, Rachel Kranton, had become an assistant professor at the University of Maryland and lived in the area. They were close. She had taken care of the family's cat, Chelsea, when Yellen and Akerlof first moved to the nation's capital.[12]

In 1995 Akerlof and Kranton struck up a conversation about the choices people made in work, school, and politics. Why did women gravitate to certain occupations, like nursing or teaching grade school, while men gravitated to other occupations, like medicine or teaching college? The skill sets weren't all that different, but women and men tended to self-select into specific groups. And why did some groups of schoolkids push each other to do well in class, while other groups ostracized their own friends for getting good grades? The economic incentives for schooling were the same, but children responded to them differently depending on their social position. And then there was this: What drew certain people to follow political parties or movements with emotional zeal, or to angrily ostracize certain groups?

Kranton had a theory that intrigued Akerlof. She believed that people defined their identities around the groups they traveled in, and that they placed great weight on their sense of identity and their attachment to these groups. This attachment drove decisions they made. The theory defied conventional economic thinking that individuals made choices simply to advance their financial standing.

They worked at the idea together for five years. Akerlof drove an old brown Toyota, which reminded Robby of his father's patchy sweaters. Akerlof would pick Kranton up at her Chevy Chase home in the morning on Fridays and work on the concept with her all day at Brookings, where he had an office. Then he would drive her home, often picking up Robby at school on the way back. Robby sat in the back seat and listened as the two hashed out a new field they wanted to pioneer, which they called "identity economics." Yellen heard about it at the dinner table at the end of her long days in the White House.

Akerlof and Kranton's research seemed irrelevant to many economists for a long time, but that would eventually change.

In 1999, after new financial turmoil sprang up in Asia and Russia, Greenspan, Summers, and Rubin turned up staring confidently from the cover of *Time*, which dubbed them the "Committee to Save the World." A financial crisis had engulfed many of Asia's fast-growing economies, with the notable exception of China. South Korea, Thailand, and Indonesia—among those hit hardest—had all gone through a period of aggressive bank lending in property markets. Many of the loans went bad, destabilizing the banks and driving the economies into recession. Russia teetered with bad loans too. It was the job of Clinton's economic team to insulate the United States from the problem and get support to wobbly countries through loans from the International Monetary Fund.

Their approach seemed to work. The US economic boom at home continued, and the unemployment rate kept falling. *Time* called Greenspan, Rubin, and Summers the Three Marketeers, supreme policy makers who navigated the economy through market turbulence to a strong and safe place.[13]

Yellen wasn't mentioned in the article. She was mentioned in a *Wall Street Journal* article on the crisis, though. Akerlof had suggested to David Wessel, a *Journal* reporter, that the world's big economies—the United States, Japan, and Europe—should collectively borrow $700 billion and lend the money directly to the poorer countries. The poor countries could spend the money to boost their economies, and pay it back when they recovered.

Yellen told Wessel her husband's idea was crazy.[14]

12

Trade in the Twilight of a Golden Age

China, Mexico, and Ricardo's Theory of Advantage
1993–2001

When Paul Samuelson was a young man at Harvard, he befriended the great mathematician and physicist Stanislaw Ulam, whose work on the Manhattan Project helped lead to the development of atomic bombs and the idea of computer simulation. The young physicist enjoyed razzing Samuelson. Ulam challenged him to name one idea in economics that wasn't already obvious to everyone, and was also verifiably true and consequential. Samuelson was stumped at first; then he told Ulam it was the idea that free trade was good for all nations.

That old idea about trade drove two important economic debates that bookended Yellen's time in Washington and defined the divisive world she inherited years later: whether to pursue trade agreements, first with Mexico, and second with China.

Clinton completed a Mexico trade deal before Yellen joined the White House, though she later played a role defending the administration's policy. The China trade debate heated up after Robby went off to college in 1999, and Yellen and Akerlof decided to return to Berkeley. Before leaving Washington, Yellen supported Clinton's decision to strengthen trade ties with China, and she later signed on to a letter of top economists supporting the policy.

In few areas in all of economics was there as much consensus as on the issue of trade, a consensus Yellen largely embraced and Akerlof doubted. Trade debates dated all the way back to the economist David Ricardo, who lived during the late 1700s and early 1800s, the Enlightenment age of intellectual ferment about economics and politics. Beyond Adam Smith and the Marquis de Condorcet, John Stuart Mill and Jeremy Bentham were building out ideas about the primacy of individual liberty in the governance of human affairs and the place of happiness in individual endeavors.

And then there was Ricardo, whose closest friend was also his fiercest intellectual rival: Thomas Malthus. The two quarreled about the simple question of how to feed Europe's growing populations. Malthus argued that European populations would have trouble growing because the region could run out of food to nourish people. Ricardo thought more food could be produced and consumed if the government got out of the way. He loathed the British Corn Laws that protected wealthy English landowners by limiting imports. Repeal the Corn Laws and the food supply would expand, Ricardo argued.

Out of these debates with Malthus grew Ricardo's theory of comparative advantage. His premise was simple: nations are better off when they specialize in producing what they're good at, and trade with each other for the rest. Ricardo saw no reason to protect landowners with laws that impeded competition from the import of grains. For the good of the broader population, he thought, imports should be embraced and not restricted.

Ricardo used wine and wool to make his point. Suppose England was most adept at making wool, and Portugal was most productive when making wine. It was in the interest of both nations to produce what they made most efficiently and trade with each other for the rest. Both sides would end up with more to consume and would be better off than if they made their own wine and their own wool and didn't trade with each other at all.

This math helps show the logic: Say 100 British workers could make 200 wool pants, or the same 100 workers could make 100 jugs of wine. Say 100 Portuguese workers could make 100 wool pants, or they could make 200 jugs of wine. Say also that one jug of wine was deemed to be equal in value to one pair of pants. Britain could make 200 pants and trade its surplus for Portugal's surplus of wine, and both countries would end up with more wine and pants in total—100 pants and 100 jugs—than either could produce on its own. Without trade, England could split its 100 workers and produce at most 100 pants and 50 jugs of wine. Portugal's 100 workers could make 100 jugs of wine and 50 pants at most on their own.

Ricardo showed the math of specializing in one product and trading for the other worked out even if one country was more productive at making both wine and trousers than the other. It was a complicated concept that defied notions of a winner-take-all world of competition. Some simple math showed that specialization and trade maximized output and consumption for everyone, no matter what.

It fell to two economists after World War II to expand on Ricardo's century-old idea.

The first was Samuelson, who formalized Ricardo's concept mathematically and examined the notion under different conditions. What if workers moved to one country or the other? What happened when more than two products were involved? What happened when prices or exchange rates changed? He essentially confirmed that trade was a win-win, but with important caveats. While one country might be better off in all by trading with another country, some people could be left behind within those countries, like laid-off winemakers in the UK or laid-off trouser-makers in Portugal. Samuelson pointed out that one challenge was deciding society's responsibility to help those left behind by free trade. What was the government's role? How much should people be expected to adapt on their own without government help when trade hurt their industries?

The second leading light in trade was Paul Krugman. Raised in suburban Long Island with an affection for science fiction, Krugman arrived at MIT quiet and self-assured. As a teen he was a fan of Isaac Asimov's Foundation novels, which conjured stories of barbarian societies tamed by scientists called psychohistorians, who used math to decode human activity and stop galactic calamities from unfolding. To Krugman, the proposition of saving humanity with scientific predictions of human behavior translated into becoming an economist, which led him to MIT for his PhD studies.

Krugman found new ways to demonstrate that trade was good. Two countries might specialize in the same product, such as luxury cars, and still benefit from trade by increasing the variety of goods available to consumers. With trade, consumers benefit from a broad menu of luxury cars, including American-made Cadillacs, German-made BMWs, and Swedish Volvos. Moreover, producing for a global marketplace gave firms incentive to build giant plants and mass-produce, increasing their efficiency and explaining the rise of cities in the industrial era, where firms concentrated masses of workers.

In modernizing trade theory, Krugman spurred a new wave of research into how the economy shaped where people lived, and he also gave the profession new ammunition with which to defend Ricardo's and Samuelson's favorite concept. The papers he wrote on trade launched him onto a lecture circuit among the field's most respected economists, a world he captured in an essay: "In the modern academic world there tends, as in any given field—whether it is international finance, Jane Austen studies, or some branch of endocrinology—to be a 'circuit,' the people who get invited to speak at academic conferences, who form a sort of de facto nomenklatura. I used to refer to the circuit in international economics as the 'floating crap game.' It's hard to get onto the circuit—it takes at least two really good papers, one to get noticed and a second to show that the first wasn't a fluke—but once you are in, the constant round of conferences and invited papers makes it easy to stay in." He was off to budget hotels in exotic places, paid for by conference organizers, a voice among what he called a "true, and wonderfully unpretentious, elite."[1]

In 1993, Clinton inherited the Bush administration's pursuit of the North American Free Trade Agreement (NAFTA) with Canada and Mexico. The agreement was politically divisive, an area where liberal consumer advocate Ralph Nader found common ground with conservative nationalist commentator Patrick Buchanan in asserting that Americans would lose jobs and income by opening up to poorer countries. The economists saw it as an obvious choice, though, and won over the new president. "Assertions that NAFTA will spur an exodus of U.S. jobs to Mexico are without basis," a group of leading economists wrote in an open letter to Clinton in 1993. "The agreement will be a net positive for the United States."[2]

For decades the Chicago economists and the Keynesians had battled each other on a vast terrain of economic ideas about markets, taxation, government spending, unemployment, inflation, stocks, central banks, and more. But Ricardo's idea was beyond disagreement among the leading antagonists in the field. Samuelson signed the NAFTA letter. So did his intellectual adversary, Milton Friedman. Tobin and Solow signed on, as did Anna Schwartz and Robert Lucas.

Yellen, then still in academia, signed the letter too. Akerlof wasn't asked for his view, and didn't sign. At home, he and Yellen disagreed. Economists always said the benefits of trade far outweighed the costs—but Akerlof suspected the costs might be greater or more acute than the economists acknowledged. He liked to say that trade was the only matter on which he ever disagreed with his wife, his idea of humor, though the joke was difficult to explain to others.[3]

A year after his election, Clinton passed NAFTA in Congress, with strong support from Republicans and a mix of support and opposition from Democrats. "We cannot stop global change," he said. "We cannot repeal the international economic competition that is everywhere. We can only harness the energy to our benefit. Now we must recognize that the only way for a wealthy nation to grow richer is to export, to simply find new customers for the products and services it makes."[4]

The 1980s and early 1990s seemed to prove the free trade advocates right. The decade had begun with the nation in fear about the rise of Japan and the threat it posed to US industries such as electronics and autos. US automakers had reeled as Honda, Toyota, and Nissan cars took over US roads. As if to rub salt in the wound, Japanese investors bought iconic US landmarks like the Pebble Beach golf course on the California coast and Manhattan's Rockefeller Center near Central Park. But Japan's economy came unglued. Its banks lent to unprofitable Japanese firms and then found themselves sitting on bad loans and reluctant to make new ones. Its stock market crashed in 1990 and kept going down for a decade.

All the while, the US economy roared back after NAFTA and the Japan battles. With the technology sector booming, manufacturing employment rose, and whole new industries in information and telecommunications emerged. Schumpeter had extolled the virtues of creative destruction—a free economy's ability to plant new industries where old ones died—and his views seemed to prove true, with the United States taking its place as the world's sole superpower, remaking old Communist powers in its free-market image.

Yellen authored Clinton's 1998 *Economic Report of the President*, which devoted a chapter to the benefits of trade and played down the impact of imports from Mexico. One concern was that competition from low-wage workers outside the United States would depress the wages of workers at home. The report acknowledged that US wage growth had indeed slowed, but said that likely wasn't because of competition from low-wage workers in places like Mexico. Instead, it argued, wage growth had slowed because of a puzzling slowdown in the productivity of American workers. To get wages up faster, US workers needed to turn out their widgets faster, too. Though productivity had declined in earlier decades, explaining the wage slowdown, the good news was that productivity was now turning up, which suggested wages would start rising, too.[5]

Then there was the argument that competition from countries like Mexico killed American jobs. That notion was hard to defend because the unemployment rate was falling. Moreover, the government had enacted programs to help workers who lost jobs to trade. In short, in the mid-1990s Americans seemed to adapt to churning in the global economy and come out on top.

The report's conclusion largely reflected the consensus thinking laid out by Ricardo, Samuelson, and Krugman, a consensus that focused in particular on how trade affected consumption. "Consumers in open economies benefit from a wider variety of goods at lower prices than do consumers in economies that resist competition from foreign suppliers," it said. "The economy as a whole benefits from an increased ability to devote its scarce resources to economic activities that it performs relatively efficiently." All one needed to do was take a walk down an aisle in Walmart, where shelves were overloaded with low-cost imports, to see the benefits.

Akerlof wasn't outspoken about his trade skepticism because it wasn't an area in which he specialized, but others who voiced doubts were shot down by the pro-trade academic consensus. Krugman was shy and somewhat awkward in person, but his writing was sharp, vivid, and withering. He lashed out at people he called "pop internationalists," among them Clinton's labor secretary, Robert Reich, who were skeptical about trade and sympathetic to protecting industries being overrun by imports. Krugman saw protectionists on the right, such as Ross Perot and Patrick Buchanan, as outright barbarians.

Harvard economics professor Dani Rodrik, a bright skeptic, was one of the people stampeded by pro-trade advocates. Economists knew that trade created winners and losers. They knew that while the overall economic pie might get larger when countries dropped barriers to trade, some segments of the population were bound to suffer. Rodrik saw signals of social tension bubbling up as work became more unstable around the world—labor strikes in France and South Korea, a revival of communism in Russia and Eastern Europe, the emergence of protectionists like Buchanan and Perot in America. The backlash shouldn't be ignored, Rodrik asserted in his slim volume *Has Globalization Gone Too Far?* "Social disintegration is not a spectator sport—those on the sidelines also get splashed with mud from the field," he warned. "Ultimately, the deepening of social fissures can harm all."[6]

Rodrik sent Krugman a copy of his book, hoping to get an endorsement, but Krugman declined. He didn't disagree with the economic analysis, he told Rodrik, but the book would only arm the barbarians, and he didn't want to be a part of that. In Rodrik's view the economists shouldn't be taking sides. "The economists had become advocates rather than analysts," he would say later.[7]

Yellen supported the Clinton administration's effort to bring China into the World Trade Organization, the Geneva-based body created as a referee for global trade, enforcing agreed-upon rules. Her 1998 *Economic Report* described the deal as a chance to open China's protected markets to US companies. So-called trade adjustment programs would help workers adapt when imports hurt their industries, giving laid-off people unemployment benefits and subsidized retraining for other industries.

In 1999, as Clinton was finalizing a trade deal with China, Yellen and Akerlof moved back to Berkeley, thinking Yellen's time in government was over. Akerlof gave his old Toyota to a bus driver who worked a route in Chevy Chase before they left.

The Clinton era drew to an end on a high note. The president rang in the new millennium at a White House New Year's Eve party with an A-list of stars including Muhammad Ali, Bono, Elizabeth Taylor, Robert De Niro, Sophia Loren, and Will Smith. Greenspan and Gene Sperling were there too. Corporate sponsors paid millions to mingle with the celebrities.[8] Five days later the president nominated Greenspan to a fourth consecutive term. With the stock market soaring, a gleeful Clinton joked that he wanted to create a website called Alan.com and take it public. "Then we could pay the debt off even before 2015," he said.

Greenspan could have been forgiven had he wanted to retire, Clinton said, but Greenspan relished the idea of another term; the job, the Fed chairman said, was "like eating peanuts. You keep doing it, keep doing it, and you never get tired." At their side was the nation's new Treasury secretary, Lawrence Summers, who ascended to Rubin's job in 1999, as had been planned at the beginning of Clinton's second term.

In September 2000, with a Senate vote of 83–15, Clinton convinced Congress to allow normal US trade relations with China and paved the way for its admission into the World Trade Organization. For years the United States had already been granting China annual, but temporary, access to US markets with low tariff barriers. Normal trade relations removed the uncertainty of renewals every year. Clinton hoped it would formalize China's cooperation with a club of rules-bound trading partners and help open the markets of the world's most populous country to US companies hungry for a billion new customers. He also hoped an open China would lead to a more democratic China, and one less threatening to others. Reformers were in charge in Beijing, and Clinton wanted to empower them.

A collection of 149 economists—including all of the luminaries who signed the NAFTA letter—banded together again to support the move.

"There is much more at stake here than our economic self-interests," Clinton said after the vote. The decision, he said, was "about building a world in which more human beings have more freedom, more control over their lives, more contact with others than ever before."[9]

It seemed the United States could do no wrong. The unemployment rate dropped below 4 percent. Wages were rising again, even with the increased competition from Mexico and other nations, in part because unemployment was so low. It was hard for companies to find available workers, so they bid up their pay to lure them. Economists James Stock and Mark Watson coined a new phrase to describe this period: the Great Moderation. After decades of battling boom-and-bust cycles that sent unemployment and inflation up and down, economists seemed to have conquered the business cycle with a combination of market-opening re-form and smart but small government interventions centered largely on the Fed's interest-rate policies. Financial turbulence bubbled from time to time—in Orange County, in Mexico, in Asia's "tiger economies" and Russia—but it all looked manageable.

The great twentieth-century debates over the ideas of Keynes and Friedman seemed to have been resolved. The market had largely won; the *Wall Street Journal* declared capitalism "giddy with triumph." But as Clinton and his young economists saw it, a lean and nimble government still had a significant role to play in smoothing out the rough edges of sometimes turbulent market forces, and they thought they had figured out how to do that. "I believe we can harness the power of the new economy to help people everywhere fulfill their dreams," Clinton said at a White House conference on the economy in April 2000.[10] Greenspan spoke later at the same conference. "Something profoundly different from the typical postwar business cycle has emerged in recent years," he began; if the United States kept inflation low and built on its trade, budget, and education policies, "I do not believe we can go far wrong."[11]

Greenspan was incorrect. A great deal was about to go wrong.

Part III

Crisis

13

Akerlof Wins
a Nobel,
Yellen Returns
to the Fed

Lessons from a Financial Bubble
and Jobless Recovery
2000–2004

In the autumn of 2001, Akerlof got an early-morning call at his Berkeley, California, home. It was October, the time of year when the Royal Swedish Academy of Sciences announced the Nobel Prize awards for economics. Akerlof was in bed in his pajamas, snoring, when the phone rang. Yellen was in the other room. Akerlof thought perhaps his friend Joseph Stiglitz had won the prize, and a reporter was calling to ask him for a comment. He was partly right. He and Stiglitz had both won the prize, together with a third economist, Michael Spence.

Over time, Akerlof's "Lemons" paper had become known as a modern masterpiece. It launched a new branch of economics that uncovered the market distortions created when buyers and sellers didn't have access to the same information. It also showed the big lessons economists could learn by zeroing in on small industries and markets. After all of its early rejections, the paper was a testament to Akerlof's perseverance and creative thinking. But he wasn't expecting this. He thought his theories were too unconventional to be recognized with the field's top prize. "This is something that happens to other people," he told a reporter in a telephone interview. "In fact, I'm not sure this is me talking to you."[1]

That December, George, Yellen, and Robby were off to Stockholm. The ceremonies included a presentation by the king of Sweden and a lavish dinner under starlit skies, attended by intellectuals dressed in long black tuxedos and gowns. Yellen wore a floor-length metallic silver-and-gold St. John knit dress. Their economist friends the Romers came along.

It was the hundredth anniversary of the Nobel Prize. The Grand Hotel in Stockholm, on the waterfront overlooking Sweden's Royal Palace, buzzed with a century's worth of prizewinners. James Watson, the American biologist who discovered the double-helix structure of DNA, strolled under the hotel's crystal chandeliers, as did Günter Grass, the German writer whose novel *The Tin Drum* traced the rise of Nazism in his hometown of Danzig. Paul Samuelson and Milton Friedman attended and debated each other loudly at dinner as others listened in.

Dressed in a dark suit and tie, Akerlof delivered a lecture to the dignitaries who descended on Stockholm. He didn't start with fancy charts or complex mathematical formulas written in Greek lettering, the common language of modern economics. Instead he started with an image from a children's book he'd read to Robby when his son was small: the cover of Richard Scarry's *Cars and Trucks and Things That Go*. It depicted cartoon animals in a parade of multicolored vehicles, including fire engines, taxis, and bucket loaders, another of Akerlof's ideas of a joke, a playful reference to his work on used cars. But he had a more serious point in mind: economists needed to use creative new vehicles to grasp reality.

Akerlof was pushing back against the conventional wisdom of a giddy era. In the real world, he said, the economy doesn't always find the fine equilibrium that seemed to emerge during the Great Moderation. He cited his work with Yellen on the complex behavior of job markets. He also cited the research of Robert Shiller, Richard Thaler, and Lawrence Summers on the inherent instability of stock markets. Behavioral economists, he argued, saw beyond theory to the true role of human folly in the working of markets. Keynes often blamed market failures on psychological propensities and irrationalities, Akerlof noted. "The economics profession tamed Keynesian economics. They domesticated it as they translated it into the 'smooth' mathematics of classical economics. But economies, like lions, are wild and dangerous. Modern behavioral economics has rediscovered the wild side of macroeconomic behavior."[2]

As Akerlof spoke, a financial bubble was already well into the process of bursting, and the giddy era was drawing to a sobering end.

The tech stock boom of the 1990s had led to an investment boom by US firms in buildings, computers, fiber-optic cables, and other gear that fueled the internet revolution. That surge of investment generated long-run benefits to the economy, but its costs were now coming due. When tech stock prices collapsed in 2000, business investment tumbled too. The United States fell into recession, ending a record-long economic expansion that had lasted a full decade. Investors, journalists, and regulators revealed how a wave of accounting fraud had fueled the preceding boom as business executives, wanting to cash in on stock incentives tied to corporate profits, cooked their books. It looked a bit like the looting Akerlof and Paul Romer had described in their 1993 paper.

The most glaring example was Enron Corporation, an energy trading company with a parking lot full of Ferraris, Maseratis, and Bentleys. Some called the executive section of the lot "bonus baby row."[3] In 2000 Enron had a market value of $70 billion, making it the seventh most valuable company in the United States. It reported more than $100 billion in revenue, some of it built up on complex sham accounting. Over the course of five months in 2001 the company collapsed, running from the resignation of its CEO, Jeffrey Skilling, in August to its bankruptcy in December. Enron's list of bank lenders was fifty-four pages long. When the lenders figured out the fraud, they bailed out. Enron, left with no cash to finance its operations, was dead.

The worst moments in a horrible year came on a mild late-summer day in New York and Washington, DC. On September 11, 2001, nineteen men trained by the al-Qaeda terrorist group hijacked four planes, flying two of them into the World Trade Center complex in Manhattan and one into the Pentagon. The fourth, retaken by passengers, crashed in a field in Pennsylvania. Thousands of Americans died. Recession already seemed to be lurking because of the tech bust; this shock made it a certainty. The nation's confidence was shaken.

The markers for economic trouble had already been out there. Akerlof noted in his Nobel speech that all it took was a reading of history to identify them.

Akerlof pointed to earlier bubbles traced out by another MIT economics professor named Charles Kindleberger in his 1978 book *Manias, Panics and Crashes: A History of Financial Crises*. Kindleberger didn't use math to do his economics; he used history books, and saw patterns in events. Bubbles, he found, tended to start with some innovation that was difficult to value but created alluring profit opportunities for those who seized them. Such bubbles were well documented going as far back as 1636, when people in Amsterdam speculated on new varieties of magnificently striped and speckled tulips. At one point during that so-called tulipmania, legend had it that a single Viceroy bulb fetched two bundles of wheat and four of rye, eight pigs, a dozen sheep, two containers of wine, four tons of butter, a thousand pounds of cheese, a bed, some clothing, and a silver beaker.[4]

Fascination with innovations turned into speculation. Sometimes this was fed by willing banks that lent gobs of money to investors. Before long, speculation became detached from reality and turned into mania, feeding frenzies for profit driven by delusion, greed, and fear of missing out. Swindlers, eager to make a quick buck, jumped in, scamming others with promises they couldn't fulfill. When reality struck, investors suddenly spurned the assets they had pushed too aggressively, and markets collapsed. Kindleberger called this the "revulsion" phase. Banks that made loans that fed the boom were then stuck with customers who couldn't pay and collateral that was worthless. The people hurt by this collapse then looked to authorities to fix the financial fallout and punish the swindlers.

Kindleberger's narrative included stories of legendary scammers including Robert Knight, who helped cook the books of the South Sea Company, an early 1700s British firm that had no profits but big plans for trade in slaves to colonies in South America. Its shares soared more than fivefold in four months and then flamed out as copycat companies multiplied and insiders sold shares before a bust they knew was coming. Knight fled England, ended up in an Antwerp jail, and then broke out.

In the foreword of the third edition of his book, released in 1996, Kindleberger warned of what looked "suspiciously like a bubble in technology stocks." On the book's cover Samuelson admonished readers, "Sometime in the next five years you may kick yourself for not reading and re-reading" the book.

The internet boom looked like booms and busts associated with railroad and canal investment in Europe and the United States during the 1700s and 1800s. Greater efficiency of transportation by rail and water transformed the American and European economies, connecting people as they'd never been connected before. Then speculators took matters too far.

The Erie Canal, completed in 1825, connected Albany to Buffalo and opened commerce from the nation's East Coast on the Hudson River to the Midwest through Lake Erie. The canal cut travel times between the two cities from two weeks to five days, and the cost of moving freight tumbled.[5] The result was a commercial renaissance, with benefits that spread down the Hudson River to Manhattan and across the Great Lakes to Chicago. Canal construction boomed across the Midwest in a frenzy of speculation. Then, when more efficient railroads came along, many of the waterways were abandoned, and boom turned into bust.

The speculative fervor unleashed by innovation in transportation bled into other markets with similar risks of collapse. For example, the Erie Canal led to a boom in Chicago real estate.[6] Between 1830 and 1836, the price of Chicago land rose from $800 per acre to $327,000 per acre in 2012 dollars, then fell to $38,000 by 1841. The Bank of Illinois went bust in 1842.

The internet transformed the US economy in much the same way as canals and railroads had before. But in its early stages it was impossible to pick the winners from the losers, so investors placed their bets everywhere. In one final frenzied leap, an eighteen-month stretch between August 1998 and February 2000, the Nasdaq composite stock index, which favored technology companies, nearly tripled. Inside the Fed, staff warnings that this wasn't sustainable became a running joke.

In 2000, investor enthusiasm turned to revulsion. The fallout was widespread. Pets.com, for example, raised $82.5 million in a February 2000 initial public offering, promising to transform the way households bought pet food and toys, the way Amazon was transforming the market for books. But the timing was off. With no revenue and the capital markets drying up, Pets.com quickly ran out of cash. The company declared bankruptcy that November.

The link between the historical bubbles that Kindleberger studied and the rigid formulas of modern economics was the band of behavioral economists championed by Akerlof during the 1980s and 1990s. For years many of their colleagues had dismissed their warnings that market rationality was a myth. Now the behavioral economists had contemporaneous proof that was hard to dispute.

Robert Shiller had been warning since the mid-1990s that stock prices were out of whack with underlying business profits. He urged Greenspan in a private meeting in December 1996 to alert people. Greenspan, who had become concerned about overvalued stocks, too, formulated a speech in his bathtub that stated he was getting worried about "irrational exuberance" in financial markets. Before he delivered the speech, he shared the text with Yellen, who thought the words came too late in the speech to get much notice. She was wrong; the markets tumbled after Greenspan's warning. Then they shot right back up.[7]

Shiller was proven right in the end. His book *Irrational Exuberance* became a bestseller. The most absentminded of professors—a man who ate cat food to test a theory—went on to even greater fortune in subsequent years selling new measurements of stock values and home prices to firms including Barclays and Standard & Poor's. He would become one of the wealthiest economists of his time, worth millions.[8]

Richard Thaler, for his part, made the rounds with an article about a market anomaly he found all too illustrative of irrational markets. In March 2000, 3Com, a company that made computer network systems, sold a small piece of its stake in Palm, which made handheld devices. Even after the divestment, 3Com still retained 95 percent of the shares of Palm. The divested piece of Palm became a hot stock, its price soaring to the point that the market somehow placed a greater value on the small stake in Palm that 3Com had sold to the public than it did on 3Com, even though 3Com still owned more Palm shares than it had sold to everyone else. In his paper Thaler asked, "Can the market add and subtract?"[9]

Lawrence Summers, as was often the case, proved to be a complex figure in this period. He was well aware of the risk of market failure. He and Andrei Shleifer had warned in the 1980s that investment fads could be driven by "noise traders" who had irrational beliefs, and that markets didn't naturally correct for these distorting impulses. Akerlof

admired his work. Then as a policy maker Summers championed deregulation of banks and the new instruments they used. To his critics, he
was on both sides of an issue; in his own mind, he was striking a better
balance between unfettered markets and government intervention. "We
have, in many ways, moved to a new paradigm of public policy in recent
years," he said as Treasury secretary in 1999, "one based on supporting,
not supplanting the market. In a sense, one that is based not only on the
invisible hand and certainly not the heavy hand, but on a helping hand
of government."[10]

Regulators did eventually crack down on the banks that fueled the
Wall Street boom, making Citigroup, Morgan Stanley, Merrill Lynch,
and other financial institutions pay $1.4 billion in settlements for pump-
ing up the bubble with glowing analyst reports about profitless companies going public.[11] Financial firms paid an additional $6.9 billion to
investors to settle class action lawsuits.[12] A new securities law authored
by Maryland senator Paul Sarbanes and Ohio representative Mike Oxley
demanded tougher rules for corporate reporting. The US Department
of Justice pursued individuals involved in the mischief, including former Enron chairman Ken Lay, who died while vacationing near Aspen,
Colorado, before his scheduled sentencing and appeal of criminal fraud
convictions.[13]

Yet those cases of criminal prosecution and government intervention were only half of the story. In several respects the financial system
proved unexpectedly resilient when the tech bubble burst. That resilience, in turn, reaffirmed to some regulators that a light touch to oversight had actually worked well.[14]

Some of the banks that lent to companies that went bust—including
Enron—had hedged themselves against losses using new financial instruments. One such instrument was called a credit default swap, which
banks used to protect themselves against losses on loans they made.

Credit default swap agreements resembled simple insurance products. If you buy fire insurance on your home, the insurer pays you if the home burns down; if it doesn't burn down, the insurer keeps the money you have paid for this protection against disaster. With credit default swaps, banks bought protection from investors and insurers on loans. When a loan went bad, the banks got paid by the investors and insurers who sold the bank the credit default swaps. If the loan didn't go bad, the investors and insurers kept the fees they earned for promising the coverage. Many Wall Street firms served as middlemen between the investors and the banks, arranging for the swap of default risks between different parties.

Regulators emerged from the tech bust more confident about big banks, not less. Greenspan said credit derivatives "appear to have effectively spread losses" from defaults by Enron and other large corporations, cushioning the financial system and economy against deep disturbances.[15] According to Fed vice chairman Roger Ferguson Jr., "the most remarkable fact regarding the banking industry during this period" was "its resilience and retention of fundamental strength."[16] The financial industry's complex new instruments seemed to have stabilized and insulated the whole system by diversifying risk. It looked like Wall Street had created its own safety net.

The Fed helped to soften the blow to the economy after the technology bust by cutting interest rates. By 2000 it had settled on a view that it couldn't spot financial bubbles and that it shouldn't try to pop them, as the central bank had done in 1929, to devastating effect. Instead, its strategy was to clean up the mess caused by a financial bubble bursting after the fact, by reducing the cost of credit. Between late 2000 and the middle of 2003, Greenspan cut short-term interest rates from 6.5 percent to 1 percent, moving most aggressively after 9/11. Low interest rates helped those in debt to refinance mortgages and business loans at lower rates, reducing their costs. It also spurred new borrowing, bolstering the economy as it recovered from the investment hangover.

Greenspan seemed to have worked his magic once again. The unemployment rate had reached 10.8 percent during the recession of 1982, and 7.8 percent in 1992. This time it only briefly exceeded 6 percent in 2003. Greenspan seemed to have engineered a soft economic landing after an array of savage shocks.

Yet puzzling forces bubbled beneath the economy's seemingly placid surface. In 2002 economic output started rising, but strangely, the job market didn't recover. The unemployment rate kept creeping higher until the middle of 2003, and then only declined slowly.

Typically a burst of hiring followed a downturn, but now analysts started talking about the "jobless recovery." In earlier downturns, firms had laid off some workers temporarily and brought them back when business revived. This time, firms fired workers for good as part of sweeping restructuring programs. *Downsizing* became a watchword of the time. When people were laid off, their spells of unemployment were longer now, because they had to find entirely new jobs.

By 2004 more than one out of five unemployed workers had been looking for a job for six months or more. During expansions in the 1950s, 1960s, 1970s, and 1980s, that ratio of long-term unemployed to all unemployed was more like one in ten or even one in twenty. Layoffs became life-changing events, not just temporary blips that resolved themselves as factories closed for a few weeks and then reopened.[17]

The economy was changing, and workers were losing power and flexibility. Companies could cut costs by moving production to China or putting technology to work that made existing workers more productive. Blue-collar workers lost power, while higher-income executives and investors reaped big gains in the first recovery of the new millennium.[18] Hotel revenue surged at luxury and upscale chains, while revenues at budget hotels barely budged. While high-end Bulgari stores sold out of $5,000 Astrale gold and diamond "cocktail rings" and Neiman Marcus sales of $500 Manolo Blahnik shoes soared, sales trudged along at Walmart and Payless shoe stores. Wall Street and executive compensation surged again, too.

Income and wealth gaps between poor, middle-class, and rich households had been widening since the 1980s. In 2004, the highest-earning 5 percent of all US households earned 21.8 percent of all US income, compared with 16.5 percent in 1980. Inequality rose through both Republican and Democrat administrations. It was nonpartisan and persistent, and during the first expansion of the 2000s it became even more pronounced.[19]

As US divides widened, China enjoyed a trade boom unlike anything the United States had experienced before. One point of reference was the Japan trade threat that preceded China. Between 1985 and 1990, US imports of goods from Japan had increased by $24 billion, adjusted for inflation. Between 2000 and 2005, by comparison, US imports from China increased $143 billion. It was as if the United States had taken on nearly six Japans all at once, except China had advantages Japan didn't, including low-wage workers whose productivity was climbing rapidly as the country opened itself to the world. Japan's advantage eventually diminished. China's rise was just starting.

While China shipped shoes, furniture, and electronics to the United States, American exports to China rose in odd categories. Its third-largest goods export in value and largest in volume was waste—the recycled paper, plastic, and metal that US households and businesses threw away. The scrap was sent off to China in large metal containers to be turned into cardboard boxes and plastic packaging that the Chinese stuffed with new goods and sent back to America. One company, Pomona, California–based America Chung Nam, sent junk every year from the United States to China that was equal in weight to seventeen US aircraft carriers. "We are the Saudi Arabia of scrap," said Robert Garino, then the director of commodity research at the Washington-based Institute of Scrap Recycling Industries.[20]

China's boom started before its admission into the World Trade Organization and accelerated after. Like the jobless recovery and fallout from the tech bust, it reshaped the world that Janet Yellen would inherit in the next few years.

More US companies closed factories and shifted production to where it was cheaper. US manufacturing employment had been falling for decades, and the decline intensified as China grew. While some people lost jobs, others benefited. Cheap imported goods poured into the United States, holding down the cost of living for many American households, as David Ricardo's theories had predicted. Between 2000 and 2004, the cost to US consumers of a set of dishes dropped 9 percent on average; men's shoe prices dropped 8.3 percent, and the cost of household appliances 7.3 percent.[21]

In building an export juggernaut, China had also built up a mountainous stash of dollars from its sales to the United States. With this money it bought US securities, including Treasury bonds and mortgage bonds. It all added up to low US inflation and a surge of demand for US securities from abroad, which had an additional effect: it held down the cost of borrowing money in the United States.

It was a perfect formula for a new financial boom. Money was cheap, and an emboldened Wall Street was revived and eager to spend it.

Greenspan thought investors would be chastened after the tech bust of 2001, and that the risk of another bubble was remote. Kindleberger, sitting alone most days in a Massachusetts retirement home, had different ideas. In 2002, at ninety-one, he was collecting daily newspaper clippings. He believed a housing bubble was building in the wake of the tech bust, and he was in search of evidence. The risk looked most acute on the West Coast, he thought. He was especially dubious of two large, private mortgage firms, Fannie Mae and Freddie Mac, that had been created by the US government. With the government's blessing, they were buying mortgages from banks. Kindleberger was wary of their activity: "Banks will make a mortgage and sell it to them. It means that the banks are ready to mortgage more and more and more and more. It's dangerous, I think."[22]

If he were thirty years younger, Kindleberger said, he'd write another book about it. He died the next year.

. . .

After Akerlof won his Nobel, Yellen settled into a quieter life in Berkeley, thinking her time in government was done. She liked to be in bed before nine, and rise by five for coffee and a couple of hours reading newspapers. She was still active. After five years in Washington, she became a fixture on a lecture circuit of academics and central bank experts tracking the global economy. It was a bit like the traveling dice game Krugman described.

She also wrote a book with Alan Blinder, *The Fabulous Decade*, on the lessons of the 1990s boom. One of those lessons, she concluded, was that restraining the budget deficit early in the 1990s had paid off. The government's restraint meant it didn't have to borrow much, which held down interest rates and made space for the private-sector investment boom that fed economic growth and created jobs before things overheated.[23]

In 2001 and again in 2003 she was invited by the Fed to speak at its exclusive annual retreat in Jackson Hole, Wyoming. Central bankers from around the world met there every August, mixing and mingling with academics, journalists, and Wall Street analysts on mountain hikes and during cocktail hour. They were always on the lookout for bear or moose. Yellen wasn't much into strenuous hikes, but the mornings were packed with formal talks about new economic research, where she became a centerpiece.

In 2001 she was given a prime spot summing up two days of discussions on the technology boom. Lawrence Summers was one of the speakers who preceded her. She focused on the pitfalls of the boom: "The dark side of tech innovations is that they tend to raise wage inequality— not just among countries but also within them. It seems clear from case studies and from firm and industry hiring patterns, that the adoption of computer-based technologies has shifted demand in favor of skilled workers." This was leaving unskilled workers, who already tended to earn lower wages, even further out in the cold. It was becoming a winner-take-all economy, and one question she posed was whether the government should do anything about it.[24]

She also warned that Wall Street banks might not be as stable as regulators liked to think: "I worry that the sophisticated risk management strategies that are now commonly used by banks and other financial institutions to monitor and manage exposure have the potential to destabilize financial markets," she said. Most were using the same risk management systems, known as value-at-risk programs, she noted. The models all had similar assumptions about how markets worked. If they were all using the same risk management systems, they might inadvertently be herding themselves into the same unseen risks. Moreover, those very systems called for firms to sell risky assets when problems mounted. That could cause cascades of selling when market sentiment about risky assets unexpectedly turned for the worse. "I believe this should be an important policy concern for central banks and other financial regulators," Yellen said. Little noticed at the time, it was a foreboding warning.

Two years later, in 2003, the thrust of Yellen's talk was that central bankers needed to stay nimble and adapt as times changed. Old rules of thumb about interest rates or inflation might not hold true as circumstances changed. Good central banking, she concluded, was like doing good detective work. You had to go where the facts took you.[25]

Yellen had another prescient observation that was largely overlooked in the moment. Her former student Larry Summers asked from the audience what might go wrong in the next ten or twenty years. Yellen said she suspected that large budget deficits—eliminated during the Clinton years when she and Summers were in power—were likely to return.

These were all little clues behind a bigger story of a shifting economy, too small to cause alarm in the moment, but glaring when looking back in time.

In 2004 Robert Parry, the president of the San Francisco Fed, was ready to retire after eighteen years on the job. The San Francisco Fed's board of directors zeroed in on Yellen. Clinton's former economic adviser Laura Tyson was on the list too, but she was moving to London to run the business school of the London School of Economics, so she took herself out of the running. Yellen, like Tyson, was a respected Washington veteran with roots in the Bay Area, and a woman who would add diversity to the Fed's mostly male ranks. Greenspan enthusiastically approved of the appointment. By June, Yellen was back at Fed meetings, monitoring the economy from her new perch on the nation's vast West Coast and running one of the central bank's biggest regional operations.

One of her first challenges was downsizing at her own institution. Technology had dried up the checking business at banks, and the Fed cleared bank checks. As that business shrank, Yellen's first task was to tour the region and lay off central bank workers.

Parry took on a new gig soon after he left the Fed. He accepted a seat on the board of directors of one of the nation's largest mortgage lenders, where he landed a job on its audit and ethics committee. By 2006 he was earning $538,824 for his services.[26] The firm was based in Los Angeles. It was named Countrywide Financial. Its chief executive officer was Angelo Mozilo.

Both the firm and its CEO would soon become Yellen's next challenge.

14

Yellen as a Regulator

An Introduction to Frankenstein Finance
2004–2006

Angelo Mozilo was the son of first-generation Italian Americans, his father the owner of a Bronx butcher shop. When he was ten years old, Mozilo started helping at the shop and at fourteen he got another job as a messenger for a small mortgage firm in midtown Manhattan. A senior executive named David Loeb joined the mortgage firm as part of a merger and liked the confident, scrappy youngster.[1]

In 1969 Mozilo and Loeb set up their own mortgage business. Mozilo was thirty-one and had worked his way through Fordham University. They invested $500,000 of their own capital—most of it Loeb's—and had ambitions so large they called their little New York start-up Countrywide. Over the next thirty-five years Mozilo and Loeb built Countrywide into the nation's largest mortgage lender, moving its headquarters to the hottest and most turbulent real estate market of all, California. Mozilo became a flashy dresser, famously tanned and coiffed, who never forgot his underdog, bootstrap identity. The big banks of Wall Street always seemed to underestimate him, and he didn't appreciate that at all.

"You need to make dust or eat dust," he often said, "and I don't like eating dust."

When Yellen arrived at the San Francisco Fed in 2004, sizing up

Mozilo's ambitions was one challenge. The other was navigating a jury-rigged bank regulatory system meant to oversee him.

Greenspan had concluded after the bursting of the tech stock bubble that banks were resilient and it was best to let them manage their own risks. The market had shown it would discipline itself and he wanted to keep the government's regulatory hand at a distance.

His worldview was reinforced by a bank regulatory overhaul enacted late in the Clinton years. Under the Gramm-Leach-Bliley Act, signed into law by the president in 1999, distinctions were blurred between traditional banks (which took deposits from everyday households and made plain-vanilla loans like mortgages) and securities firms (which bought and sold billions of dollars at a time in bonds, stocks, and new financial instruments of much greater complexity). As part of that overhaul, Congress changed how regulators treated a wide range of financial institutions. "Fed lite" provisions in the law constrained the central bank's oversight of banks when some other regulator, such as the Securities and Exchange Commission (SEC), was already overseeing the firm or its subsidiaries. "Fed lite" became an appropriate description of how the central bank, from the very top at least, saw its job as a regulator when Yellen returned to the Fed in 2004.

At the same time, low interest rates were helping to fuel a mortgage boom. Between 1999 and 2005, US households took on an additional $4.5 trillion in mortgage debt, accumulating in six years more debt than they had taken on in all the time before that.[2] In 2006 home prices started falling, a signal that debt-driven bidding wars for homes had reached their limits. Yet households took on another trillion dollars of mortgage debt in one final burst of borrowing mania that year.

The banking industry and its customers fell in love with unconventional mortgages. The banks offered a range of different flavors, like treats lining the shelves of a sweet-smelling doughnut shop. Borrowers could try hybrid adjustable rate mortgages, which promised low interest rates in the early years of repayment and then higher rates later. Or they could have interest-only loans, which allowed borrowers to delay paying back what they had initially borrowed. Then there were option adjustable rate mortgages, or option ARMs, which gave borrowers the option of choosing how much to pay at first, and negative amortization loans that tacked on debt at the end of the loan in return for not paying enough to cover interest at the beginning.

Tailoring a loan to a person's unique needs made some sense. In this case, however, many of the loans went to borrowers with checkered credit histories. Some were known as "subprime" borrowers because their income or credit history suggested they were at higher risk of not paying than most others.

That was like selling doughnuts with extra icing and sprinkles to people with diabetes.

Countrywide was at the center of the boom, the nation's biggest mortgage originator from 2004 through 2007. Its mortgages were fed into an elaborate Wall Street securities machine. After Countrywide originated mortgages, it sold them to Wall Street firms that packaged them into securities and sold them to investors around the world. Also among the customers for its mortgages were the two Washington firms that worried Kindleberger so much, Fannie Mae and Freddie Mac.

In a September 2003 story, *Fortune* dubbed Countrywide "the 23,000% stock," the best performing financial company over two decades.[3] Mozilo had outdone even Warren Buffett, the legendary founder of Berkshire Hathaway. Countrywide's profits were on track to exceed those of McDonald's and Walt Disney. Mozilo believed he was engaged in a noble cause, no less a highly profitable one. The home was a symbol of the American Dream. With innovative mortgages, he believed he was bringing access to that dream to people who hadn't been able to reach it before, and in fact had long faced discrimination from lenders. The federal government, with laws like the Community Reinvestment Act of 1977, encouraged banks to do just this. Countrywide didn't take federally insured deposits and thus wasn't subject to that law. Still, Mozilo believed he was advancing the cause of social justice on his own. "Countrywide was one of the greatest companies in the history of this country," he said.[4]

Along the way, Mozilo accumulated friends in high places. A Countrywide VIP lending program known as "Friends of Angelo" provided mortgages at attractive rates to favored customers. Among the recipients of these mortgages were senators Christopher Dodd of Connecticut and Kent Conrad of North Dakota, and two former CEOs of Fannie Mae.[5]

Mozilo wanted market share. Other industries had become dominated by giant leaders, embodied then by Walmart's position in retailing. The swaggering kid from the Bronx wanted to be the dominant player in mortgages. To do that, he wanted to take over more and more of the mortgage origination marketplace and squeeze out competitors. In 2004 he announced he was gunning to control 30 percent of the marketplace for originating mortgages by 2008. At the time Countrywide was already producing more than $350 billion in new mortgage credit a year, more than any other financial institution in the nation. It controlled 13 percent of the whole market, and Mozilo was sure he could take more.[6]

To reach the goal, Countrywide dropped its lending standards and broadened its offerings to reach more people. Borrowers with little chance of repaying gobbled up credit. What Mozilo described as a path to the American Dream became an impossible burden.

Mozilo wasn't blind to the problem. In one private email he acknowledged that some of the loans his firm was behind were becoming toxic. In another he said the firm was flying blind in its lending.[7] But he kept going.

When Yellen became president of the San Francisco Fed in 2004, she was initially worried about the commercial real estate market—the market for buildings and office towers, not residential homes. California had a long and painful history of overdoing it in commercial real estate, for instance during the savings and loan boom that Akerlof examined in his 1993 paper on looting. It took years for the California economy to recover after that bust. By 2004 commercial real estate lending in the region was booming again. Yellen had the bank's examiners look into it and warned publicly that local banks might be getting too exposed to that risk yet again.

Within a year she realized the problem might be somewhere else. Fed officials had been debating the risk of a housing bubble for years. Yellen saw a problem, though like many others she was initially slow to pick up on its complexity and gravity. Home prices were unusually high and a "serious issue" for the Fed, she said in a speech a year into her term.[8] But she talked herself out of calling for more serious action from the central bank to stop it. Instead she embraced the standard view at the Fed: if there was a bubble and it burst, the central bank could manage the fallout by lowering interest rates to boost the economy during the bust, as it had done after the internet bubble ended. In the meantime, she said the best way for the Fed to manage a bubble was to use its regulatory powers to push banks to stop lending so freely. The flaw in her argument was that Greenspan wasn't inclined to do that, and even if he had been, the regulatory system underneath him wasn't set up to bear that responsibility.

The Fed's Jackson Hole symposium in August 2005 was arranged to celebrate Greenspan's legacy. Raghuram Rajan, then the International Monetary Fund's chief economist, warned the central bankers at the meeting that financial innovation might be making the banking system riskier. The audience wasn't very supportive. Summers called Rajan's premise Luddite and misguided.[9]

While Washington's top regulators weren't interested in cracking down, Yellen's dinner companions back at home were.

Mozilo became the subject of regular conversation in the Yellen and Akerlof household in 2005. George and Robby started reading about him and found him to be a strange character, in his resplendent suits and colorful handkerchiefs, big gold cuff links, and deep orange tan. The family had a long talk about him during a trip to the wine country, and George and Robby routinely brought him up over dinner.[10] What was it that drove this son of a Bronx butcher to such extravagance, and made him so determined to become the biggest guy in finance? His drive for recognition and dominance seemed dangerous to them, and that drive seemed to pervade the culture of the firm.

The psychology of the man and the company culture fascinated George and Robby. They saw danger, and started pestering Yellen to crack down on him. It got to the point where she got tired of hearing it from them.

"C'mon, stop about the suits," she shot back when they kept prodding her. She couldn't crack down on a man simply because he wore gold cuff links and had a chip on his shoulder. She had to follow processes. But she knew they had a point. Yellen and her examiners were worried too.

Fed examiners in Washington and San Francisco were constrained, but behind the scenes they tried to tame Countrywide's appetites. In September 2005 the central bank sent Mozilo a formal letter telling him he should set limits on his growth plans and how much risk he was prepared to take. The regulator was uncomfortable with Countrywide's exotic mortgages and whether it was managing the risk carefully. They referred to the company by its stock ticker symbol, CFC: "CFC's growth profile makes having a comprehensive risk management framework essential. And by being the leader in the mortgage industry, it is incumbent on CFC to be a first class corporate-wide risk manager," Fed officials wrote.[11] They sounded some alarm that Countrywide had set out an aggressive growth strategy without also planning to set aside more money for potential losses. Such a cushion, known as capital, was barely keeping pace as the bank's lending became riskier.

Fed supervisors also pressed Countrywide on the exotic mortgages it was underwriting. How would these mortgages behave if market conditions changed? Nobody had much experience with them. The Fed "did not like some of these products," said John McMurray, a Countrywide executive, in a later interview with investigators.[12] This bothered Mozilo. Unconventional mortgages were a growth area for the firm that he didn't want to give up. To dominate the market, he had to innovate.

Yellen shook up her staff in San Francisco to strengthen its oversight of banks. When she joined the San Francisco Fed in 2004, its head of bank supervision, Terry Schwakopf, wore other hats, including helping to manage public outreach of the central bank. In 2004 one of Schwakopf's projects was launching FedVille, a website meant to teach grade-school kids about money.[13] Fed officials in Washington reviewed the San Francisco oversight bank operation and found it lacking. Schwakopf left the job and Yellen brought in Stephen M. Hoffman Jr., an old hand in bank supervision whose experience ran back to the 1970s, before Greenspan's embrace of light-touch oversight.

There were limits to how much Yellen could do, though. The Fed was a balkanized regulator. Fed supervisors in Washington, not Yellen or her staff in San Francisco, were in charge of bank oversight. While many of the Fed's Washington supervisors shared Yellen's concerns, the man in charge until early 2006 was Greenspan, who stuck to the view that the market could police itself.

The Fed chairman did take one step toward slowing the mortgage boom. After holding interest rates down for years after the tech bust, the Fed started raising them in 2004. In small increments, the central bank kept raising them as the housing boom kept building.

An array of other regulators competed for power and fees earned for regulating financial firms. The Office of the Comptroller of the Currency regulated banks. The Office of Thrift Supervision (OTS) oversaw savings and loan institutions, which were like banks but had a narrower scope of lending that centered on mortgages. The SEC examined securities firms. The Federal Deposit Insurance Corporation was in charge of closing banks when they failed. The Commodities Futures Trading Commission looked after derivatives instruments. At a minimum this jumble of regulators had to coordinate and cooperate. Instead some jockeyed for influence.

Yellen and Mozilo met in a San Francisco Fed conference room every three months. It was a businesslike atmosphere, where she and Fed examiners from San Francisco and Washington politely prodded the Countrywide executive about his growth strategy. "Our supervisory folks that I met with were alerting me to underwriting practices that were a huge concern. They were telling me about low-doc and no-doc loans, about the rising prevalence of ninja loans, no income/no jobs/no asset-type loans," Yellen said later. "The San Francisco Fed was quite concerned about what was going on. We tried to insist on tighter risk controls."[14]

Fed oversight became a source of tension within Countrywide, where a power struggle was in play over who would succeed Mozilo. Stanford Kurland, the low-key company president seen as the heir apparent, was sympathetic to the concerns of regulators. David Sambol, the chief operating officer, saw the regulators as a nuisance. Mozilo had a falling-out with Kurland over the Fed, which Mozilo saw as an obstruction to his growth plans. "The Fed just didn't understand our organization," Mozilo said in a court deposition later.[15] Kurland quit.

Countrywide was being courted by another Washington regulator at the time. The Office of Thrift Supervision saw in the giant California mortgage lender a chance to dramatically increase the fees it collected from financial firms as part of its oversight of them. OTS supervisors weren't paid based on how much fee income they brought in, but they saw value in the expanded influence that came with it. Countrywide could in theory change its organizational structure so that it was a thrift holding company, which focused more narrowly on mortgages than conventional banks did. That would put it under the purview of the OTS and take it out from under the Fed's glare.

During the summer of 2006, Mozilo's Countrywide lieutenants prepared a sixty-nine-page memo ahead of a meeting with OTS officials. The firm seemed to want assurance that its aggressive growth plans and unconventional mortgages would be blessed. The memo included an assessment by Countrywide's lawyers that "OTS regulation of holding companies is not as intrusive as that of the Federal Reserve." It also highlighted a public speech that February by OTS director John Reich, who touted his agency as a "regulatory alternative" for financial firms and highlighted his flexibility toward unconventional mortgages. "Products like these have long been offered by the thrift industry," he said.[16]

"The only way we could move forward was going to the OTS," Mozilo said later.

In November 2006 Mozilo flew his company jet to San Francisco to break the news to Yellen. Her new head of supervision, Stephen Hoffman, was with her at the meeting. Mozilo told them he had decided to change Countrywide's organizational structure, and was thus dumping the Fed as his regulator.

As Yellen retold it, "One day Angelo came up and we had our regular quarterly meeting and he said to me, 'Janet, I have to tell you, it's been terrific to be supervised by you. You guys are really on top of your game and we really appreciate all of the valuable advice that you've given us. But, you know, we've realized that we don't actually need to be a bank holding company. We realized it would be okay to be a thrift holding company. And so we're changing our charter.'"[17]

Yellen and Hoffman were flabbergasted. The regulatory system was set up in a way that allowed Mozilo to shop for regulators and bolt when he didn't like what he was being told. Now he was going to be the problem of the OTS, and there wasn't much they could do about it.

Countrywide's fate might have been sealed even before Mozilo ditched the Fed. Between 2002 and 2006, the share of nonstandard loans that it generated grew from 25 percent of all of the loans it originated to 45 percent. That meant more risk. Moreover, it held more of these loans itself, rather than originating and selling them to Wall Street firms and thus dispersing the risk to others. Between 2002 and 2006 Countrywide's own mortgage holdings grew from $6 billion to $78 billion.

Where had the money come from to make the loans it kept as investments? For the most part Countrywide borrowed the money. In four years its borrowing ballooned from $19.8 billion to $71.5 billion. Much of that borrowing had to be paid back regularly in very short time frames every few months.

To keep the machine running, Countrywide routinely paid back its old short-term loans and took out new ones to replace them. But this strategy posed another question. If the loans it made to homeowners went bad, would its own lenders keep feeding it money? The answer to this question was about to become a very serious problem for Angelo Mozilo.

15

Yellen and Akerlof
See Storms
from the Lighthouse

Nursing the Economy and
Robby's Damaged Back
2007

While a financial crisis brewed inside Countrywide, Yellen and Akerlof faced a health crisis in their own family.

Robby graduated from Yale in 2003 and decided to become an economist like his parents. During his third year of graduate studies at Harvard, a time when most students are finishing their coursework and writing papers themselves, nerve pains shot down his left leg to his foot.

Doctors discovered a herniated disk in the lumbar region of his spine. Robby liked to run and had an old case of modest scoliosis, which may have set off the problem. The doctors advised him to wait it out—cases like this often went away after a few months. But after six months Robby's had only gotten worse. He couldn't sit for more than fifteen minutes at a time. He stopped showing up for seminars and receded from view of his classmates. By December 2006 he had had enough. He opted for surgery to remove pressure on a disk in his spine. The surgery went poorly and the pain grew even more intense. It got to a point where he couldn't walk.

Akerlof flew east to Cambridge to take care of his son for a few months. The Nobel winner slept on a foldout couch in Robby's small apartment and brought him pizza and Chinese takeout to eat. He ventured to the basement with bundles of Robby's laundry, sticking quarters in coin-operated washing machines and dryers. While Robby lay immobile, they read, watched movies, and talked about economics. Robby took cortisone shots to relieve the pain and disappeared from his studies for long stretches. Yellen later joined them in New York, after Akerlof took the early lead in caring for their son.

As Akerlof nursed Robby back to health, Yellen watched Mozilo's creation sink into a deepening downward spiral. In 2007, households were delaying or skipping monthly payments on mortgages in growing numbers. A measure of these delayed payments—called the delinquency rate—rose nationally from 1.6 percent of all mortgages in mid-2006 to 2.7 percent by mid-2007. That might not sound like a lot, but for a nation by then sitting on more than $10 trillion of mortgage debt, every percentage point increase in the delinquency rate amounted to roughly $100 billion of additional debt at risk of defaulting. The rate peaked at more than 11 percent in 2010.[1]

Countrywide's mortgages fared worse than others. On June 30, 2007, nearly 5 percent of the debt it underwrote was delinquent, up from less than 4 percent just six months earlier. From January 2007 through July 2007, Countrywide's shares lost more than a third of their value.

Yellen used Fed policy meetings to air her growing concerns as Countrywide cracked. Fed officials gathered eight times per year in formal meetings to discuss how the economy was performing and to set an interest-rate policy to keep inflation and unemployment in balance. The twelve regional Fed bank presidents and the Washington-based governors packed together with staff into the Fed's boardroom for one or two days of discussion and debate, led by the central bank's chairman. A rotation of regional bank presidents got to vote along with the Washington board governors and New York Fed president on decisions. They called the voting group the Federal Open Market Committee.

For the Fed chairman, building a consensus in such a large group was always a challenge. Greenspan had been in full command when he retired. Ben Bernanke got Greenspan's job in early 2006, and he was still getting the hang of it.

Fed meetings had become a bit like Sunday in the National Football League. It was game day, when long days of preparation and behind-the-scenes strategizing were put to work. At the conclusion of discussions the central bank put out a statement summarizing its thinking and announcing any change in its plans for interest rates. The statements had been an innovation introduced by Greenspan in the 1990s, when he was under pressure from Congress to become more transparent. Even the hint of a change in its thinking about rates in these statements could send stocks or bonds into spasmodic swings, with repercussions that rippled around the world.

Yellen changed the way her economics team back in San Francisco prepared for these Washington meetings. Under her predecessor, Parry, the staff had come up with economic forecasts that often mirrored the forecasts produced by Fed economists in Washington. "I already know that," Yellen told her team back in San Francisco. She pressed her economists to come up with material that would bring new analysis and new ideas to the high-stakes discussions in DC.

Her briefings back in San Francisco went on for hours and drew on new research her San Francisco team worked up. When she left for Washington, she was armed with stacks of briefing materials bundled together in dark binders. When it was her time to speak, she pulled out prepared statements and read them in a slow, hypnotizing cadence. Her presentations were always topical and backed by reams of research. "The room hushed when she spoke," Bernanke said of Yellen's performances.[2]

She sometimes drew on quirky California anecdotes, delivered in a steady deadpan voice, which registered bursts of laughter from her colleagues. During the boom, she reported, her contacts in the private equity business were becoming disgusted that overly eager investors kept throwing money at them. During the depths of the crisis, she would relate, sales of cheap wine from Napa Valley soared, while the expensive stuff trailed. East Bay plastic surgeons later reported that cash-strapped rich people were canceling elective procedures. The Silicon Valley Country Club, with a $250,000 entrance fee and seven-to-eight-year waiting list, saw its waiting list shrink to a mere thirteen.

Yellen developed another habit around her Fed policy meeting routines. While sitting for hours in airport waiting lounges, she became somewhat addicted to the Brick Breaker game on her BlackBerry phone, in which a player smashes down walls of bricks by deflecting a ball with a paddle. The game had thirty-four levels that became progressively harder to complete. She got so good at it that she managed to get through them all.

By mid-2007, however, the time for games was over.

"I still feel the presence of a 600-pound gorilla in the room," Yellen said at the Fed's June 2007 meeting. "That is the housing sector. The risk for further significant deterioration in the housing market, with house prices falling and mortgage delinquencies rising further, causes me appreciable angst."[3] She turned to an analysis by her San Francisco team of economists. Around the country, home prices were falling, and in the same places, mortgage delinquencies were also rising. This had the potential to feed on itself.

Many households had taken out loans requiring very low down payments. As home prices fell, they were left with less at stake, and less incentive to repay the loans. "Subprime borrowers, especially those with very low equity stakes, have less incentive to keep their mortgages current when housing no longer seems an attractive investment," Yellen said. A related problem was that people depended on refinancing mortgages at lower rates so they could keep paying them. When price declines deepened, banks stopped playing the refinance game that had kept many borrowers afloat. "These results," Yellen said, "highlight the potential risks that rising defaults in subprime could spread to other sectors of the mortgage market and could trigger a vicious cycle in which a further deceleration in house prices increases foreclosures, in turn exacerbating downside price movements." The housing problem, in other words, could feed on itself and destabilize banks.

In August, panic spread.

It started in an unlikely place: Düsseldorf, Germany, where a little-known bank called IKB Deutsche Industriebank AG sat near the Rhine River. Since 1924 IKB had focused on lending money to small and mid-size German companies that it knew well. Then in 2002 it decided to broaden its portfolio and began investing in securities tied to subprime US mortgages.[4]

How could a small German bank possibly have felt comfortable making such a risky leap?

Imagine a vast plumbing system. Wall Street had turned the US mortgage market into such a system that the money from mortgages ran through. The design of the mortgage-backed-securities market was meant to spit out very safe investments and also more risky investments, tailored by bankers to the tastes and needs of different investors.

It started with investment banks pooling together thousands or even tens of thousands of mortgages of varying risk. Out of the mortgage pools came regular streams of cash from the monthly interest and principal payments that households made on their loans. The cash from the mortgage pools flowed like water to faucets that were directed into collections of different giant tubs. The banks organized the streams of money that went into these tubs based on the risk and returns that investors in the mortgage pools were willing to accept. Some investors got high returns, along with the understanding that if the money stream dried up, then the first place it would stop flowing was into their tub. The investors who wanted access to the tub that would keep getting water even in the worst circumstances accepted lower returns as their tradeoff.

Credit rating businesses like Moody's and Standard & Poor's asserted that those in line at the most liquid tubs were as safe as investors in AAA-rated US Treasury bonds.

IKB believed them.

One problem was that this piping system stopped working when mortgage defaults rose to unimagined levels. In those cases, the water dried up and even investors who had placed their bets on the most liquid tub were at risk of losing their money.

That wasn't IKB's only problem. The other problem was that it was borrowing a lot of money itself, and its lenders could demand their money back at almost any moment. IKB got money to make its investments through a $2 trillion global market called the commercial paper market, where financial firms made loans to each other for very short periods of time, such as three, six, or nine months at a time. When commercial paper loans came due every few months, borrowers like IKB typically borrowed again, repaying the old loan and replacing it with new short-term debt.

In the summer of 2007, Wall Street firms began spurning IKB's efforts to raise money in the commercial paper market, fearful that its mortgage investments were heading toward default, and it wouldn't be able to repay its borrowing the next time around. Unable to borrow money, it couldn't pay off the expiring commercial paper loans and faced overnight collapse. It had to be bailed out by one of its shareholders with the encouragement of German regulators.

The IKB meltdown was a sign of trouble on many levels. First, it showed the global nature of the US mortgage boom, which had found its way to the banks of the Rhine, where an institution that knew very little about the US mortgage market was suddenly highly vulnerable to mortgage defaults in places like Phoenix and Las Vegas. Second, it exposed a major ingredient to a financial crisis. IKB held assets that didn't pay off for years, but it got the money for those investments by taking out loans it had to repay every few months. If its own commercial paper lenders wouldn't let it keep rolling over its borrowing, it was sunk.

On August 2, three days after the IKB rescue, Angelo Mozilo realized he had the exact same problem. He couldn't roll over commercial paper and other short-term borrowing. More than a third of all of Countrywide's $78 billion in debt was short-term in nature, including more than $13 billion of commercial paper.[5] Mozilo said it felt like a terrorist attack. "Fear in the credit markets is now tending towards panic," he wrote to a former Fed governor, Lyle Gramley, who had served as a Countrywide director years earlier. Gramley had already reached out to Bernanke's office to warn the central bank of a problem.[6]

On August 14 Countrywide reported that foreclosures and delinquencies on its portfolio of mortgages were rising and it was facing unprecedented disruptions in financial markets. On August 16 a Countrywide branch in Calabasas became home to a scene right out of the Great Depression—depositors standing in lines to get their money out of the bank, fearful it might collapse without government support.[7]

John Reich, the OTS supervisor who had won the Countrywide account nine months earlier, had a rosy view of Countrywide's prospects. Countrywide's competition was melting away, he told worried Fed officials. Its long-term prospects were good. But fear was showing up in other corners of the globe. BNP Paribas, a French bank, barred investors from taking money out of funds it managed that also held US subprime mortgages. There was a growing stampede out of these instruments, and it didn't know what they were worth anymore. Two Bear Stearns hedge funds exposed to subprime mortgages had already collapsed.

Bernanke canceled his August vacation plans.

Mozilo asked the Fed for help. The central bank made emergency loans to banks in panics like this. Mozilo wanted access to those loans, even though he had walked away from Fed oversight months earlier. "Mozilo seemed overwhelmed and unclear on what was going on," said Timothy Geithner, who then ran the Federal Reserve Bank of New York and reviewed the request. "Like many of the more desperate CEOs I would deal with during the crisis, his main focus was what the government could do to help his firm, and what we could say to get markets to stop fretting about it."[8]

Yellen's lieutenants in San Francisco thought there was no way the Fed should help Countrywide. For Yellen, it wasn't so simple. If Countrywide collapsed, it could bring down other banks and spread to the broader economy. At the same time, Yellen believed Mozilo was in denial about the disrepair in his company. She told the Fed's number-two official in Washington, Donald Kohn, that the best solution was for Countrywide to be sold to another firm that could fix it. The Fed spurned Mozilo's pleas for help. Instead he agreed to sell a $2 billion ownership stake in his firm to Bank of America as a new source of funds.

As Countrywide melted, Yellen, George, and Robby gathered in New York to prepare for Robby's back procedure at the Hospital for Special Surgery in Manhattan. For two years Robby and George had been pestering Yellen about Countrywide; now they all realized that the problem in financial markets was much bigger than that one firm. The housing market, the mortgage market, the economy, the banks; they were all tied together in dangerous ways. What they were witnessing were the beginnings of a serious, system-wide shock that could cripple the whole economy.

Akerlof tended to think in images and stories—the creatures in Koren's cartoons, the used-car market, the dam sites as metaphors for the job market, the Richard Scarry metaphor in his Nobel speech. All of these years, as he sat in academic seminars watching researchers lay out rigid mathematical proofs on boards, he had listened and wondered how the formulas might fit into some larger and more vivid story, or some larger map of a landscape he was building in his mind.

The image in his mind now was that of a terrible storm. Back in the 1990s he wrote that paper about looting, which examined how individuals took advantage of shoddy regulation and accounting to loot society for short-term profits from firms they drove toward bankruptcy. He suspected that the new financial instruments on Wall Street were amplifying the problem. They were conceived as vehicles to diversify risk, but instead they were being used to increase and hide risk. All those years he had been staring at clouds on horizons, as if viewed in the distance from a lighthouse. Now he saw that the storm was right there, directly overhead, letting loose in dangerous ways.

His wife, Janet Yellen, was one of the lighthouse keepers, tasked to manage the ensuing fury. Nearly everywhere Yellen looked, complex instruments she hadn't heard of before were in some state of turmoil, and bad mortgages were almost everywhere underneath the trouble. The names attached to these instruments were a jumble, but they had common ingredients that exposed large parts of the financial system.

Banks created products called structured investment vehicles (SIVs) that invested in mortgages and amplified how much they could invest by borrowing money. They also created collateralized debt obligations (CDOs), giant bundles of mortgage securities packed with risky debt and sold to investors or held by the banks themselves. Supposedly safe money market mutual funds—investments where households parked their savings and expected safe and modest returns—had been loaded up with "asset-backed commercial paper," short-term investments also stuffed with suspect mortgage investments.

Egged on by financial firms run by executives who were all too eager to grow and reward themselves with big bonus packages, American households had stretched themselves too far, taking on too much debt. Now the financial firms were breaking up like damaged ships in turbulent water. The executives wanted lifeboats.

Yellen saw a broader problem in their cries for help. A damaged financial system would starve the economy of funds, which could cause recession and unemployment. "If liquidity isn't quickly restored in these markets, we are looking at a credit crunch," she said in an August conference call with Fed officials as Countrywide teetered. "Signs of it are everywhere. Just to see that, Countrywide itself is 20 percent of the market, and it announced that it is tightening credit standards. Every day we hear about companies that are trying to finance prime quality jumbo mortgages and cannot get the financing to do that and are tightening standards. Although we may not have yet seen data suggesting that these changes in financial conditions are having an effect on economic growth, I think any forward-looking assessment would suggest that tighter credit conditions have to have that effect."[9]

The Fed was in a complicated situation. Inflation had started rising in the months before the August financial mayhem. Half a world away, China's industrial machine was growing stronger. For years the exports it produced with cheap labor had pushed global inflation down. Now it was gobbling up commodities like steel, wood, coal, oil, and other raw materials to feed its giant factories, which had the opposite effect on inflation. But Yellen thought a financial crisis would reverse an inflation problem quickly. The Fed didn't need to raise interest rates to fight inflation, as some officials wanted. She concluded it needed to cut rates to prepare for an inevitable downturn.

To some of her colleagues Yellen might sound alarmist, but she was developing a knack for making prescient calls on where the economy was headed, and also on how the Fed would have to respond. In the market's simplistic formulation, she tended to be a "dove" who favored low interest rates to boost economic activity and reduce unemployment. Less obvious was that she wasn't dogmatic about how she viewed a shifting economy or about whether old ideas in economics were holding up in changing circumstances. *Dove* was too narrow a definition. She now realized the housing boom had been built upon a fragile financial architecture that was prone to crack under a housing bust. She wasn't the Fed's central decision-maker; that was Bernanke. But she was a voice people started noting.

"She was on the right side of the internal debates," said Timothy Geithner, Bernanke's lieutenant in New York. "Always worried it was going to get worse. Early advocate of forceful action."

At its September meeting, the Fed cut its benchmark interest rate by half a percentage point. Yellen described a scene of "utter devastation" in mortgage markets and warned that the financial system wouldn't return to normal soon. It was not the time for a wait-and-see approach, she said. More rate cuts would be needed. Moving slowly, she said, "would be misguided and fraught with hazard because it would deprive us of the opportunity to act in time to forestall the likely damage."[10]

The Fed cut interest rates again in December, and again Yellen pushed for more. "At the time of our last meeting, I held out hope that the financial turmoil would gradually ebb and the economy might escape without serious damage," she said. "Subsequent developments have severely shaken that belief." The credit crunch was worsening. The risk of recession was now "all too real."[11]

The National Bureau of Economic Research later determined that a recession had started that very month. When Fed officials trimmed short-term interest rates by a quarter of a percentage point at that December meeting, Yellen said it wasn't enough and they might need to meet again before the next official meeting, an unusual step for the regimented central bank and a sign of emergency.

A few weeks later, with financial markets reeling and new signs emerging that the job market was slowing, the Fed slashed rates before its regularly scheduled meeting. "There are times when events are just moving too fast for us to wait," Bernanke told his colleagues in an emergency conference call.

Yellen backed him. "The risk of a severe recession and credit crisis is unacceptably high," she said. "We need strong action."[12]

As the Fed scrambled to keep up with the worsening storm, Mozilo jumped a second time for a life preserver. A few days before the Fed's emergency rate cut in January 2008, he sold the rest of his firm to Bank of America. Over the next decade the big Charlotte bank waded through billions of dollars in losses and legal settlements surrounding shoddy Countrywide loans it had inherited in the purchase. Bank of America's share price exceeded $51 when it made its initial investment in Mozilo's firm. Fourteen years later, it still hadn't recovered the ground it subsequently lost.

Mozilo blamed the Fed, in part, for his problems. Back in 2006 the central bank was deep into a cycle of interest-rate increases, a process started by Greenspan and carried on by Bernanke for a few more months after he became chairman that year. Mozilo thought the Fed rate increases went too far, making adjustable rate mortgages more costly and harder for households to repay.

"The Fed knowingly—knowing that well over fifty, sixty, seventy percent of the loans made in 2003, '04, '05, and '06 were indexed variable-rate loans, indexed one way or another to the fed funds rate, increased the fed funds rate seventeen times, seventeen consecutive times, with most of the product out there being variable-rate product," he told Wall Street analysts in a 2007 conference call. The rate increases triggered the subsequent wave of delinquencies, he believed. "You never knew when they were going to stop increasing. But the fact they did that had a material impact on affordability, as people went to refinance or people went to buy. Major, major impact."[13]

When contacted years later for his reflections on Yellen, Mozilo said he had no problems with her, though he said he did have problems with journalists who seemed intent on making him look bad. "She was a terrific woman and an excellent regulator," he said. "She was extremely helpful to me and Countrywide."[14]

Yellen offered her reflections to the Financial Crisis Inquiry Commission, a federal body set up to examine the crisis. She seemed to have figured out what was coming sooner than many others, her inquisitors noted during her testimony.

In truth, she said, she hadn't put the pieces of the puzzle together fast enough to stop it.

"I'm sorry," she said. "I wish I had, but I didn't."[15]

16

Financial Panic

Bernanke's Loyal Field Commander
2008

Imagine for a moment that you are a Civil War historian with a comfortable academic job. You have read the battlefront letters and know what happened in the minds of generals, their tactical brilliance and their fateful blunders in places like Chancellorsville, Virginia, and Gettysburg, Pennsylvania, the fear that ruined some and the audacity and grit that drove others. You know the terrain of battlefields, the slope of a Gettysburg hill called Little Round Top that Union troops charged down with bayonets fixed to push back advancing Confederate soldiers. You know the mechanics of the artillery used to slay men in open fields, how far cone-shaped minié ball bullets flew in the rain, how many men it took to pack and fire a cannon. You know how Washington politics shaped the positioning of troops and the men who led them, how political calculations drove the seasons of war.

Imagine then that you take a job as an adviser at the Pentagon. Things go well. Your imagination and your ability to connect history to the present and to events around the world impress others. You seem calm and levelheaded in a town that usually sees only through the next news cycle. Things go so well that you get the job of defense secretary.

Imagine then that a new civil war breaks out under your command, a war nobody saw coming, including you. It happens almost overnight. Now you need to fight it, not with muskets and cannons but with drones and laser-guided missiles. The fate of a nation hangs on your ability to apply lessons of the past to a fast-moving and unexpected modern crisis.

This is what happened to Ben Bernanke. His battlefield was finance.

Bernanke's path to Washington looked a bit like Yellen's. Like her, he was raised in a comfortable Jewish home of modest middle-class means. Also like her, he was motivated to become an economist by childhood stories of the Great Depression.

Bernanke's father was a pharmacist in the small town of Dillon, South Carolina. As a boy, young Ben visited his grandmother Masia in Charlotte, North Carolina, and listened on her front porch as she recounted her experiences of the Great Depression, which sparked his interest in history.[1] An interest in baseball turned into a love of statistics. His family, skittish about the $4,600 annual cost, reluctantly sent him off to Harvard. There, an adviser encouraged Bernanke to go to MIT for his advanced studies. At MIT he read Milton Friedman and Anna Schwartz's *Monetary History*, which turned his attention to the Federal Reserve. His teachers included Robert Solow and Paul Samuelson; his peers Paul Krugman and a collection of other young math experts flocking to MIT in its heyday.

"I guess I am a Great Depression buff the way some people are Civil War buffs," Bernanke said in a book of essays he assembled on the subject.[2] "The Depression was an incredibly dramatic episode—an era of stock market crashes, bread lines, bank runs, and wild currency speculation, with the storm clouds of war gathering ominously in the background all the while. Fascinating, and often tragic, characters abound during this period, from hapless policy makers trying to make sense of events for which their experience had not prepared them, to ordinary people coping heroically with the effects of the economic catastrophe. For my money, few periods are so replete with human interest."

Bernanke started his career as an academic, and he distinguished himself as a professor at Stanford and Princeton. Like Yellen, he was invited to speak to Fed officials at the central bank's exclusive annual gatherings in Jackson Hole. Then in 2002 he landed an offer from President George W. Bush to serve as a governor on the Washington, DC, Fed board, in the shadow of Greenspan. In the 1990s Yellen had helped to start an influx of academics to the Fed, then Bernanke became a beneficiary of that trend in the 2000s.

Bernanke's work as one of several Fed governors under Greenspan was smart and provocative, his writing approachable and audacious. He explained things in ways that seemed clear and coherent, a contrast to the intentional muddle that sometimes came from Greenspan's public pronouncements.

In one speech Bernanke challenged Japan's central bank, the Bank of Japan, to be more aggressive in battling a long period of economic stagnation with creative interest-rate policies. In another he explained how China's economic emergence had led to an ocean of global saving that held down interest rates everywhere. As China and other developing countries got richer, he explained, their people socked away more income. Their glut of saving led to a demand for investments, including US Treasury bonds, which held down interest rates. That helped to explain a riddle that puzzled Greenspan in the 2000s: How come the Fed was raising its benchmark interest rate, but other interest rates kept falling? Rates usually went up and down together.

From his perch as a Fed governor, Bernanke—like Yellen—landed the job of chair of the White House Council of Economic Advisers, where his job was to advise the president on economic policy. President Bush liked to tease the academic about the tan socks he wore unfashionably with his dark suits in the Oval Office. During his years at Stanford and Princeton, Bernanke hadn't been used to dressing up at all.

When Greenspan retired at the age of seventy-nine in 2006, Bush elevated Bernanke to the most powerful economic job in the world: chairman of the Federal Reserve.

The big question when Bernanke became chairman was whether anyone else could handle a job Greenspan had dominated for two decades. Investors and politicians had come to revere Greenspan. Senator John McCain joked more than once that when Greenspan died, somebody should prop him up in a chair and pretend he was still running the central bank.

Bernanke was a quiet man. Maurice Obstfeld, his classmate at MIT, remembered sharing an office with Bernanke when they were graduate students together in the 1970s. They liked and respected each other, yet barely exchanged a word for the whole academic year. When other Fed officials visited his office as governor and later chairman, Bernanke wasn't much for small talk. His taciturn nature intimidated some people, while others saw it as a reflection of a cerebral mindset that was simply different. His lip sometimes quivered when he testified before Congress, not because he wasn't sure what to say but because speaking publicly was uncomfortable for him, especially in front of lawmakers whose motivations made it seem like they were of a different species.

The new Fed chairman sometimes forced himself to be social. At lunchtime he walked through an underground tunnel that connected the Fed's two main buildings beneath C Street, and up an elevator to the same Fed cafeteria where Yellen and Akerlof had first gotten to know each other years earlier. When staff waited for that elevator to the cafeteria, they lined up politely to give others a chance to get off before boarding. Bernanke lined up with them. In the cafeteria, he wandered with his food tray in two hands, asking staffers if they minded if he sat with them. He often started by asking what research they were working on.

Bernanke had an unusual ability to focus and concentrate. He could read about a page a minute in a book and stay focused on the task for hours on end, absorbing information as he went. It allowed him to knock off several books a week, for fun or work. In August 2007, before canceling his summer vacation to deal with market turmoil, he planned to take *The New Bill James Historical Baseball Abstract*, more than a thousand pages, to the beach in South Carolina to read.

He had a wry sense of humor. When Elizabeth Duke, a Fed governor with roots as the leader of a small bank in Virginia, met him in his office to discuss the economy, she commented to him that she couldn't believe she was sitting there talking to the actual Ben Bernanke. "You'll get used to it," he quipped in a steady monotone voice. "I did."

Once, when introduced to two children on "Take Your Child to Work Day," and asked to explain to them how he had achieved such a lofty position, he joked, "You need to be in the wrong place at the wrong time."

When mortgage markets started melting down, Bernanke was combating a gluten allergy that sapped his hunger. His colleagues noticed the cuffs of his pants fraying because he was losing weight, and the legs of his pants were hanging low to the ground over his shoes. He abandoned the cheesy frozen Hot Pockets sandwiches he liked to warm in a microwave oven and went on a gluten-free diet with the help of his wife, Anna.

To manage the ensuing crisis, the subdued general had to marshal all of the Fed's forces quickly, and his own internal forces too. He had set out to be a less domineering leader than Greenspan became in his later years, but Bernanke soon discovered he was going to need to move the Fed with his own quiet will.

The central bank played two different roles, one in normal times and one in crises. During normal times its main job was to guide interest rates up and down to keep inflation low and job growth steady. During crises, it had the additional and perhaps more important job of stopping bank panics. That role was the reason the Fed was created in 1913.

Banking is a simple business at its core, but one with built-in features that makes banks especially vulnerable to collapse. Banks take deposits from households and businesses and then invest that money by making loans to other households or businesses that want mortgages, car loans, or funds to start new business projects. In taking money from depositors and lending it to others, a bank is playing a critical role, moving the resources of society from savers to investors, from places where people have spare money to places where people believe they can put money to work productively. The bank makes profits by charging more for the loans it makes than it pays to the depositors who put their money there for safekeeping.

But there has always been a danger in this arrangement. The health of the bank hangs on its depositors' trust that they will get their money back when they want it. During the 1800s, depositors routinely got worried that they wouldn't get their money back because of some sign of instability around the banks that took their money. Bank loans to railroads or canals might go bad, or rumors might swirl of some swindle, arousing fear in the people who deposited their money there. When depositors rushed to get their money out all at once, and that money was tied up in long-term loans or investments, the bank had a problem known as a run. When people lined up for their money and the bank couldn't deliver, it was threatened with sudden ruin.

The last straw after a century of these crises was the Panic of 1907, which pushed Congress to create the Fed in 1913 as a bulwark against bank runs. The Fed set up something called a discount window: when bank depositors demanded their money all at once, and the banks didn't have the cash on hand to satisfy the unexpected demand, they could go to the Fed's discount window for help. Regional Fed banks had actual windows through which they conducted business.[3] Bankers pledged their loans as collateral and got cash from the Fed that they returned to depositors to calm their fears. When the panic subsided, they would repay the Fed, which became known as the financial system's lender of last resort.

One of Bernanke's critiques of the Fed's behavior during the Great Depression was that it allowed too many banks to fail—more than ten thousand during the 1930s. At a celebration of Milton Friedman's ninetieth birthday in Chicago in 2002, Bernanke turned to the aging professor, whose *Monetary History of the United States* blamed the Fed for the Depression, and said, "You're right, we did it. We're very sorry. But thanks to you, we won't do it again."[4]

In 2008 Ben Bernanke had a modern-day bank run on his hands.

This time the problem wasn't inside banks, at least not at first. It was distributed throughout the financial system, in securities firms, insurance companies, money market mutual funds, hedge funds, and other institutions dealing in strange new mortgage bonds. These instruments typically paid off in the long term, and financial firms borrowed money in the short term to purchase them. Fed officials called this a shadow banking system.

One of the Fed's problems was that it had no infrastructure in place to stop a collapse when panic struck. Bernanke had to create that infrastructure in the middle of an unfolding crisis, at the same time deciding which firms would survive with the Fed's support or die without it.

It was destined to be a messy—and politically fraught—process.

Bernanke's reading of history was that he needed to act boldly to avoid remaking the mistakes of the 1930s. His watchword became "blue sky thinking." No idea, no matter how unorthodox, was off the table.

In March 2008, Bear Stearns fell into a spiral like the one Countrywide had experienced months earlier. As a securities firm, Bear wasn't regulated by the Fed, so it had no access to the central bank's discount window. Yet it behaved like a bank in complex ways: it got short-term funding through lending arrangements with money market mutual funds, commercial paper lenders, or hedge funds, and it invested the money they gave it into real estate instruments. When the institutions that lent to it got scared, they withdrew their funds.

Bernanke set up programs designed to get funds into the hands of securities firms in exchange for collateral, but it was too little, too late for Bear. To prevent its collapse, the Fed lent funds to J.P. Morgan, which in turn bought Bear, with the Fed's agreement that it would take on some of the risk by holding some of Bear's mortgage loans itself.[5]

"An old-fashioned bank run is what really led to Bear Stearns's demise," William Dudley, who ran the New York Fed's market operations, told his colleagues when officials gathered after the collapse. "In this case it wasn't depositors lining up to make withdrawals; it was customers moving their business elsewhere."[6]

Bernanke built an inner circle of advisers in Washington and New York. Dudley was one of them. So was the president of the New York Fed, Timothy Geithner, and a small collection of senior Washington staff and officials.

Yellen wasn't in his inner circle, in part because breakneck decisions had to be confined to a small group of people. In San Francisco Yellen was far removed from the center of action taking place on Wall Street. That was Geithner's ground. To learn more about the Fed's bailout of Bear Stearns, she listened silently to a conference call Fed officials in Washington held to brief news reporters on developments. She didn't want to call Bernanke directly, because he and his staff were already overwhelmed dealing with the crisis.

Another person even further on the outside and looking in that March was Barack Obama, then a senator fighting Hillary Clinton to win the Democratic nomination for the presidency. After the Bear rescue, Obama's campaign adviser Austan Goolsbee arranged for him to talk to Yellen to learn what had happened. In a thirty-minute phone call, she explained that something like a modern-day bank run was spreading like wildfire through financial markets. Her explanation was concise and coherent, which impressed the aspiring president.

Bernanke quickly ran up against resistance to his actions. Jim Bunning, a Republican senator from Kentucky, said that in protecting Bear from collapse, the Fed was picking winners and losers in financial markets and veering toward socialism. Even Paul Volcker, the popular ex–Fed chairman and a Democrat, said the central bank was acting at the "very edge" of its legal authority.[7] In executing the Bear rescue, the Fed depended on a Depression-era law that permitted it to lend widely during "unusual and exigent circumstances," a provision that it would have to cite over and over again in the months ahead.[8]

Inside the Fed a collection of Bernanke's colleagues resisted too. Some didn't like the central bank extending the reach of its programs to new firms. Where would it stop? They argued that its rescues encouraged firms to take more and more risk, the idea known in economics as "moral hazard," which could lead to even bigger problems down the road. Some Fed officials also didn't like the fact that the central bank was cutting interest rates when inflation was still high. Interest rate reductions risked sending inflation higher and destroying the credibility the central bank had established since its mistakes of the 1970s, they believed.

"I have yet to see a plausible case for market failure that would warrant such intervention by a central bank here," Jeffrey Lacker, president of the Richmond Fed, said in a Federal Open Market Committee conference call on March 10, as the central bank expanded its lending programs.[9] "I believe we need to adopt a strategy of easing much less aggressively going forward," he said on March 18, a few days after the Bear bailout, when the Fed yet again cut interest rates to prop up a sinking economy.[10]

Bernanke came to see that he could count on Yellen's support for the risky interventions he was undertaking. While many others expressed doubts, she saw the problem the way he did. At times, in retrospect, she even looked a step ahead. Risks to the whole financial system were large and building rapidly, she argued against Lacker in the March 10 conference call, as Bernanke tried to sell his plans to lend more widely to firms in need of funds: "A dangerous dynamic has set in."

Yellen often framed decisions as a balance between an action's costs and benefits. That was how she had handled the intense Kyoto debates in the White House years earlier. Important choices were rarely simple. They had to be weighed, so she was routinely measuring the world around her. In this case, she calculated, the risk of moral hazard was outweighed by the benefit of preventing a financial system meltdown.

When Bernanke wanted to cut interest rates after the Bear bailout, she agreed with that too. High inflation shouldn't be a constraint, she said. With the economy in such peril, she argued that inflation was bound to fall substantially. It hadn't happened yet, but it likely would. Like Bernanke, in a time of crisis she believed the imperative was to act boldly. "I don't believe in gradualism in circumstances like these," she said at the March 18 meeting. "I think it is important to move as much as we can."

These were transformative times for Yellen. Like Bernanke, she'd been drawn to economics by stories of the Great Depression. Now she was staring at the potential of a repeat of that disaster, and she was part of a group of people uniquely placed to have a chance to prevent it. They had failed to see it coming, but it wasn't too late to contain the damage. The moment, in her mind, called for maximum effort and an appreciation of the lessons of history.

The Bear bailout stabilized markets for a time, but it didn't last long. In the months ahead the financial system became something like a wartime triage tent, with patients spread etherized on tables in shock, convulsing at times, calming, and then convulsing again. With only a fractured and archaic system in place to manage a fast-moving modern meltdown, the regulators were forced to make ad hoc decisions about which financial firms to save and how to put to rest the ones it didn't or couldn't. Part of the calculation was this: If the firm collapses, how many others will it take down with it?

One of the next to go was another California mortgage lender in Yellen's backyard, this one named IndyMac. Like Countrywide, it was regulated by the Office of Thrift Supervision, not the Fed. Also like Countrywide, when it went into its tailspin, it came to the Fed for help.

Under the Fed's expanded programs IndyMac was eligible for loans from the central bank, but Yellen's supervisors worried that it wouldn't have the resources to repay. The Fed was mandated to lend widely, but only when firms had collateral of value. Unbeknownst to Yellen, the OTS had downgraded its assessment of IndyMac's health without telling the Fed. She was also unaware that the Federal Deposit Insurance Corp. was preparing to close the firm. Yellen's team tightened the terms of the central bank's loan and was lucky the Fed wasn't on the hook for more, she told her colleagues during a discussion that summer. "Troubled banks can be downgraded and fail very rapidly," she warned.[11] Making decisions about which firms to help was even harder when the Fed depended on the judgments of other regulators about the health of banks getting central bank money.

IndyMac was closed by regulators two weeks after it came to the Fed for help.[12] "San Francisco did a really good job in a difficult situation," Bernanke told Yellen at the meeting.

"I don't think that IndyMac is going to be the last failing bank," she said. It was a point she would repeat to colleagues all summer. This was going to get worse.

In Washington, Fannie Mae and Freddie Mac were an even bigger concern.

Congress had created Fannie Mae in 1938 to bolster the housing market during the Great Depression. With the government's backing, it purchased mortgages insured by the Federal Housing Administration.

In 1968, Congress and the Johnson administration didn't like the debt Fannie was adding to the government's ledgers. They turned it into a hybrid beast—a private corporation with private shareholders and highly paid executives, off the government's ledgers, but blessed with the implicit backing of US taxpayers. The government connection helped it borrow at lower interest rates than private firms, an immense advantage. Congress also granted it new powers to buy mortgages and package them into securities. Freddie Mac was created two years later with a similar role.

The two mortgage behemoths collectively sat on more than $5 trillion in mortgages that they owned or guaranteed by the time of the crisis. They were among Angelo Mozilo's best customers. Feeling threatened by private-sector competition in the 2000s, they expanded into riskier mortgages, in the process earning their executives enormous sums. Fannie's chief executive, Daniel Mudd, made about $65 million between 2000 and 2008.[13] All the while, Fannie and Freddie were lobbying lawmakers to keep regulators at bay. Between 1999 and 2008 they spent $164 million convincing officials not to impose tougher oversight of their activities. They also demanded they be allowed to rack up huge amounts of debt to fuel their mortgage lending. By the end of 2007, they had about $74 of debt for every $75 of loans they backed, making each among the most leveraged of any financial institution in the nation. John Kerr, one of Fannie's regulators, called it "the worst-run financial institution" he had seen in his many years as a bank regulator. Another regulator likened its internal processes for managing mortgages to a bowl of spaghetti.

Yet Fannie and Freddie were too big to fail. Their portfolios accounted for about half of all US mortgages. If either collapsed, it would take the rest of the financial system with it. After months of trying to find some other way out, on September 7, US Treasury Secretary Hank

Paulson announced the inevitable. The federal government was taking both Fannie and Freddie over. Paulson hoped the Treasury's explicit backing would calm investors by showing that there was a firm floor under the mortgage market. But it did the opposite. If Fannie and Freddie could collapse, who was next?

On September 8, investors turned their attention to Lehman Brothers.

Fed officials had spent the summer game-planning for the storm to hit the investment bank. Geithner liked to talk about "spraying foam on the runway" for its prospective crash, meaning programs to prevent the fallout from hitting other financial institutions. But that was going to be a challenge. Lehman was a large player in markets for complex financial instruments, including credit default swaps that exposed hedge funds and other financial institutions to its potential failure. If it collapsed, they wouldn't get their money back. It also depended on outside lenders for short-term funds; a default would expose them too. Another problem: Lehman said it owned $54 billion worth of real estate assets, but few believed its holdings were worth anywhere near that amount. This meant its collateral wasn't worth much.

The US Treasury was exhausted by bailouts. "I just can't stomach us bailing out Lehman,"[14] Paulson's chief of staff, Jim Wilkinson, wrote to a press aide a few days after the Fannie and Freddie bailout. Paulson asked the chief executive of Bank of America, Ken Lewis, to put on his "imagination hat" and try to find a way to buy Lehman on his own, but Lewis wasn't buying without government help. When Lehman's chief executive, Richard Fuld, called Lewis to try to talk about a deal, Lewis's wife answered. Her husband wasn't going to pick up the phone, she told him; please stop calling.

Paulson summoned the heads of Wall Street's big firms to meet at the New York Fed to sort out Lehman's problems on a Friday, telling them the Treasury wouldn't participate in a bailout. "Not a penny," he said.[15]

Lewis turned his attention to the next investment bank likely to fail, Merrill Lynch. That weekend he bought it for $50 billion, two-thirds of its value a year earlier.[16] Another potential buyer, the British bank Barclays, backed out of a Lehman bailout when its regulators refused to approve the transaction.

Early Monday morning, days after the Fannie Mae takeover, Lehman Brothers filed for bankruptcy protection. Within hours an impossible array of other firms, including a money market fund called the Reserve Fund, the insurer AIG, industrial firms including General Electric, and more banks, including Morgan Stanley, Wachovia, and Washington Mutual, all found themselves under intense pressure from customers and lenders who wanted to get their money out.

The Lehman collapse was Ben Bernanke's Battle of Antietam, the nation's bloodiest day in four years of harrowing civil war, the day Union forces suffered grievous losses and drove Abraham Lincoln to bold and aggressive action on and off the battlefield. "This is the economic equivalent of war," Paulson said on a call with Bernanke and others. "The market is ready to collapse."[17]

Americans had long harbored a distrust of banking and the people who did it, which helped to explain the backlash Bernanke knew was coming. Thomas Jefferson, author of the Declaration of Independence and third president of the United States, was also an indebted Virginia plantation owner who described banks as more dangerous than standing armies. President Andrew Jackson called bankers vipers and thieves. Henry Ford, founder of the Ford Motor Company, was quoted as saying, "It is well enough that people of the nation do not understand our banking and money system, for if they did, I believe there would be a revolution before tomorrow morning."

Yet finance also was essential to the workings of a market economy. At its core, money was the means by which humans escaped inefficient barter. Banking was the means through which men and women with good ideas found resources to put those ideas to work, to develop inventions, and to build new industries. It was also the means through which savers prepared for the future. In the simple notion of interest on loans was the essentially hopeful idea that money and ideas put to work today might be worth even more in the future when properly employed.

Finance, in short, might be ugly to some, but it was also necessary to all.

Bernanke understood that if the wheels of finance came to a halt, so would the wheels of commerce, including the creation of income and jobs that sustained families. In the aftermath of Lehman's collapse, he saw that his worst fears had been realized. Panic spread, and a full-blown financial meltdown was now potentially on his hands.

He turned to the theories of a nineteenth-century British writer named Walter Bagehot for guidance. In his book *Lombard Street: A Description of the Money Market*, Bagehot argued that the job of a central bank in a panic was to lend aggressively: "A panic, in a word, is a species of neuralgia, and according to the rules of science you must not starve it." Central banks "must lend to merchants, to minor bankers, to 'this man and that man,' whenever the security is good. In wild periods of alarm, one failure makes many, and the best way to prevent the derivative failures is to arrest the primary failure which causes them." Bernanke put Bagehot's rules of financial warfare to work, unleashing all of his cannons. Heedless of the unpopularity he was surely inviting, the mild, unlikely general became perhaps the boldest financier in human history.

Bernanke and Paulson agreed to bail out AIG a day after the fallout from Lehman's collapse spread to other firms and markets. Then Bernanke created new lending programs never used before to keep banks and other modern-day financiers—like money market mutual funds and commercial paper lenders—from getting caught in the vortex. Without these loan programs, big industrial firms, including GE and US automakers, would also be vulnerable.

With Bush's permission, Bernanke and Paulson went to Congress and said they needed $700 billion to prop up the banking system and avoid disaster. A presidential election was just two months away. After one contentious meeting in the White House with Bush and lawmakers, Paulson got down on one knee. "Don't blow this up," he begged Nancy Pelosi, House speaker and a Democrat.

"We're not the ones trying to blow this up," she shot back, noting Paulson's own party was resisting the plan.[18]

The vast majority of funds dispersed under the program were eventually recouped; the ultimate cost to the federal government was estimated to be $31 billion.[19]

At every turn, Yellen, like a loyal field commander, supported Bernanke's moves and urged him to stay on a bold course while others wavered, second-guessed, and dissented. "It is time for all hands on deck when it comes to our policy tools," she said in October.[20] The next month, the Fed announced that it would buy hundreds of billions of dollars' worth of mortgage bonds issued by Fannie Mae and Freddie Mac to calm the mortgage market and breathe life back into lending. A few weeks after that, the Fed pushed its main lending rate to near zero, more grease to get the financial system moving again.

Yellen started her presentation at the Fed's final policy meeting of the year with an accounting joke: On the left side of bank balance sheets, where their assets were recorded, nothing was right, she said. On the right side of bank balance sheets, where their access to funds was recorded, nothing was left.

Then she turned serious. Fed officials were going to have to figure out how to restart an economy that had cratered. A deep and painful recession loomed. But Yellen wasn't ready to relent. Her words from the earlier October meeting became her watchwords for the coming years.

"We need to do much more," she said, "and the sooner the better."

Janet Yellen at the birthday party of a childhood friend
(Courtesy of Barbara Schwartz)

A note from Yellen to a childhood friend
(Courtesy of Barbara Schwartz)

On a cruise with her family, circa 1960
(Courtesy of Janet Yellen)

Robby's second
birthday party in
Berkeley, California
(Courtesy of Janet Yellen)

Wedding day with George, 1978
(Courtesy of Janet Yellen)

The LM Curve

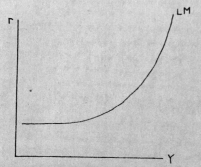

Last time we introduced the notion of an LM curve, which is a locus of values of r and Y which, for given values of M and P, satisfy the equilibrium condition in the money market, $M/p = L(r, Y)$. The LM curve is usually drawn as a concave function of r. This reflects the belief that <u>the interest elasticity of demand for money is a decreasing function of r.</u> At some sufficiently low value of r, the interest elasticity of demand for money may become infinite, in which case, a liquidity <u>trap</u> is said to exist, and the LM curve is horizontal in this region.

Graphical Derivation of the LM Curve

If we divide the demand for money, $L(r, Y)$ into two portions, $L(r, Y) = L_s(r) + L_T(Y)$ where L_s is the speculative demand for money and a function of r alone, and L_T is the transactions demand for money and a function of Y alone, then we may derive the LM curve from the underlying behavioral relationships, given values of P and M, in the 4-quadrant diagram below.

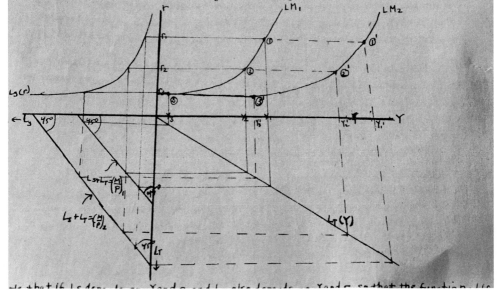

A sample of Janet Yellen's notes from the classes of James Tobin

(*Courtesy of Heidi Hartmann*)

Yellen in the Rose Garden, 1997, flanked from left to right by Lawrence
Summers, Al Gore, Bill Clinton, and Frank Raines

(AFP via Getty Images)

Nobel ceremony for George, with Robby, in 2001

(Courtesy of Janet Yellen)

Hiking in New Hampshire, 2006
(Courtesy of Janet Yellen)

Yellen debating economics with her friend and mentor Joseph Stiglitz, 2013
(Bloomberg via Getty Images)

Yellen as Fed chair, with Vice Chairman Stanley Fischer, 2015
(Courtesy of Federal Reserve)

With Alan Greenspan, Ben Bernanke, and Paul Volcker,
living Fed leaders of her time
(Courtesy of Janet Yellen)

Yellen having a
laugh at the British
embassy, 2017
*(Getty Images North
America)*

Yellen saying farewell to the Fed staff, 2019
(Courtesy of the Federal Reserve)

Yellen meeting with President Joe Biden, November 2021,
to discuss the debt ceiling
(Official White House Photo by Cameron Smith)

Visiting her favorite spot in Hawaii with George
(Courtesy of Janet Yellen)

17

"These Are
Fucking People!"

At the Center of a New Way
of Central Banking
2009–2010

In late 2009, Mary Daly sat with Yellen and other San Francisco Fed staff economists to prepare for another central bank meeting. Daly had taken an unusual path to the central bank. The Missouri daughter of divorced parents—a postman and a stay-at-home mother—she had dropped out of high school at fifteen and supported herself delivering doughnuts and selling lingerie at a Target store.

A friend suggested she finish her general equivalency diploma. She did, and then took classes at the University of Missouri.[1] In college Daly considered pursuing a career in psychology, but a professor suggested that she might be too blunt to interact with people, so she decided to become an economist.

Daly earned her PhD at Syracuse University and then set out to understand the lives of people living at the margins of the economy, where she once resided. By 2009, she had been a little-known staff economist at the San Francisco Fed for more than a decade. She specialized in research that probed the fringes of labor markets, including the fortunes of people with disabilities, Black men, and the elderly. She was also working on papers that examined the economic and social underpinnings of suicide.

The financial crisis had been tamed by then, but the economic aftershocks had not. After the bailouts of 2008, Fed officials and a new president, Barack Obama, expected an economic recovery to begin in the summer of 2009. It did, but with no vigor. The unemployment rate kept rising. In October that year it hit 10 percent. Among fifteen million unemployed Americans, more than six million had been out of work for six months or more.

Yellen's staff presented her with forecasts showing that they expected the jobless rate to decline slowly over years. She was unsatisfied. There were lives underneath these statistics; that was one of her mantras. The recovery wasn't good enough. The Fed had a lot more work to do, and Yellen had a message for her team.

"These are fucking people!" Yellen exclaimed, banging her fist on the table at a San Francisco Fed meeting. She wanted to know more about what was happening underneath the high unemployment rate. If she was going to make a case that the central bank needed to do more, she needed to understand the contours of the problem and where it reached. Her staff had to dig deeper. She had no patience for complacency.

Mary Daly's work was more relevant than ever.

"It was a defining moment in my career," the former high school dropout said. "This was a call for me to have a place at the table. I had an epiphany that day. This was exactly what I wanted to be for the rest of my career."

Yellen's character also took on new shape in the aftermath of the crisis. She was already known as methodical, precise, calm, approachable, perhaps a little neurotic about deadlines and preparation and traveling with her own pillow. She also had a light side that bubbled up in laughter, and a compassionate side that showed when she earnestly checked in on colleagues dealing with ailing family members, or even pets. In the aftermath of the 2008 financial crisis, she projected a sense of urgency and intensity that struck others around her. James Tobin's moral passion drove her more than ever. She expected that urgency in her colleagues, too.

Yellen and Akerlof were both drawn to economics by stories of the hardships suffered by people without work. As a girl sitting at the dinner table with her father, the neighborhood doctor, Yellen heard about patients who fell into spirals of depression, alcohol abuse, and divorce when they lost a paycheck and the dignity that came with it. She was drawn to Akerlof in part by his preoccupation with the same issue, and together they set out to study it and find ways to combat it. They seemed to have the same moral compass. They were drawn to Keynes because he offered answers, and central to his answer was that the government needed to get involved during economic crises.

If ever there was a time in her life to put her knowledge to work, Yellen believed, this was it. It became the period that defined her.

The problem after the financial crisis was that the Fed had shot all of its normal artillery. Back in December 2008, Bernanke had already convinced his colleagues to cut the Fed's main interest rate to near zero to help households and businesses ease the burdens of debt, or take out new loans to encourage dormant spending and investing. If the Fed was going to encourage economic activity, it was going to have to find new ways to do it.

The Fed could theoretically try to engineer a negative interest rate, essentially charging banks money if they didn't lend out the funds it gave them. But that was so far from the realm of its experience, and seemed so hard to pull off when so much of American finance didn't even happen in banks. Fed officials were reluctant to even try, though central bankers in Europe and Japan later embraced that tactic.

There were two other courses of action the Fed could take. One was to promise investors and banks that rates were going to stay near zero for a long time. That would pull down borrowing costs not just on a three-month loan or six-month loan but also on loans for two years, three years, or even longer. By pulling down borrowing costs for longer periods, the Fed might encourage more activity immediately, and even more refinancing of old and expensive debt.

Another way to pull down long-term interest rates was to buy bonds that didn't mature until years down the road. Bernanke liked to call that "long-term securities asset purchases," but Wall Street tends to gravitate to simple two-word terms. So instead, in the bowels of Manhattan, that idea became known as quantitative easing, or QE. Japan had tried to do something like this during its long economic malaise, but Bernanke believed that Japanese central bankers had botched the effort, and suspected he could do it better.

Over the next few years, Yellen became one of Bernanke's leading advocates for both actions, not only a vote he counted on to support contentious policies but also a voice pushing others to join.

Even though it had set aside the most radical actions—including negative interest rates—the Fed was still entering an unknown new world. What if it promised to keep rates low but then had to go back on its promise? Would investors even believe the central bank? The Fed cared so much about its credibility, and this could squander it. Would it cause even more uncertainty by leaving investors to guess exactly how long it would keep rates low?

As for quantitative easing, the risks and unknowns were enormous. The Fed was pumping trillions of dollars into the financial system as it gobbled up long-term bonds from investors and banks. Would that set off a new inflationary fire? Would it cause a new financial bubble? Would it crush the value of the US dollar in global markets by flooding the world with an oversupply, perhaps even render the dollar worthless as the US central bank engulfed the world with funds? Wasn't it inadvertently punishing savers who put their money away for safekeeping, and were now being hit with tiny returns on those investments? Was any of this a job to be outsourced to unelected officials?

The Fed started down a path with these policies during the crisis. After pushing its benchmark interest rate to near zero in 2008, the central bank announced in early 2009 that it expected to keep the interest rate near zero for an extended period of time. The mortgage bonds the Fed started buying in 2008 were pumped up to more than $1 trillion and expanded to include long-term Treasury bonds.

Yellen wanted Bernanke to double down on everything; what the central bank had done wasn't enough. He was sympathetic to that view, but had a divided committee to bring along. Yellen made her case to colleagues at a December 2009 meeting in Washington with stories from back in California. "My contacts are more likely to be considering continued layoffs rather than any substantial hiring," she said. "They remain shell-shocked and traumatized from recent events. A couple of them emphasize that they're making plans based on what they see over the next three to six months, since they have little confidence looking beyond that horizon. They remain focused on ensuring their survival and are hesitant to hire or invest beyond replacing essential equipment."[2]

Officials on the San Francisco Fed's board of directors worried that the economy was so weak that "we will end up with a lost generation of people whose skills and labor market attachment atrophy from disuse," Yellen told her colleagues. Her son, Robby, had it much better than most Americans, but even he saw the impact of a tough job market up close. He finished his PhD studies at Harvard and explored a brutal academic hiring market in which few university departments were adding to their ranks of professors. His problem was compounded by the fact that his back problem had set back his research. He decided to wait it out and spend two more years researching before trying the job market again.

...

As Yellen rose in public life, Akerlof tried to stay out of her way, and she his. In February 2009, Akerlof and Robert Shiller published a book called *Animal Spirits*, a reference to Keynes's argument that human emotion had to be taken into account when considering economic behavior.[3] The profession had scrubbed emotion from its mathematical formulas; Akerlof and Shiller believed it needed to be put back in to understand and respond to the financial crisis and its aftermath.

What had caused the banking panic? That was simple: fear.

How did you address it? That was simple too: the Fed.

Their book was covered with drawings of hairy creatures climbing up and down the unpredictable wiggles of an economic chart, their faces displaying a range of feelings including euphoria, confidence, fear, and confusion. Ed Koren, the *New Yorker* cartoonist whose drawings had inspired Akerlof to think about economics differently, drew them for the project.

The book made a few glancing references to Yellen's academic work, but Akerlof sought to avoid any mention that his wife was a top official at the institution he was calling to action. In the acknowledgments, he singled out and thanked Koren, the Canadian Institute for Advanced Research, and the National Science Foundation for their input and support, but not Yellen. He didn't want his affection for far-out ideas to become her problem, and she didn't want her public life to stop him from writing what he wanted to write.

He was a theorist and she was a practitioner. He trafficked in a world of ideas and technical research. She trafficked in a world of putting ideas to work. They tried to pursue both on their own terms. At the dinner table he tested ideas, and she often shot them down. But you didn't need to dig deep to see how the work of each was driven by a common worldview.

Yellen and Akerlof both believed the government had a role to play in times just like this. Though Fed officials were exhausted, and the tools they had at their disposal were constrained, the central bank couldn't wait on the sidelines for conditions to improve, they each thought.

Animal Spirits likened the government's job in a crisis to that of the cat in Dr. Seuss's book *The Cat in the Hat Comes Back*. In the children's book, the cat tries to solve the problem of a ring in the bathtub. "He tried Plan A, and then Plan B, and then Plan C, and then even Plan D." If the Fed found its plans weren't working, it needed to go to Plan E, Akerlof and Shiller wrote. It was their version of Bernanke's "whatever it takes" mentality, largely contrary to the teachings of the Chicago school that Yellen and Akerlof had fought as young researchers decades earlier.

As Chicago school economists might note, there was an irony in Akerlof's choice of metaphor: in the Cat in the Hat story, it was the cat who caused the ring in the tub in the first place while stuffing himself with cake. And this was exactly what was behind a backlash that brewed in the aftermath of the financial crisis. In the eyes of many opponents of the Fed, the government was the problem and not the solution.

Bernanke bore the brunt of this backlash. The *Wall Street Journal*'s editorial page made him the focus of routine criticism.[4] Bernanke had encouraged Greenspan to keep interest rates too low before the crisis, fostering the disastrous housing boom, *WSJ* editorials charged. Now the Fed was repeating the exact same mistake, the opinion pages asserted, while warning this would lead to any number of bad outcomes—another bubble, a collapse in the value of the US dollar, an upsurge of inflation.

At its most scathing and unseemly, the *WSJ* editorial page cheered when Texas governor Rick Perry accused Bernanke of treason and warned he'd be treated "pretty ugly" if he ever showed up in Texas. The editorial page acknowledged that Perry might have chosen his words a bit poorly—particularly the point about treason—but called the point of his broader attack on Bernanke a public service.[5]

Lawmakers also went after Bernanke. When *Time* recognized his audacity by naming him Person of the Year in 2009, Republican senator Jim Bunning replied that Adolf Hitler had also won the award, as had Joseph Stalin and Richard Nixon, twice. Richard Shelby, the Alabama Republican on the Senate Banking Committee, blasted the bailouts. "For many years I held the Federal Reserve in very high regard," he told Bernanke at a hearing. "I fear now, however, that our trust and confidence were misplaced."[6]

Democrats also heaped on scorn. Vermont senator Bernie Sanders, a socialist who caucused with progressives in the party, joined with Texas Republican Ron Paul in demanding that the Fed's interest-rate decisions be subjected to closer scrutiny by Congress through annual audits.[7] Bernanke saw that as an attack on the Fed's independence, and an invitation to the kind of political meddling that had led to a disastrous outbreak of inflation in the 1970s.

Bernanke was a stoic man, but he was also proud. The backlash wore on him. His term was set to expire in 2010, and Obama considered giving the job to Lawrence Summers, one of the president's top economic advisers. Obama had promised Summers as much when he convinced the Harvard professor to join his administration. Bernanke, meanwhile, wasn't sure he even wanted another term.

"I understood that criticism was part of the job, but it bothered me nonetheless," he reflected in his memoir later. "On darker days I wondered whether I was the right person for the job, and if remaining in the post was the right thing for the country and for the Federal Reserve."[8]

Despite the blowback, he decided he needed to finish the job, told Obama as much, and was nominated by the president and confirmed by a recalcitrant Senate for a second term. In giving Bernanke four more years, Obama went back on his word to Summers, but he believed the times demanded it.

The blowback that plagued Bernanke came to Yellen's San Francisco Fed, too. The central banking system had gone through its own building boom in the 2000s. In 2007, after two years of delays, the San Francisco Fed opened a gleaming new waterfront tower in the city's financial district, eighteen stories tall, wrapped in stainless steel, and described by the *San Francisco Chronicle* as "daunting and dazzling."[9] President Donald Trump, a former real estate mogul, in an executive order later called it one of the ugliest structures in the city.[10]

A progressive protest movement called Occupy Wall Street stationed itself with tents and placards outside the building after the crisis. Before encampments were stationed there, Yellen heard stories of economists and other building workers being harassed or challenged on their way to work or in grocery market checkout lines. Ron Paul's new book, *End the Fed*, became popular on the right, fueling blowback across the political spectrum.

Yellen always believed that people should take some sense of pride and belonging in their jobs and workplace. It was common sense, and it was also borne out in the research she and Akerlof had done together. For most people, work is more than just a paycheck. People belong to a culture in a workplace, and if the culture is strong, they will be more satisfied and more productive. After the crisis, she held town-hall-style meetings inside the building and started a regular routine called "Java with Janet" with local Fed employees to explain what the central bank was doing and why it mattered.

The Fed had clearly erred before the crisis—Bernanke, Greenspan, and others acknowledged that its regulation was lax—but many of the criticisms leveled against it after the crisis turned out to be wrong for years after the crisis. Despite the many warnings that the Fed's policies were going to spark an outbreak of inflation, consumer prices actually retreated, a sign of the economy's lasting weakness after more than two years of recession and financial mayhem. Consumer prices fell in 2009, the first sustained decline since after the Korean War ended in the 1950s. After that, for a decade, annual price changes rarely kept up with the Fed's 2 percent goal.

Warnings of a collapse in the dollar also didn't play out. The currency strengthened because the rest of the world was in even worse shape. Europe in particular was headed toward deepening crises in Greece, Portugal, Italy, and Spain, all heavily indebted and plagued by unhealthy banks. Many of the Fed's critics wanted higher interest rates from the central bank, austere tax and spending policies, and a rejection of bank bailouts. Europe was a case study in what happened with those policies: it tried them, went back into recession, and then abandoned its most austere policies because of the disastrous effects.

Nor did another discernable financial bubble appear. As for whether the Fed was punishing savers with its policies, Bernanke and Yellen argued it would have been even worse for savers if the central bank had acted differently. If it wasn't as aggressive, the United States might have gone back into recession, which would have punished savers even more. That's the exact problem Europe faced. It ended up with negative interest rates and higher unemployment.

"I continue to see a persuasive case for further policy easing," Yellen told her colleagues in a late 2009 policy meeting.[11] At the very least, she said, the Fed needed to resist the temptation to start raising interest rates prematurely, which could strangle an already weak expansion. This was a mistake the central bank made in the 1930s, and it extended the Great Depression. The Fed's bond purchase programs were on track to expire in 2010, and she said that the central bank should consider resuming them. "I always felt like she was a bit ahead of everybody else," said Brian Sack, who ran the New York Fed's powerful market desk.

The decision on resuming bond buying came to a head in the middle of 2010. The unemployment rate seemed to be stuck above 9 percent.

Even though the Fed sought a predictable rate of inflation around 2 percent, official readings kept coming up short. If allowed to continue, the United States risked falling into the upside-down world that had plagued Japan for nearly two decades, where the economy was so weak that prices fell broadly and routinely, something called deflation, not inflation.

In normal times it is manageable or even healthy to have prices fall in a few discrete sectors, like televisions or women's dresses, but when it happens across the economy broadly, it can be a sign that an unhealthy anemia plagues the marketplace, a sickness that produces symptoms that get increasingly hard to treat. When prices fall broadly, for instance, household and business debts become harder to pay off. That's because household and business incomes get sucked down with the broader trend of consumer prices, leaving people with less money to pay fixed interest costs on their loans.

In mid-2010 Bernanke realized that he might need to restart the bond-buying programs, as Yellen had urged six months earlier. The action was bound to be deeply unpopular, not only to many in the public but also inside the Fed. The central bank was delving deeper into this unknown world, experimenting with untested theories on a subject so abstract that nobody knew exactly where it would lead.

"What are the long-term implications of doing more, or even of maintaining the current level of monetary stimulus?" Thomas Hoenig, president of the Kansas City Fed, asked at a tense August meeting. "Can we actually improve the economy faster by keeping rates at zero, or are we perhaps adding to the uncertainty by taking actions that are, in my opinion, unsustainable in the intermediate and long run? Are we, in fact, damaging the long-run economy, as our last experiment with low rates, in my opinion, might have done?"[12]

As that debate unfolded, Yellen and Akerlof prepared for another move. Donald Kohn, a veteran of the Fed and Bernanke's top lieutenant during the financial crisis, was retiring as vice chairman. Obama asked Yellen to replace him. Geithner, who became Obama's Treasury secretary, saw her as the obvious choice. Obama had been impressed with her when they spoke by phone after the Bear Stearns collapse, though he didn't know much about her beyond that.

It had been more than a decade since Yellen and Akerlof left Washington. They had no plans to return when they left in 1999. They were coming back to a much different place, a more bitter and more partisan place, boiling in intractable problems, far away from the optimism of the 1990s.

Yellen would be Bernanke's number two. She got the job by being a smart and steady hand during the worst of times, exceptionally prepared, with her eyes open to the next problem that might be lurking around the corner. She also got it with a view that this was no time for timidity.

After Yellen left the San Francisco Fed, her research director, John Williams, became the bank's new president. When he left to run the New York Fed a few years later, the San Francisco Fed hired a new leader. Her name was Mary Daly.

18

Yellen as #2

Palace Intrigue
2010–2014

Every organization has its own unique culture, shaped by the style of its leaders and by its own history and foundational stories. The Fed's culture is quiet, formal, and regal.

The Fed's chair, like a king or queen, is the center of its attention and formalities. The chairman's second-floor office is spacious, with high ceilings, long windows, dark built-in bookcases, and an elegant chandelier. Bernanke worked at a nineteenth-century wooden desk and met visitors at a brown tufted leather couch that sat near his fireplace, flanked by flags of the United States and the Fed's symbolic eagle. He slept on the couch some nights during the worst days of the crisis.

The room felt a little bigger than a squash court. A small wood-paneled library was nearby, as was an anteroom for larger meetings. Visitors to the court waited in a comfortable greeting room with two large upholstered couches, a coffee table, and a receptionist before being escorted down the long hallway to the chairman's office. People spoke quietly.

Spacious governor's offices lined the hallway around the chairman, but activity in the building buzzed around the chairman, not them. Yellen had joked at Harvard that she could die in her office, and people wouldn't notice for days. She made the same joke at the Fed when she

was a governor in the 1990s. Her new office as vice chair was at the end
of the hallway, in a corner of the building.

One floor up, an army of researchers quietly tapped away at their
analysis. The Fed is the largest employer of economists in the nation.
Every year when new PhDs are coming onto the market, it is among the
most active and dependable recruiters. The cream of the crop tend to go
to MIT, Harvard, Chicago, or other top universities as assistant professors, but the Fed is also a sought-after alternative.

In Washington, information flows to the Fed leader, a fact that has
rankled governors for decades. In the 1990s the heads of the Fed's various research divisions were dubbed the central bank's barons, serving
at the center of the chairman's court. When Karen Johnson was named
director of the Fed's division of international finance in 1998, Donald
Kohn, then head of the monetary affairs division, where interest-rate
policies were formulated, jokingly gave her a scepter to mark her eleva-
tion into the inner sanctum.

Some economists would get a chance to present to the Federal Open
Market Committee or to present to the board in its regularly scheduled
weekly meeting. When she was a governor in Greenspan's Fed, Yellen
and Alan Blinder, then vice chairman, ruffled the power structure by
reaching out directly to researchers. Bernanke also tried to loosen up
the culture when he took over from Greenspan. He gave governors and
regional bank presidents a chance to speak first at Federal Open Market Committee meetings before handing down his conclusions, a move
other decision-makers saw as an attempt to empower them. Then he
tried to summarize and incorporate their thinking into his formulations.

At the same time he seemed to take on a lot of work himself before official gatherings, a trait reinforced by the intensity of the financial
crisis and Bernanke's circumscribed personality. Senior staff worked in
loyal overdrive for him through the crisis, feeding him ideas and analyses
to the point of their own exhaustion. Brian Madigan, the head of mone-

tary affairs, which designed interest-rate policy, started looking pale and gaunt. William English, who succeeded him, developed intense back pain and worked around the clock, often while lying down. A gentle giant—six feet, ten inches tall, quiet, deliberate, and as wonky as the rest—he often showed up at meetings with a large cushion to relieve the pressure on his lower spine.

As vice chair, Yellen was the first person to arrive at most board meetings. She became part of Bernanke's inner circle, along with William Dudley, who had succeeded Geithner as president of the New York Fed when Geithner became Treasury secretary. That group of three top officials was known inside the Fed as "the Troika," which formulated plans to bring to the other governors and bank presidents for debate and approval. Bernanke drove the process and worried about convincing others to follow his lead. Yellen and Dudley pushed him to stay the course with his unconventional policies amid internal and external resistance. They also pulled him back when he dreamed up ideas they didn't think could be turned into action.

Being a number two in any organization is not easy. You are near power but don't hold it yourself. You are expected to be loyal to the leader and thus need to be careful about speaking out too aggressively. You might lead the place someday, but it's not in any way clear you will. Your job is to help the number one, even if that means subduing some of the very talents or impulses that got you into the number-two spot to begin with. When Yellen became vice chair of the Fed, no previous number two had ever been elevated to the top spot. She wasn't gunning for the top spot, anyway, though she was aware it was possible, with Bernanke likely stepping down after his second term ended in two years.

Yellen arrived with a fire in her that surprised some of her new colleagues in Washington. She had a sense of mission that wasn't obvious in the methodical presentations she made in policy meetings or public speeches, or when she milled comfortably with others at official dinners.

Serving as vice chair was going to mean striking some balance between working loyally as a lieutenant in the shadows, and pushing aggressively toward outcomes she viewed as imperative. She and Bernanke had similar goals—to push as hard as they could to get the economy going again—but operated from much different perches and with different personal styles. Bernanke was remote, and also trying to play the role of a consensus builder. Yellen was warm, and also driven to counter intense opposition to get the policy she thought was right.

They were friendly with each other, but not too friendly. Bernanke invited Yellen to sit with him at a Washington Nationals baseball game. He was a big fan. She had lost interest in baseball after the Dodgers decided to leave Brooklyn in 1957. During a rain delay she thought it might be time to leave, but he thought the game would resume quickly. They stuck around and had a beer together under cover. When the Nationals rallied, Bernanke was thrilled, Yellen not so much.

Yellen and Akerlof rented a home in Georgetown, a cozy Washington neighborhood for some of the city's political and media leaders. Their friend Robert Shiller warned them not to buy, because he thought home prices might fall further. They filled their rental with furniture from two large chain retailers, IKEA and Crate and Barrel. As a young woman, Yellen had developed an interest in abstract expressionist painting, particularly the work of Robert Motherwell. But she didn't have time to shop for anything elaborate, and George didn't have interest. Robby sent them some framed posters with scenes from Berkeley to hang on their walls. They returned in 2010 with two cars, a 1992 Acura Legend driven by Yellen and a 1998 Volvo driven by George. Both cars initially failed inspection when they applied for district license plates.

Akerlof was on to his next book, *Identity Economics*, an exploration with his former student Rachel Kranton of how social division played into economic life. He also took a job as a researcher at the International Monetary Fund, which he walked to from Georgetown in the morning.

Robby was getting ready for another entry into the job market after the disappointments of 2009.

The debate over more bond purchases—quantitative easing, as it was known—drew to a close when Yellen arrived in the fall of 2010. One of her friends at the Fed was Elizabeth Duke, the polite Virginia banker nominated to be a governor by George W. Bush. Duke, Yellen, and another Fed governor, Sarah Bloom Raskin, often went for lunch at the Fed or near the building. Yellen understood as well as anybody the feelings of isolation and frustration sometimes associated with being a Fed governor in Washington, having served in the role herself. Still, a governor's vote mattered a great deal to the chairman, and she went to work on Duke.

Duke had a small-town sensibility and was skeptical of the central bank's unusual bond-buying programs. Yellen wanted to win over her support. One night in the fall of 2010, Yellen and Duke were at a dinner at the Fed's Martin Building, across the street from the chairman's office. They started talking about the bond program after dinner as they walked to their cars in a parking garage below the Fed, where the vice chair parked her old Acura. There was an intensity in Yellen that struck Duke. She and Bernanke had been studying events like this their entire lives, Yellen told Duke. It is what they'd always prepared for. She was sure the Fed needed to do more, and they needed her support. At one point it almost looked like tears welled up in Yellen's eyes, Duke noticed.

"She was just incredibly passionate and emotional about it," said Duke, who reluctantly voted for the program.[1] When Yellen believed in something, Duke said later, "She was a bit like a dog with a bone."

In October 2010 the Fed launched what came to be known as QE2: $600 billion of additional purchases of Treasury bonds to keep long-term interest rates low.

The Fed was a tired institution after the crisis. Bernanke hired a management consultant, Carl Robinson, who ran a firm called Vantage Leadership, to help him think through how to run the place better.[2] Yellen became one of Robinson's main points of contact.

Yellen worried that Bernanke and his top staffers took on too much themselves and she pushed English to delegate more of his work. She wanted to build a more orderly process for formulating ideas in the monetary affairs division so it didn't depend so much on a few overworked people. She came down on one of English's deputies, Seth Carpenter, for being hard on two younger coworkers, though she could be hard on subordinates too. One junior staffer in another division remembered leaving in tears after a heated discussion with Yellen related to bank regulation. "Janet could laugh at life," Carl Robinson said. "She could also be tough. There is no question about that."[3]

In San Francisco, as a regional bank president, Yellen had an entire staff to herself. At the board she had no one. Unsatisfied with this arrangement, she asked senior Fed economist Andrew Levin to serve as her special adviser. Levin was a smart Stanford-trained monetary strategist. He was also aggressive—a loose cannon, in his own words—and, to some others in the Fed's cloistered research and monetary divisions, intrusive.

Some staff grumbled about Yellen's surprisingly intense style and her polarizing sidekick. She thought carefully about work culture and understood the Fed's culture as well as anyone, yet some staff came to worry about what the place would look like if she were ever in charge. The stakes were high, and the job wasn't easy or fun. "By 2010, when Janet came in, there was some hope that everything was going to kind of settle down, but then it didn't," Levin said. "We got this very long, slow recovery."[4]

All the while, Bernanke and Yellen were remaking modern central banking. For decades the Fed had operated behind a curtain, shrouding its thinking about the economy, its goals, and its policies and often leaving market traders and bankers to figure it out for themselves. This mysteriousness felt empowering to the central bankers and gave them a sense of latitude when making decisions. But academics, including Bernanke, came to a conclusion that secrecy was counterproductive. It was better to state your goals clearly and explain your thinking, not to leave the markets constantly guessing what you might do next. What was the benefit of intentionally creating uncertainty? Other central banks were already opening up.

Bernanke placed Yellen in charge of a communication committee, with Levin assisting her, to find new ideas on how to open up. They formulated a mission statement that clearly stated the Fed's desire to achieve regular and predictable 2 percent inflation, along with low unemployment. The inflation target was a promise to households that the central bank wouldn't let the purchasing power of their paychecks melt away as it had during the 1970s. Why 2 percent inflation instead of zero? Because zero inflation was so close to deflation, which, as Japanese officials discovered, was an unhealthy state of affairs. As long as household incomes were rising, a little inflation at a predictable rate left people better off. Yellen had made that argument to Greenspan all the way back in 1996. More than a decade later, they finally formalized the goal.

Yellen pressed to ensure that jobs were mentioned in the mission statement too. The Fed couldn't focus on inflation without thinking about the impact of their policies on unemployment; the law chartering the Fed stated as much. With inflation low and unemployment high, she and Bernanke believed they had a clear mandate to push the economy toward faster growth to encourage hiring, if only they had the tools.

Yellen's committee paved the way for Bernanke to conduct regular press conferences, opening himself up to public scrutiny and giving him a forum in which to explain himself. Other central banks were going in this direction, too. Tied to the press conferences, the Fed started releasing forecasts for where officials thought interest rates were heading. The

Fed's "dot plot"—as Wall Street traders called it, in their relentless push to boil everything down to catchy two-word phrases—would serve as a new window into the central bank's thinking.

These moves all looked technical from the outside, but their broader purpose was big: to bring the mysterious central bank out from the shadows for a skeptical and increasingly angry nation to view in fuller light. They had an additional purpose. Bernanke wanted a more vocal Fed to convince the public that interest rates would stay low to support the recovery.

The strategy led to some messy moments. In an August 2011 meeting, with little notice, Bernanke sprung an idea on colleagues: he wanted to state publicly that the Fed wouldn't raise interest rates for two more years. The debate caused by this surprise proposal dragged on so long that his lieutenants worried they wouldn't have a statement out at 2:00 p.m., the appointed time. That surely would have left markets abuzz with rumors about intrigue inside the palace.

Bernanke's chief of staff, Michelle Smith, prodded him to wrap the discussion up. "We have to get this done by one thirty," he warned colleagues as they went back and forth over the language attached to his promise to keep rates low. "Michelle tells us we need to get this done as soon as possible." As the clock ticked down, three regional bank presidents said they couldn't go along with the Fed's statement. Bernanke won approval from the others, but with three dissents from the presidents that made it harder to convince investors the Fed was really committed to the policy.[5]

On a different occasion, Bernanke was scorched by stories related to a third central bank bond purchase program in 2012. A *Wall Street Journal* article uncovered details of internal deliberations about the program, with descriptions of behind-the-scenes discussions about the policy as well as confidential details about the research conducted and options considered by the staff.[6] In a letter to other officials, Bernanke complained of "a number of items in the article that seemed clearly in violation of our guidelines."[7] His underlying message to the Fed governors and bank presidents: be careful what you tell reporters about internal talks.

A few days later, a market research firm named Medley Global Advisors put out a report with additional details about the Fed's deliberations. Its author, Regina Schleiger, was an experienced journalist, but Medley's audience wasn't broad like the *WSJ*'s; it served mostly hedge funds that placed trades on the direction of interest rates. The hedge funds sometimes had billions of dollars at stake in these trades, and paid handsomely for information from private advisory firms that promised them an advantage in the marketplace.

The Fed had a long and uncomfortable history trying to strike a balance when talking to people outside the institution. Officials wanted to hear from people in finance so it could understand how its decisions might affect markets. One miscalculation in reading market expectations could cause the Fed's interest-rate decisions to backfire. The central bank did as much back in 1994, when it misread market expectations for rate increases and Orange County went bankrupt after being on the wrong side of a trade. For years Fed officials invited a few Wall Street analysts to its Jackson Hole retreat, where they rubbed elbows during mountain hikes. But the Fed's own views were potentially of great value to the same people. Where to draw the line about whom they talked to and what officials said or asked?

After the financial crisis, scrutiny intensified. Yellen had talked to Schleiger months before the Medley report came out. Other officials clearly had too, and it looked like some person or people had said too much. Critics accused the Fed of making inappropriate leaks.

The case dogged the Fed for years.[8] A Fed policy—written by the Yellen communication committee in 2011—called for inappropriate disclosures to be referred to the Fed's general counsel and its secretary

of the Federal Open Market Committee, who was Bill English, and then
to an independent inspector general if warranted. Bernanke sent the
case to his general counsel, Scott Alvarez, and English. While they were
examining the case, the Fed's inspector general received an anonymous
tip and started looking at the matter, too. One internal report at the inspector general's office in 2014 suggested delays might have impeded its
investigation, though the inspector general did conduct a long review.[9]

Republicans in Congress saw the case as evidence that the central
bank was too cozy with people in financial markets. The Republican-
controlled House Financial Services Committee investigated, and lawmakers accused the Fed of covering up leaks. The Justice Department,
the Securities and Exchange Commission, and the Commodity Futures
Trading Commission also looked into it. No charges resulted, though
Jeffrey Lacker, the Richmond Fed president, resigned from his post
years after the investigations started, after acknowledging that he had
talked to Schleiger without revealing it.[10]

Yellen maintained she wasn't a leaker. While she did talk to Schleiger,
she told House investigators, nothing she said in June could have been
material in Schleiger's October reporting about a meeting that occurred
in September. "Let me assure you," she said, "I did not convey any confidential information."[11]

It was a public embarrassment at a time when the public distrusted
the place, but Bernanke and Yellen had a bigger preoccupation during
those years. Their primary worry was the tax and spending plans of the
US government.

Keynes's ideas had gone in and out of fashion for many years. Now
they were central to the economic direction of the nation. His prescrip-
tion for crises like this was tax cuts and spending to boost economic
activity when the private sector stalled. Early on, Republicans and Democrats had some disagreements about which was more effective at promoting economic growth, tax cuts or spending increases. Republicans

said tax cuts had a bigger impact—a "multiplier effect," in economics lingo—while Democrats said spending increases were more useful. But they generally agreed that in a time of crisis, a budget deficit shouldn't be a restraint on supporting the economy.

The debate switched in 2010, after Obama won the White House and Republicans took control of Congress. Then the debate was over whether the government should do anything at all.

Republicans seemed to fall into a peculiar pattern. George H. W. Bush successfully brought down budget deficits in the early 1990s, but after him Republicans tended not to worry much about deficits when they occupied the White House. Vice President Richard Cheney famously said that "deficits don't matter" during George W. Bush's presidency in the 2000s, when tax cuts and spending increases were pumping up deficits. In 2000, Clinton's last year as president, the United States ran a budget surplus of $86 billion; it ran a deficit during every year of Bush's presidency, which ended in 2008 on a then-record $641 billion shortfall. Annual government spending increased by more than $1 trillion during the second Bush's presidency.

When Republicans were out of the White House, they tended to resurface concerns about deficits and attacked Keynesian support of spending programs. Deficit hawks, described as being part of a patriotic Tea Party movement, swept into Washington in 2010, when the annual deficit hit $1.3 trillion, expressing alarm at the rapid growth of government debt during and after the financial crisis. In just two years Keynes seemed to have been revived and then vanquished all over again.

Bernanke's final years as Fed chairman were consumed by battles over government budgets. The Fed was caught in the middle of these debates and its critics took a new line of attack against the central bank. They argued that its low-interest-rate policies were enabling large government budget deficits by keeping the cost of government borrowing so low. When the government spends more money than it brings in from tax revenues—which is almost always—it amasses the missing money by issuing Treasury bonds. The interest on that borrowing, as with the interest paid by households and businesses, is affected by Fed policies.

Bernanke and Yellen disagreed with the new line of criticism. They wanted smaller budget deficits in the long run, but believed this was no time to be making that push. Spending cuts restrained already-anemic economic growth and forced the Fed over and over again to do even more to keep the United States out of another recession. Then the policies the Fed advanced to keep the economy growing invited even more backlash. It was a vexing paradox. The Fed was being blamed for policies that Bernanke and Yellen believed they had no choice but to enact as the rest of the government grew more austere.

From time to time Republicans in Congress threatened to enforce a law that set arbitrary caps on how much the government was allowed to borrow, known as a debt ceiling. It was a strange law. The lion's share of government spending was tied up in already-promised Social Security and Medicare benefits, military contracts, and interest on the debt. These were long-standing commitments. If government borrowing was stopped in its tracks without warning, as these arbitrary limits sometimes required, the nation would either have to default on its debt, skip promised payments to elderly households, or skimp on planned military spending.

Beyond this risk of sudden and chaotic disruption, the law simply didn't work at all in creating the budget discipline it was meant to instill. Despite its existence in various forms for decades, debt kept rising year after year; the only recent exception being in the late 1990s, when the United States ran budget surpluses. As debt rose, Congress simply reset the cap at higher levels. All the debt ceiling did was create occasional market uncertainty, which made financing the debt more expensive, because investors demanded higher interest payments as a hedge against the risk of self-imposed default.

The end result of these budget battles: Congress came close to defaulting, but stepped back at the last minute, causing confusion in financial markets. Budget deficits shrank, but only temporarily. Obama and his Republican opponents in Congress failed to agree on a plan to manage deficits in the long run. Temporary spending cuts slowed the recovery. They also likely inhibited progress on reducing unemployment; in the early months of 2014 the unemployment rate still exceeded 6.5 percent, higher than at any point in more than a decade before the financial crisis.

Again and again Bernanke and Yellen turned to unconventional policies that they thought would help keep the expansion going. Again and again they faced internal and external resistance.

After launching a third round of bond purchases in 2012, Yellen confronted Fed governors. She wanted to press ahead, and several of the governors wanted to stop. Elizabeth Duke was one of these governors; another was Jeremy Stein, a Harvard finance professor who had advised Summers and Geithner during the crisis. Stein worried that the Fed programs gave investors too much incentive to bid up stock or bond prices and would spur another boom-and-bust financial cycle that would haunt the central bank. He pressed Bernanke to stop.

"What are we supposed to do, just go oars up?" an exasperated Yellen asked Stein in a tense discussion in her office.

A third reluctant governor was a low-key Republican named Jerome Powell, appointed by Obama as a compromise to win Republican support in Congress for his other nominees. By early 2013 the Fed had increased its holdings of bonds and other assets to nearly $4 trillion, up from less than $800 billion before the financial crisis, all in the name of keeping interest rates down to boost the expansion. Powell asked how much further the central bank was prepared to go. "We're headed for five trillion dollars," he said at a meeting in March 2013. He said he found that chilling. "We need to regain control of this."[12]

Powell's office was next to Yellen's and the two became close. A lawyer by training, he often popped into her office to quiz her about her economic ideas. Though she was a Democrat and he was a Republican, he didn't think her convictions were shaped by politics. He thought she just wanted to get her answers right and found her an easygoing neighbor beneath her bookish demeanor. He was prepared to change his mind if the facts supported her arguments.

Bernanke's chief of staff, Michelle Smith, called the three dissident governors "the Three Amigos."[13] Yellen thought they were focused on the wrong problem: the real problem remained that unemployment was too high, and the risks of sticking with their programs weren't that great, she argued. The Fed had committed to keeping the bond programs going until the jobless rate fell further, and she wanted to stay at it. "It is just critical that we not degrade our credibility by failing to make good on a promise that we made," she said at the March 2013 meeting.

The central bank kept the program going for several months before slowing down, finally stopping with its holdings at $4.5 trillion. To put the enormity of this amount in perspective, it was more than enough money to buy all of the public companies listed in Canada, Germany, and Mexico combined. And still the warnings about the dire consequences of the Fed's perceived recklessness proved wrong. Inflation remained subdued; the dollar remained the centerpiece of global finance; no obvious new bubble emerged; and a frustrating expansion persisted.

Looking back, Stein said later, he had scored some debate points against Yellen, but she and Bernanke were right about the big picture. The financial stability risks that concerned him back then didn't bear out. "They were the right people to lead the Fed at the time," he said.[14] Powell also acknowledged that his worries had been overdone. "Let's let the data speak," he said in 2015. "The evidence so far is clear that the benefits of these policies have been substantial, and that the risks have not materialized."[15]

As his eight years as Fed chairman wound down, Bernanke was ready to exit center stage a frustrated man. His deepest frustration, he reflected in his memoir, was the government's political dysfunction. "The founders had designed a system to be deliberative; instead it was paralyzed. Too often, the system promoted showboating, blind ideology, and malice. Nothing could be done, it seemed, until all of the wrong approaches were tried first."

Obama needed to find a replacement for Bernanke. As the president saw it, he had two choices. One was his friend and former adviser Larry Summers, who had been promised the job years earlier and then spurned. Summers had left Washington, but he was ready to come back if offered the job.

The other was Janet Yellen.

19

Yellen Becomes Leader

A Summer of Summers
2013–2014

Lawrence Summers played a consequential role in nearly every major economic debate of the past half century. As a young man he considered becoming a lawyer, but from childhood his skills had been honed in economics, and he chose to put his debate instincts to work there instead. Confident, combative, ambitious, pedigreed, intelligent, and numerate, this was bound to take him places and also cause him trouble, and it did.

Summers was the child of two economics professors, Bob and Anita Summers, who taught at the University of Pennsylvania and Swarthmore College and raised three boys in a Philadelphia suburb. From a young age, Summers was trained to think in numbers and probability, to make reasoned decisions he could justify while considering the range of outcomes he might be forgoing with his choices. When Bob Summers took Larry to the train as a boy of maybe three, his father used the track numbers at stations to teach his son the difference between odd and even numbers. Bob later developed a bidding system for the children to make choices about apportioning television time, then scrapped the system when they outbid him for time he wanted.[1] Anita took young Larry to her economics courses at Swarthmore when he was in high school.

Summers had two uncles who were giants in the field. One was Kenneth Arrow, Anita's brother. Arrow was cerebral and kind. Two of his major contributions to economics were revelations in their time and won him a Nobel Prize in 1972. One, the first welfare theorem, used advanced mathematics to show that Adam Smith was right at a core level. If one put aside all of the known frictions and anomalies in human behavior—which of course were numerous—markets really did work at maximizing and efficiently distributing all of the goods and services that humans create. In other words, the invisible hand of markets was the best way to fulfill basic human needs and wants. Arrow worked some of his proofs out with Gerard Debreu, Akerlof's colleague at Berkeley.

Arrow's other theorem was related to democracy and led toward darker conclusions about American life. Known as the impossibility theorem, it showed, again using advanced mathematics, that it was impossible to design an effective system for making group decisions short of dictatorship. In other words, while markets worked, democracy was fundamentally flawed and messy.

Arrow was more than intelligent. He seemed to know everything. When assistant professors challenged him to discuss how dolphins communicated, he was up on the latest literature on the subject. He could recite the Declaration of Independence by heart. He could discuss in detail biographies of the poet Emily Dickinson. His challenge as a teacher was that from his own Olympian intellectual place, he sometimes didn't grasp how little others comprehended of what he was saying.

More than anything, though, Uncle Kenneth was patient and kind with Summers. He liked taking young Larry for spins in his red convertible when the family came to visit. He was struck by his nephew's love of debate. "He liked to argue. He was very well-informed," Arrow told the *Wall Street Journal* about his nephew.[2]

The other uncle was Paul Samuelson, the brother of Robert Summers, who had changed his last name at a young age. Samuelson took a life-long interest in his precocious nephew, alternatively chiding him, provoking him, spurring him on, and embracing him. The relationship was not only a window into the character of Summers; it was also a window into that of Samuelson, who was demanding, social, and not always very nice.

Uncle Paul heard about Larry's intelligence when his nephew was young. Once the Summers family visited Cambridge when Larry was around ten. Samuelson sent him off to decipher where on the thermometer the Fahrenheit and Celsius scales converged.[3] Not yet knowing algebra, Larry worked it out in the back seat of the family's car by trial and error on sheets of paper—it was minus 40 degrees, the preteen reported back to his acclaimed uncle.

By the time he was in the sixth grade, Larry had created a system to calculate the probability that a baseball team would make it to the playoffs in October based on its performance through the Fourth of July. In 1965 the *Philadelphia Bulletin* described Summers as the most qualified eleven-year-old oddsmaker in baseball.[4] At sixteen he went to Uncle Paul's MIT as an undergraduate student. "Many children are taught to believe in God. I came to believe in the power of systems analysis," Summers wrote later in a graduate school application.

At MIT he studied physics and quickly discovered that he had innate instincts about economics that he hadn't yet acquired in physics, a sense of how to get to the heart of a question at once. He had a similar problem with the study of law; he realized it would take him years to climb through the ranks of some law firm to get to where he wanted to be, which was in courtrooms arguing cases on center stage. So at MIT Summers turned to economics, where he had aptitude and a head start. He also led the school's debate team to national standing. One of his favorite debate tactics was to argue against opponents based on the business uncertainty their proposals might create. Through debate Summers learned to look at both sides of an argument, how to poke holes at either side, and also how to make a case for either side when asked, all tools he employed in his careers in academics and politics.

Summers went to Harvard—where he first met Yellen in 1975—for his PhD, and then returned to MIT as an assistant professor. At MIT, students and faculty put on an annual skit for fun. His colleagues likened Summers in the show to a racehorse bred for personal success. He didn't appreciate being measured solely based on his bloodlines; he thought he had his own intellect to stand on by then. Another time, Summers sat with Samuelson and other faculty members for lunch and got into a debate. His uncle shredded him in front of everybody for making a bad argument.[5] "Larry," Samuelson said, "I just wrote a eulogy for Art Okun. And in that eulogy I said that in all the years I had known Art Okun I had never heard him say a stupid thing. Well, Larry, I won't be able to say that about you." Summers was deflated by the insensitive public rebuke from his acclaimed uncle.

"Paul could be tough, but he also knew the old thing about afflicting the comfortable, and he did," Summers said of his uncle. "Nobody punctured pretense or pomposity better or more decisively than he did."

Summers became quite adept at this skill, too.

He returned to Harvard, helping to lead a revival of its economics department and reverse a decline in its stature that traced back to when Samuelson left decades earlier. At Harvard, Summers navigated himself to the center of many of the most important economic debates of the 1980s, often taking nuanced and unconventional views that moved the field in new directions.

He crossed paths with Yellen once again. As she and Akerlof developed theories about inefficient labor markets, Summers developed parallel theories that complemented theirs. While Chicago school professors advanced the notion of efficient financial markets, Summers helped to

puncture those ideas, too, putting his stamp on the behavioral economics theories that challenged the notion of efficiency. At seminars that
they both visited, Summers liked to wander off with Akerlof to discuss
ideas meant to shake the economic establishment.

Summers was a whirlwind. Taxation, consumer behavior, the primacy of using actual data to back up abstract ideas—you name a subject,
and he was often there. Students began lining up outside of his office for
time with him, as they had done with Solow in an earlier era, and he
engaged with them enthusiastically. One of those students was David
Wilcox, a graduate student at MIT in the 1980s who was struggling to
work out a dissertation on social security programs and the economic
effects of government tax and spending policies.

"It was a mess. I had run aground," Wilcox said later. An MIT adviser
suggested he go see Summers at Harvard. Summers flipped through the
paper quickly—casually, it seemed—and in about thirty minutes got to
the heart of the matter and straightened the paper out. "I left his office
with a sense of direction and hope," Wilcox said. "I literally owe Larry
my career."[6] Wilcox would go on to become the head of the Fed's research and statistics division, one of its top economists, at the center of
its interest-rate decisions.

The list of Summers's protégés grew, among them Sheryl Sandberg,
later a billionaire and chief operating officer of Facebook; Timothy
Geithner, later secretary of the Treasury; and James Poterba, later president of the National Bureau of Economic Research.

Summers became a tenured professor at Harvard in 1983 at the age
of twenty-eight, among the earliest tenure appointments the university
ever made. He hired a team of research assistants to help him with the
many projects he had running. He served a stint working in Ronald Reagan's Council of Economic Advisers as an assistant to his mentor Martin
Feldstein, a moderate Republican.

"I thought I was conquering the world," Summers said later, when asked to reflect on the event that next altered his life.[7] In 1984, at the age of twenty-nine, Summers was diagnosed with stage IV Hodgkin's disease, a cancer of the lymphatic system. He beat it and emerged with even greater drive. If he was going to do anything in life, he thought, he should do it right away, while he could.

In 1993, when he was thirty-eight, the American Economic Association awarded him its Clark Medal for top young economists. His uncles Samuelson and Arrow had won the Clark Medal too, before their Nobel Prizes. So had Friedman and Tobin. Neither Akerlof nor Yellen ever had.

But writing papers and debating abstract ideas wasn't enough for Summers. He wanted to put ideas to the test, formulate and fight for them in the arena of politics and policy making. He wanted to slug it out with others where ideas turned into actions. In 1988 he signed up to advise the presidential campaign of Michael Dukakis, a Massachusetts Democrat. There he met Robert Rubin and Gene Sperling. After Dukakis lost, rivals in the administration of his opponent, George H. W. Bush, blessed the World Bank's decision to hire Summers as its chief economist. The fact that a Republican hired him was testament, again, to his aptitude, and also to the fact that his ideas weren't easily pigeonholed by any ideology.

Summers stepped into trouble in public life. In 1991 he signed a World Bank memo written by a subordinate that argued, in an intentionally provocative tone, that rich countries should ship their pollution to poor countries because it was an economically efficient way of distributing the costs of the problem. Summers didn't write the memo, and the author, Lant Pritchett, later said that somebody else had doctored it, but Summers took the blame and the episode took on a life of its own.[8] It found its way to the *Economist* magazine, outraging Al Gore, who pushed against Summers as a candidate to run the Council of Economic Advisers when Clinton was elected a year later.

"When I make a mistake, it's a whopper," Summers said.

Clinton instead put Summers in a lower-profile but influential US Treasury job. Yellen later got the CEA job, and they crossed paths yet again, working on the same side in White House debates about climate-change policy. They both wanted to address climate change but use market-oriented measures to do it.

Over time, Summers set his sights on the even bigger job of running the Treasury. He served loyally at the side of Lloyd Bentsen, Clinton's first Treasury secretary, and then worked for Robert Rubin for four years, earning Rubin's trust along the way. Summers was intellectually boisterous and personally sloppy; Rubin, a Wall Street veteran, was buttoned down and deliberate with every word. But the two had similar worldviews, an abiding belief in markets and a belief that the government had a role in managing them with restraint and a sense of its own limitations.

Rubin admired the mind of Summers. At the beginning of Clinton's second term, both were thinking about leaving the administration. Rubin wanted to stay only if Summers stayed, so he worked out a deal with the president.[9] He would stick around for a couple more years to lead the Treasury, with the understanding that Summers would get the job when he left. In 1999, at the age of forty-four, Summers became the youngest US Treasury secretary since Alexander Hamilton, who was in his thirties when he served in the role.

"He definitely was not a late bloomer," Solow said of Summers at the time. "He was probably born in full bloom."[10]

However, his sharp-elbowed style left lasting impressions, and some bitterness, on many people. After a debate about the fate of Fannie Mae and Freddie Mac in the mid-1990s, one staffer recalled, "Nobody has bullied me in my adult life the way that Larry did on this one."[11] Summers would become a prescient public critic of Fannie and Freddie before their collapse. Along the way, Samuelson cheered his nephew on from afar. "I never told you how great I thought you were at the Treasury," he wrote to his nephew in 2001.[12] "So I'll just say you were only perfect—in there with Hamilton and Gallatin," a reference to Albert Gallatin, who led the Treasury after Hamilton under Thomas Jefferson and James Madison.

After Clinton's second term ended, Summers became president of Harvard, where he took on an imperious style that rubbed some faculty members the wrong way. In tenure discussions, for instance, he sometimes challenged or demeaned the work of other professors, alienating colleagues in the process. One of his conflicts was with Cornel West, an African American Studies professor who recalled in his memoir a 2001 meeting with Summers in which he said the new university president criticized his work habits, his grading style, and his dabbling in hip-hop music. Summers wanted to meet more regularly, to which West replied, "If you think that I'm going to trot in here every two weeks to be monitored like a miscreant graduate student, I'm afraid, my brother, that you've messed with the wrong brother."[13] West left for Princeton. Summers later said he had numerous concerns with West.

When Summers made impolitic remarks about the dearth of women in science—suggesting that among other possible reasons, this might be because their brains were wired differently than men's—it was the final straw for a legion of colleagues. Faculty rallied against him. Summers discovered he had lost allies among them and stepped down in early 2006. "I grieve for you," Samuelson wrote to his nephew. "Mob psychology can be much the same on college campuses as elsewhere." He counseled Summers to avoid bitterness. "I am mindful of negative aspects of grudges and of acting rashly in anger," Summers replied.[14]

Samuelson harbored bitter feelings about Rubin, who served on the board of the Harvard Corporation, one of the university's two governing boards. He thought Rubin gave bad counsel to his nephew. In private Samuelson also gossiped about Summers. "Rubin taught Larry some tact—but nobody could keep his shirt tails firmly tucked in," Samuelson said in a letter to Stanley Fischer, the former MIT professor.

Summers stayed on as a professor at Harvard after resigning the presidency there, but he craved a return to Washington, as either Treasury secretary or Fed chairman. He worked for Obama during the 2008 presidential campaign and impressed the Democratic nominee. "Larry could hear your arguments, restate them better than you could, and then show why you were wrong," Obama said in his memoir.[15] He then sized up Summers rather bluntly: "As I got to know him, I'd come to believe that most of Larry's difficulties playing well with others had less to do with malice and more to do with obliviousness. For Larry, qualities like tact and restraint just cluttered the mind. He himself seemed impervious to hurt feelings or the usual insecurities."

Obama wanted Geithner at the Treasury in 2009. Geithner had worked with Bernanke through the crisis as president of the New York Fed and would be a steadying hand. Obama also wanted the intellect of Summers close to him to think through the complicated tasks ahead, so he offered the Harvard professor a White House job and a commitment to make him Fed chairman when Bernanke's first term was up in 2010. The arrangement was the idea of Obama's chief of staff, Rahm Emanuel.[16]

"I needed him, his country needed him," Obama said.

However, Obama changed his mind and decided to keep Bernanke in the Fed job. After Obama broke the news to him, Summers called Emanuel to vent while Emanuel's family was on vacation. Emanuel's wife, Amy Rule, told her husband he could either spend his vacation with her or with Summers, but not both. Two years into Obama's first term, Summers returned to Harvard, where he built a new life as a public intellectual. From that perch he spoke his mind about economics without worrying as much about the problems he caused himself by offending others.

Summers and Yellen had crossed each other's paths again and again.

He was her student at Harvard in the 1970s. They plowed similar ground on labor market research in the 1980s. They developed a web of mutual connections, such as with Andrei Shleifer, who wrote papers with Summers in the 1980s and then asked Yellen and Akerlof to help with his ill-fated Russia work in the 1990s. Yellen and Summers were on the same side of debates in the Clinton White House in the 1990s. When Robby Akerlof went to Harvard for his PhD studies in the 2000s, Summers was president and welcomed Yellen's son. Shleifer became one of Robby's thesis advisers.

Yellen and Summers respected each other. Yellen understood as well as anyone what it meant when somebody said, "That is just Larry being Larry." They weren't rivals; they were more like siblings, entangled in a long and complex relationship.

Yellen and Summers emerged from the 1980s debates between Friedman, Samuelson, and Tobin with a view that markets were necessary but imperfect, and that the government had a role to play in managing business cycles and other economic problems. That role, moreover, had to be handled deliberately. They believed in backing up ideas with data and analysis. They saw the central bank as an imperative player in the economy. They understood from the 1970s that one of the worst mistakes a central bank could make was to tolerate sustained and rising inflation, something it had the power and the tools to prevent. They also believed that a central bank could help when the economy sank.

But they had much different temperaments. One example was how they went about giving speeches. Yellen prepared, footnoted exhaustively, and rarely strayed from the script. Summers liked to wing it, which sometimes landed him in trouble. They also had vastly different approaches to the mundane issue of traveling to the airport. Summers found airports annoying and sought to minimize the time he spent in them. He often arrived late, hustling to gates. "If you've never missed a plane, you're spending too much time in airports," he liked to say.

Yellen's airport theory was framed around the concept of crisis management. She wanted to minimize the possibility of major disruption, such as missing a flight. She didn't mind being in airports; she took reading with her that she would want to do somewhere anyway; she might as well do it in the airport while she waited. By getting to the airport early, she got the best seats for reading in the passenger lounges, early boarding, and the best choice of overhead compartment space on the plane. Some of her travel companions also came to think that Yellen simply liked being first.

The fact that each had a discrete, thought-out theory about how to travel to an airport said something about their intellects. It also provided a view into much bigger issues in economics. Economists believe that an individual's goal is to maximize his or her utility. When it came to airport travel, Yellen and Summers had completely different views about what they were trying to maximize, which led to different behavior and different explanations for their actions. Their contrary airport theories were proof that humans are complex and different in their aspirations and dispositions. This is exactly what Akerlof had been arguing for nearly half a century. To understand markets, he believed, economists needed to dig deeper to understand the varied impulses of humans themselves.

Obama's choice came to a head in the summer of 2013. Bernanke was preparing to move on. Obama was again leaning toward Summers for the job. At this point, though, Summers didn't believe he would get it, nor was he as hungry for it as he had been four years earlier. Geithner reflected in his memoir that when Yellen became vice chair, Summers told him she was certain to be the next chair. She was too compelling a figure not to get it.[17]

That summer, Washington buzzed with gossip and chatter about who would get the position. Obama got a memo from Gene Sperling, who was once again serving as the head of the president's National Economic Council, and Jack Lew, the new Treasury secretary, noting that Summers had more experience managing crises, going back to the Asian financial crisis in the 1990s, but that both candidates were strong choices. Yellen, in particular, had built a record and reputation as an intelligent forecaster of economic problems lurking around corners. A *Wall Street Journal* study of the forecasting records of every Fed official in recent years showed that her public premonitions most often turned out to be true.[18] At the same time, however, word of her sometimes stressful relations with staff at the Fed as vice chair also found its way to White House advisers and to the ears of reporters.

As the summer dragged on, Yellen and Summers were both in the awkward position of being the subjects of a public debate that they couldn't speak about publicly, objects of the criticism and judgments of other people who tended to talk about them anonymously. Obama dragged the decision into August, and when Yellen didn't hear from the White House, she started telling people she figured she wouldn't get the job.

In the end, Obama's choice was made easy by one simple fact: Summers lacked support in the progressive wing of the Democratic Party in the Senate. In addition to his sometimes-intemperate style, his positions supporting free trade and financial sector deregulation in the 1990s had become subjects of progressive scorn. Summers was among the most consequential economists of his generation and perhaps the most gifted, but Janet Yellen, the careful and methodical one, got the job he had once coveted.

Yellen rose up in a period of crisis with conviction and purpose, more than personal ambition or political bent. After the crisis ended, she was at Bernanke's side over and over again, pressing him to carry on with unpopular policies that others doubted and spurned. She was simply convinced they were the right thing to do.

As Bernanke departed the scene, Yellen said to him, "I believe the most remarkable aspect of your achievements of the last eight years has been your courage." Despite the criticism heaped on him and the doubts expressed by others, she said, "you remained determined, open-minded, and creative in your effort to do what was best for the country."[19]

Of his own experience, Bernanke reflected that it was like being in a car wreck. "You're mostly involved in trying to avoid going off the bridge, and then later on you say, 'Oh my God!'"[20]

Part IV

Leader

20

Identity Crisis

Akerlof's New Theory of
Reds versus Greens
2014

Janet Yellen was sixty-seven years old, two years past the nation's historic retirement age, when she became chair of the Federal Reserve in 2014.

The optimism that lit the nation in 2000 was gone, replaced by fourteen years of crisis. An internet-stock-bubble crashed. Terrorist attacks that took down Manhattan's signature Twin Towers and dented a nation's feeling of invincibility. A housing bubble that grew beneath the noses of bank titans and then crumbled upon them. A mortgage meltdown that nearly took down the entire financial system. Unpopular bailouts. Surging imports from a revitalized Chinese manufacturing leviathan that washed over American towns and destroyed jobs. Slow recoveries that took too long for millions of families who waited without financial resources or the dignity of work while the economy healed in a new age of turbulence.

Yellen had started the millennium an accomplished economist, but by no measure a historic one. Her career looked conventional for a person with her smarts. Then she rose up as crisis unfolded, her voice, vision, and conviction becoming more acute as she puzzled out shifting problems and adapted to them. She hadn't set out to become the most powerful woman in US economic history. She became that person out of necessity.

Fourteen years of crisis didn't just change Yellen. It also took a toll on the social fabric of the country and defined her days as a national leader. And as had been the case many times before, Yellen's husband was ahead of many other people, developing theories that helped to explain what was happening beneath the crashing waves of economic upheaval.

To understand this shifting social landscape, move the lens for a moment far from the machinery of money and power Yellen wielded in Washington, to a map of western North Carolina, near the Appalachian Mountains. Across that map runs North Carolina 321, a state highway that traces old Native American trading routes through rolling forest-land near the Appalachians. At one intersection of Route 321 is Hickory, a beehive of furniture manufacturing that was decimated during the 2000s by competition from China. At the other intersection, just fifty-two miles away to the south and east, is the approach to Charlotte, the state's largest city and a growing financial center.

Between those two dots on a map was a story that explained Akerlof's new theory of social discord, and Yellen's next crisis.

Hickory thrived in the late 1990s. Migrant coal miners and steel-workers from the Virginia and West Virginia mountains in the north poured into town in search of jobs. Hickory's unemployment rate during the boom dropped below 2 percent, among the lowest jobless rates in the nation. Locals thought the town's economy was diversified; it had factories in a range of industries, including fiber-optic cables and textiles, in addition to furniture.

Charlotte thrived too, transformed by a brash banker named Hugh McColl, an ex-Marine who spent the 1990s gobbling up small North Carolina banks like a general on a campaign for regional domination. His North Carolina National Bank became NationsBank. In 1998 Nations-

Bank purchased San Francisco's giant Bank of America. McColl kept the merged bank's headquarters in Charlotte and took the Bank of America name, securing his city's place as a national financial center. The CEO kept a crystal replica of a hand grenade on his desk as a reminder of his military days and gave out copies of it to his best-performing employees. In 1999, Charlotte's unemployment rate fell under 3 percent.[1]

In 2001 Catawba County, the home of Hickory, still had more manufacturing jobs, at forty thousand, than Mecklenburg County, home of Charlotte, had finance jobs, at thirty-four thousand.[2]

Then they went in different directions.

Over the next decade a US import boom of Chinese-made furniture washed over Hickory like a tsunami.[3] Furniture making was a labor-intensive business, with all the cutting, stapling, sanding, and gluing that was required. A $12-an-hour job in Hickory could be replaced by 50-cents-an-hour workers in China. North Carolina furniture executives shifted low-end production overseas; then Chinese producers started competing with their suitors, selling tables and dressers directly to big US retailers like Walmart and Home Depot.

It was a disaster for Hickory. Between 2000 and 2014, the metro area lost nearly forty thousand jobs.[4] The percent of the population living under official poverty thresholds in Hickory's Catawba County rose from 9 to 16 percent. Those collecting food stamps and federal disability benefits rose, too.[5] "We kept thinking, 'It's gonna come back,'" said Warren Wood, the Hickory city manager in 2021. But it never did.[6]

The government set up programs to help workers transition from jobs disrupted by trade competition, offering funding for people to go back to school. For thousands of middle-aged men and women with little schooling to begin with, the programs didn't help much. Many people who went through these programs ended up in lower-paying health service jobs, cleaning bedpans or taking blood from the arms of patients in local hospitals for a few dollars an hour.[7]

"Those trade policies really decimated a lot of families," Wood said.

David Autor, an MIT economist who studied trade and labor markets, called China's economy a "500-ton boulder perched on a ledge." At some point it would tumble and splatter what was below. "You just didn't know when," he said.[8]

By 2014 the boulder had splattered Hickory. Economists had long argued that while free trade created winners and losers, the net results would be beneficial for the country as a whole. Americans did gain from inexpensive Chinese imports, filling their homes with low-price kitchen tables and deck furniture. Cheap imports kept inflation and interest rates low. That helped millions of Americans take out mortgages and buy bigger houses. But Autor's work showed that the China shock was different from previous import booms—more devastating to communities that were especially vulnerable to low-wage manufacturing competition from abroad, like Hickory. Chinese competition destroyed 2.4 million US jobs between 1999 and 2011, he found.[9]

Trade theory was the one area where many economists agreed, but they had misjudged how trade would impact the United States when a counterpart as large and poor as China developed so quickly. One of the leading theorists, Paul Krugman, had accomplished a rare feat by the time Autor's work was published. In 2008 he won a Nobel Prize for the win-win trade theories he'd produced as a young researcher. Then in 2009 he was a finalist for a Pulitzer Prize for opinion columns he'd written for the *New York Times*. The opinion columns didn't focus much on the pitfalls of trade. Mostly they were attacks on the Republican Party and conservatives, which made him popular with progressives and an object of derision from the right.

Over time Krugman came to realize he was part of an economic consensus that misjudged the painful underbelly of trade liberalization. "To make partial excuses for those of us who failed to consider these issues 25 years ago, at the time we had no way to know that either the hyperglobalization that began in the 1990s or the trade-deficit surge a decade later were going to happen," he wrote. "Without the combination of these developments, the China shock would have been much smaller. Still, we missed a crucial part of the story."[10]

While Hickory suffered, Charlotte thrived, creating more than a quarter of a million new jobs. A tech- and finance-driven national economy was creating service-sector jobs in densely populated cities like Charlotte. As Hickory's manufacturing sector contracted, an army of management consultants and other white-collar professionals clustered around Charlotte's financial sector. Charlotte became a place where young people with college degrees wanted to work, live, and socialize.

After the nation's financial sector was nearly wrecked in 2008, Bank of America in Charlotte, fresh off its purchases of Countrywide and Merrill Lynch, got $45 billion investments from the federal government to keep it strong and stable, and plenty of time to pay the money back if it wanted. Hickory got little federal support.

Why didn't people in Hickory just move to Charlotte, where work was abundant? It wasn't that simple. Jobs in the two places demanded different skills, and people in these two places had different interests and personal connections. Many younger people went, but older dislocated manufacturing workers stayed home and suffered.

A divide grew between Hickory and Charlotte that wasn't purely economic. Between 2000 and 2014, Charlotte became more racially diverse, more educated, more affluent, more densely populated, and more politically progressive. Hickory became less educated and less diverse, with an older and less mobile population that was more politically conservative by comparison. They were fifty-two miles away from each other, but worlds apart.

In the year 2000, 93 percent of people in Hickory's Catawba County had been born in the United States, and that statistic remained near 92 percent fourteen years later. During the same period, the native-born population in Charlotte's Mecklenburg County dropped from 89 to 84 percent. Mecklenburg's share of the population that spoke only English at home dropped from 87 to 81 percent; in Catawba it held over 88 percent. More people moved from out of state to Mecklenburg, while out-of-state migration to Catawba changed little.[11]

The political leanings of the two populations changed rapidly as well. In 2000, both counties sided with Republican George W. Bush over Democrat Al Gore. By 2012, Democrat Barack Obama took 60 percent of Charlotte's Mecklenburg County vote, while Republican Mitt Romney took 64 percent of the Catawba County vote. In fact, Catawba was shifting further to the right of Romney. By 2014 the area had a vibrant Tea Party movement that positioned itself in opposition to the nation's leaders and embraced the name a local newspaper used to describe it, "the lion's den." People in Hickory came to resent the banks in Charlotte for getting bailouts. They also came to resent the federal government for opening them to trade with China.

"We never got anything," Wood said. "There's just been a disconnect between elites and working folks."

By the time Yellen ascended to the top economic job in the nation as chair of the Fed, Akerlof had spent nearly two decades working on theories that helped to explain a social divide developing between Hickory and Charlotte, and around the nation in similar ways. The divide was deeper and more pervasive than any economic data point or election outcome could explain. As Akerlof saw it, social division was embedded in human nature and programmed in the way individuals interacted. This programming was evident in markets and throughout history.

Modern economists had always boiled their formulas down to the motivations and actions of individuals. People acted rationally and in their own interest, they believed, and individual choices could be aggregated together in markets into a collective wisdom of crowds. Akerlof came to a much different view. He believed that humans were group animals. They cared deeply about how they fit into groups on matters relating to gender, race, religion, politics, work choices, and any number of other issues, even allegiances to sports teams. People tended to define themselves around big group allegiances and associations. Group identification, in turn, drove many decisions.

Among other things, group identification was a formula for conflict. Akerlof's friend Amartya Sen had experienced such oppositional culture in the most violent way in post-independence India, when a Muslim man burst through his family's gate, bleeding from knife wounds, after being stabbed for wandering into a Hindu neighborhood looking for work.

Sociologists had long seen a tendency for group conflict in human nature. In a 1954 experiment, Muzafer Sherif, a Turkish American social psychologist at the University of Oklahoma, took about two dozen eleven- and twelve-year-old boys to Robbers Cave State Park, 150 miles from Oklahoma City. The boys bonded in two separate groups that were kept apart from each other. One group killed a copperhead snake and called itself the Rattlers. The others identified themselves as the Eagles. When the two groups were introduced to each other for four days of competition, they were overwhelmed by group feelings for and against each other. The Rattlers were intensely loyal to each other and intensely opposed to the Eagles, and the Eagles felt the same way about the Rattlers. Beyond formal competitions, they raided each other's huts. The Eagles burned the Rattlers' flag. The groups taunted and name-called to the point where the warring factions had to be separated physically by adult supervisors.[12]

Henri Tajfel, a sociology professor at the University of Bristol, England, extended this work in the late 1960s. He asked teens to examine the paintings of two abstract artists, Paul Klee and Wassily Kandinsky, and told them he was breaking them into two groups based on their preferences for abstract art. In truth, they were sorted randomly. Tajfel found the Klee supporters became rivals of Kandinsky supporters even though there was absolutely no difference between the people in each group, not even their preferences for abstract art. The mere act of labeling people as part of a group set them against each other, he explained in a 1971 paper.[13]

This kind of sorting intensified in postcrisis America, and Akerlof had already spent nearly two decades trying to understand how it worked.

Akerlof's former student Rachel Kranton approached him in 1995. She thought economists were missing something important in overlooking how group identity shaped individual behavior. She had spent time in the 1980s studying in Egypt. She was struck there by how street markets for tomatoes sometimes worked. When tomatoes were in short supply, vendors didn't raise tomato prices, as standard economic theory said they would. Instead they hoarded them, setting scarce tomatoes aside for favored customers or for people in their neighborhoods and charging them regular prices. The vendors weren't driven by economic incentives alone; they were also driven by a strong sense of connection to groups in their own communities. Because of these connections, their behavior defied conventional economics.

During the 1990s, Akerlof and Kranton started wandering tree-lined streets on long walks near the Brookings Institution, several blocks north of the White House, talking about her ideas. It struck them that group identification was almost everywhere they looked, including in economics.

One clear example was the way men and women separated themselves into categories in the labor market. Some jobs were seen as "men's jobs," and some jobs were seen as "women's jobs," even when natural differences between men and women didn't necessarily define who was best suited for a task. When women became lawyers, they often felt a need to behave aggressively, like men, to fit in. When men worked as nurses, some others saw their work as women's work and demeaned them. Some women felt ostracized for working at all and not staying home with children, while men felt ostracized for doing just the opposite.

Akerlof had seen these norms about work and gender up close in Berkeley when he picked up his son, Robby, from grade school in the 1980s. Puzzled mothers didn't understand why he wasn't at his job. Some thought he must be unemployed.

Social customs often weren't economically efficient. In the case of gender, they often kept capable people out of jobs they might do well. Yet group identifications shaped the choices people made and how they defined themselves. They shaped the most important market of all—the market for work.

There was something radical about what Akerlof and Kranton were trying to do. The primacy of the individual in economics traced back to Enlightenment-era writer Jeremy Bentham, who theorized that economics and public policy were ultimately about maximizing an individual's sense of well-being, or what he called utility. Akerlof thought the whole idea of individual utility needed to be redefined. It wasn't always economic interest that defined the decisions individuals made, even decisions like what job to seek. Utility and decisions were often driven by a person's sense of social identity and group allegiances.

Before Akerlof and Kranton published their paper, "Economics and Identity," Akerlof gave a talk at the University of Chicago on the subject. The talk was mostly dismissed by his peers. While he spoke, Chicago professor Sherwin Rosen interjected, "Well, we've all heard bad seminars before." But Gary Becker, another Chicago professor who won a Nobel Prize for using economic analysis to examine social issues such as marriage or feelings such as altruism, supported Akerlof. "I think you have something here," Becker said as they walked back to the university faculty club together after Akerlof's talk.

Akerlof and Kranton built mathematical formulas that broke hypothetical groups of people into "Reds" and "Greens," then showed how

group dynamics and biases could be modeled to explain and predict behaviors. They used this group identity model to dissect discrimination
in the job market.

The model also extended to politics, which Akerlof and Kranton
said amplified group dynamics, sometimes for better and sometimes
for worse. Politicians were expert at playing to and reinforcing the tendency of individuals to align themselves to groups with tightly bound
beliefs, and to lash out at groups in opposition to them. "Fascist and
populist leaders are infamous for their rhetoric fostering racial and eth-
nic divisions, with tragic consequences," they wrote. "Symbolic acts and
transformed identities spur revolutions. The ringing of the Liberty Bell
called on the colonists' identities as Americans. Gandhi's Salt March
sparked an Indian national identity. The French Revolution changed
subjects into 'citizens,' and the Russian Revolution turned them into
'comrades.'"[14]

Akerlof and Kranton kept digging. They released their book *Identity
Economics* in 2010.[15]

The original paper hypothesized groups of Reds versus Greens inter-
acting in opposition to each other. By 2014 the real world was dividing
into Reds versus Blues.

Echoing Akerlof and Kranton's ideas, a wedge was growing between
Hickory and Charlotte, summed up by the Hickory city manager as
working people versus elites. Jobs were concentrating in one place and
not the other. Underneath that, intense group dynamics were building
division between the two places. One pressure point for this division
was in the marketplace for politics. In places like Hickory, Tea Party
followers called themselves "patriots," like those who called themselves
"citizens" in eighteenth-century France. Also like French citizens of the
turbulent Enlightenment era, some Tea Party followers liked to talk
about revolution.

Economic interest and social identity were colliding in clusters around the country. Rural versus urban, conservative versus progressive, manufacturing versus services, traditional family versus modern family—in-groups and out-groups increasingly defined themselves in opposition to each other. The United States was becoming a nation of Rattlers and Eagles.

Though Akerlof and Kranton had a hard time getting their work accepted among economists, they did have the attention of one young professor in London who set out to draw upon their theories.

That professor was Robert Akerlof.

All those years earlier, as a teenager sitting in the back seat of his father's old Toyota on his way to and from school, Robby had listened to and participated in the discussions between Rachel Kranton and George Akerlof. He then made the work his own.

Few economics departments at top US universities were much interested in the subject when he started looking for jobs again in 2010. Robert Akerlof, with an undergraduate degree from Yale, a PhD from Harvard, and postdoctoral studies at MIT, landed a spot on the faculty of the University of Warwick in London. He found a place to live a few blocks away from where Yellen and George thought about settling in the early 1980s. Like his mother, he was orderly and liked to cook. Like his father, he was intent on prodding his field into a new way of thinking.

Many economists still weren't paying attention in 2014, but the forces that George Akerlof and his son described would soon alter Janet Yellen's fate as leader of the Fed, and the nation's fate, too.

21

Yellen Leads the Fed

Flying a Plane with No Gauges
2014–2015

Some of Yellen's colleagues found a change in her when she became the institution's leader in 2014. After all of the stresses that consumed the Fed during her four-year term as vice chair, after all of the confrontations and crises, she seemed more relaxed in the big office.

As the recovery trudged along, the unemployment rate had finally dropped below 7 percent. It had taken too long to get there, but Fed officials were beginning to see a future in which their extraordinary policies might no longer be necessary. This removed some of the pressure that burdened Bernanke and some of the urgency that drove Yellen. Her job would be different from Bernanke's; circumstances had changed. Her job was to move the Fed back toward some state of normalcy, and she figured she had plenty of time to do it.

Yellen adapted her style. As vice chair she had positioned herself as an advocate for uncomfortable policies in a divided institution operating under intense pressure. In that role she sometimes clashed with people who disagreed with her. As chair, she decided it was her job to unify. That meant spending more time pulling people together and less time pushing others toward her view.

Yellen's views of leadership were shaped in part by George and Robby's work on identity. Her husband and son believed work wasn't just about a paycheck. People wanted to feel a sense of purpose and belonging at work. It was common sense and was also borne out in their research. The Fed had been through difficult times and Yellen concluded it was up to her to build an environment that felt rewarding to others. The institution needed work. Bernanke had chipped away at the Fed's monarchal traditions and pushed policy makers to be more consensus-oriented than they had become during Greenspan's long run in power. Yellen had to move further down that path, she decided, which meant running the place without dominating group decisions.

The Fed still had an insular quality. Bernanke worked a lot by himself and was sometimes visibly uncomfortable with others. Yellen was more social. She was comfortable milling around at events and scheduled lots of meetings with colleagues. She wanted to widen the array of people airing out ideas. "It's important for people to feel like they have a say," she said at the time. "I place a lot of emphasis on talking to people."

Yellen was as ready to do this job as anyone who preceded her. She had served in the institution at almost every level possible—as a researcher in the 1970s, a board governor in the 1990s, a regional bank president in the 2000s, and then vice chair. Nobody knew the central bank better. The straight-A student and class valedictorian also had a quiet competitive streak. In her low-key way, Janet Yellen appeared to like coming out on top.

She looked different, too. Washington gossips noticed that she wore the same black outfit when President Obama announced her nomination as at her confirmation hearing in the Senate. The observation made its way to social media and turned into a debate about whether such observations were sexist. People didn't keep track of Alan Greenspan's dark suits. Why did Yellen face such superficial scrutiny?

In fact, Yellen had been thinking about her wardrobe. She liked wearing knit outfits by St. John, but the brand had shifted toward a younger audience when she was still president at the San Francisco Fed. There weren't many other options. She had pestered Blake Nordstrom, president of the Nordstrom retail chain and a director on the San Francisco Fed's board, to convince executives at St. John to keep designing clothes for mature professional women. When that didn't work, she stopped buying the brand. She hadn't updated her wardrobe in years.

After being called out by the online gossips for wearing the same black suit twice, she decided it was time to take a trip to Bloomingdale's in Chevy Chase for a fashion upgrade. On her way there, she noticed a small retail store that featured the clothing of Nina McLemore, a designer she liked. McLemore made colorful suits with short pop-up collars on the jackets. The designer saw the collars as a way to convey confidence and leadership with a little bit of style. Yellen bought a few, and they became her new signature, dressed up sometimes with large, beaded necklaces. She looked bolder on the surface and more stylish than before.

Yellen's first act as a nominee in the fall of 2013 was to convince the White House to ask Stanley Fischer to become the Fed's new vice chairman, and to convince Fischer to take the job. Fischer was widely seen as the dean of modern central banking, a front-row fixture at the Fed's annual gatherings in Jackson Hole, where former students regularly lined up to greet him. He taught economics in the 1970s and 1980s at MIT, where his students included Bernanke and many of the Fed's senior staff. Fischer went on to become the number-two official at the International Monetary Fund in the 1990s, and leader of the Bank of Israel in the 2000s.

Bernanke saw Yellen's choice as another act of self-confidence. Some leaders surround themselves with weak subordinates to avoid threats to their authority. In bringing Fischer to the Fed, she showed she intended to surround herself with the best and the brightest without fear of being overshadowed by anyone in her new role. She also built bridges to the staff by bringing in somebody who taught many of them.

Two weeks before running her first policy meeting in March 2014, Yellen gathered with Washington-based Fed governors and some staffers in a wood-paneled library across from the Fed's main boardroom. She blocked out three hours for a videoconference call with regional bank presidents. She wanted to plot out the Fed's communications on interest rates, she told them, and she wanted them all involved well in advance. She listened quietly as they debated, summing up their views at the end, and then told them that Fed staff in Washington would begin working on formulations that took their different views into account.

Yellen wanted an orderly process and lots of interaction. In all, during her first six months as Fed boss, she spent more than fifty-five hours on phone calls and private meetings with Fed governors and the twelve regional bank presidents, according to her calendars. She scheduled large chunks of time for one-on-one calls with regional Fed bank presidents before each policy meeting. Staff planning around meetings became more collaborative.

"I feel very listened-to by Janet," said Richard Fisher, then-president of the Federal Reserve Bank of Dallas.

Fisher liked Yellen even though he disagreed with top officials, fearing their policies would backfire and cause inflation. He saw a playfulness in Yellen that only rarely showed up in public. In one speech he compared her to Mae West, the seductive Depression-era movie star who said in the 1940 movie *My Little Chickadee* "I generally avoid temptation, unless I can't resist it." Sizing up the risks that Yellen would succumb to the temptations of inflation, Fisher assured an audience in Houston that Yellen was no Mae West. She wouldn't succumb. It was an odd comparison, but Yellen took the bait. At his retirement party Yellen mustered a Mae West impression and purred to Fisher, "Why don't you come up and see me sometime?" It was an echo of the famous line from another West movie, *She Done Him Wrong*.

Yellen bounced back from early setbacks. She traveled to Australia to attend a meeting with foreign finance officials just before the March gathering. After spending days shaking their hands and cooped up on airplanes, she returned to Washington with a bitter cold that sent her temperature soaring to 104 degrees. On the Sunday before the gathering, she told her chief of staff, Michelle Smith, to make preparations in case she missed the meeting. It would have been an embarrassing start, with the potential to unsettle markets.

Yellen's temperature receded and she attended as planned, then fumbled a question on the big stage of her first press briefing after the meeting. Press briefings were broadcast on major cable television networks and watched closely on Wall Street. Markets tended to tumble and rally as Fed leaders spoke. Reporters pressed Yellen about when the Fed might start raising interest rates and she suggested it could happen within several months. That was more specific than she had intended, and a shock to nervous investors, who sent stock prices tumbling before the press conference ended. They weren't ready for the Fed to move and didn't think the economy was either.

The day after the press conference, Yellen knocked on the office door of Jeremy Stein, the Fed governor she had once battled, and poked her head in.

"I'm sorry," she said sheepishly. "I fucked that up."

She didn't dwell on it, though, and moved on.

The problem at the time was that many of the Fed's old models for how the economy behaved once again didn't work. That made it hard to know when to raise interest rates and how much.

An old rule of thumb known as Okun's law related the growth of economic output to changes in unemployment. It held that it took fast growth to bring unemployment down. The idea was named after Art

Okun, the economist Paul Samuelson cited to chide his nephew Larry Summers at MIT years earlier. During expansions in the 1980s and 1990s, economic output had grown at an annual rate near 4 percent, adjusted for inflation, and then during the slower 2000s it grew at a rate near 3 percent. After the financial crisis it grew at a much slower rate, closer to 2 percent. Under Okun's law the economy wasn't growing fast enough for the unemployment rate to fall, but it did. That meant Okun's law was broken.

The Phillips curve—which related inflation to unemployment—also didn't work. Broadly speaking, the theory held that high unemployment was a sign that the economy's resources were underutilized, and the inflation rate should fall. A low unemployment rate meant the economy's resources were scarce, so inflation should accelerate. But the high unemployment rate early in the expansion didn't lead to lower inflation, and then as the jobless rate fell to lower levels, the inflation rate didn't pick up. Instead, though unemployment went up and down, the inflation rate remained stuck under the Fed's 2 percent target for years. The Phillips curve was thus broken too.

It was like flying a plane near the ground and the gauges went out. Yellen was going to have to test the wind, size up the landscape, and adjust as she went.

In the view of many Republicans in Congress, the easy-spending policies of Obama and the Fed were the problem that kept the economy growing so slowly. But that wasn't a satisfying diagnosis; across the Atlantic many European countries had adopted more austere policies and they did even worse. The European Union went back into recession in 2012, and in 2014 it was just starting to climb out of it. Unemployment in the European Union in 2013 was higher than it ever got in the US downturn.

Summers, back at Harvard, had his own theory. In his mind, the United States had entered a new period he dubbed "secular stagnation," borrowing a phrase from the Depression-era economist named Alvin Hansen.[1] The United States had fallen into this anemic new era, Summers said, for an array of reasons that couldn't easily be boiled down to suit the simplistic politics of the moment. The banking system was fragile after the financial crisis; aging populations around the world were spending less; the world didn't need as many giant manufacturing plants in a new information era where clicks on digital tablets and cell phones meant more to some people than tangible goods they bought in stores. And where plants did go up, globalization and new technologies meant the plants didn't need to be in the United States, and often didn't need many workers in them running the machines.

In this low-growth era, Summers surmised, the economy couldn't bear high interest rates. If the Fed tried to raise them, it would push the economy back into recession. In addition, he argued, the Obama White House should have pushed for even more expansive public spending projects to fill the hole the private sector wasn't filling on its own.

Yellen was sympathetic to his views. For years at the Fed she had been puzzled about why interest rates and inflation remained so low for so long after the crisis ended. Even interest rates the Fed didn't directly control—in corporate bond markets, overseas markets, and markets for a wide range of US Treasury bonds—remained unusually low. There was just no sign that anything was going back to the way it had been a decade or two earlier. For a while she figured this was due to lingering headwinds after the financial crisis—people, businesses, and banks were jittery about moving too aggressively.

Summers helped to explain why the recovery was dragging on so long. In his view secular stagnation had been going on for years, and probably started before the financial crisis. If this were true, it meant the Fed might have raised interest rates too much early in Bernanke's first term, exactly what Angelo Mozilo accused the central bank of doing back then. That couldn't have accounted for the severity of the financial crisis, but it was a potential mistake Yellen didn't intend to risk repeating.

She had her own theory about how to respond. As long as inflation didn't pick up, she didn't need to hurry to raise interest rates. She could stay out of the way as unemployment fell. She didn't know how low it could go, but she could probe to find out. She suspected that workers would become scarce and companies would bid up wages, improve benefits, and add training to attract them. That might draw even more people back into the labor market. A vicious cycle might finally turn virtuous, and she wanted to stay out of the way and give it a chance to happen.

After years supporting a policy of high-stakes risk-taking, the Fed's methodical new leader chose the most boring policy possible. She did nearly nothing at all.

By 2014 the Fed's bond purchase program was on course to end. Officials eventually wanted to reduce these holdings, but Yellen was in no hurry to start. She was also in no hurry to raise interest rates. Instead she waited, and prepared for some unknown day down the road when the Fed would need to move.

Staff dove into planning for technical challenges. They had to develop a strategy to dump mortgage and Treasury bonds without disrupting financial markets and causing a new crisis. Should they sell them quickly, or allow them to mature and wind down slowly? The Fed also faced challenges influencing interest rates. After flooding banks with more money than the banks were willing to lend, the Fed's old techniques for influencing interest rates were obsolete and in need of refiguring. While staff worked to adapt the Fed's plumbing to meet these challenges, senior officials debated and deliberated, but by design they changed little of any substance.

Markets and news cycles are built for action and change, but boring worked. The jobless rate kept falling. As Yellen predicted, pay raises crept up. Also as she predicted, people who had stopped looking for work started looking for jobs again. All the while inflation held steady, as she had expected.

Even boring excited the passions of opposition in a public arena increasingly oriented toward conflict. In October 2014, Yellen was scheduled to speak at an annual conference hosted by the Federal Reserve Bank of Boston. The subject that year was inequality. Fed leaders had spoken at the Boston Fed conference before and she accepted. As always, she started working on the speech months before it was set to be delivered.

She stuck mostly to a dry recitation of facts. The average inflation-adjusted income of the top 5 percent of households grew by 38 percent from 1989 to 2013, while incomes for everybody else grew less than 10 percent. By 2013, the bottom half of American households held just 1 percent of all of the nation's wealth, down from 3 percent in 1989.[2]

The United States has always had its divide between rich and poor, as would any capitalist country, but there were two problems demonstrated by these numbers. The first was that the divide seemed to be growing. There was something in this new high-tech, global era that concentrated the spoils of capitalism in the hands of smaller and smaller shares of the population. This was bound to frustrate and anger growing proportions of the population. The second problem was that Americans also had become less mobile. Children born into families with low levels of income and wealth had fewer chances to get rich than children born in generations before them. When it came to mobility, the United States was behind many other countries, including Australia, Norway, Canada, and even France. It suggested that the American Dream—the idea that any American with brains, grit, or initiative could succeed—had come unglued.

"I think it is appropriate to ask whether this trend is compatible with values rooted in our nation's history," Yellen said in Boston.

Republicans roasted her when she went to Capitol Hill a few months later. They thought she was picking up on campaign issues being pushed by Democrats, trying to help her party by shining a light on inequality. "You're sticking your nose in places that you have no business to be," Mick Mulvaney, a South Carolina Republican, lectured her.[3]

Yellen's predecessors at the Fed had spoken about broad economic issues, she pointed out. "I am entitled to do the same," she shot back sternly.

It wasn't just Republicans who came after her. Ralph Nader, the progressive consumer activist, thought Yellen's policy of keeping interest rates low was hurting Americans who kept funds in interest-bearing savings accounts that were the only income for many households. "I think you should sit down with your Nobel Prize winning husband, economist George Akerlof, who is known to be consumer-sensitive," Nader wrote to Yellen. "Together, figure out what to do for tens of millions of Americans who, with more interest income, could stimulate the economy by spending toward the necessities of life."[4]

Nader's letter annoyed Yellen's easygoing husband, who understood that she knew much more about interest rates than he did, even with his economics Nobel.

She responded to Nader herself. "It may help to review a few basic facts," she started, reciting the damage caused by recession. "Would savers have been better off if the Federal Reserve had not acted as forcefully as it did and had maintained a higher level of short-term interest rates, including rates paid to savers? I don't believe so. Unemployment would have risen to even higher levels, home prices would have collapsed further, even more businesses and individuals would have faced bankruptcy and foreclosure, and the stock market would not have recovered. True, savers could have seen higher returns on their federally insured deposits, but these returns would hardly have offset the more dramatic declines they would have experienced in the value of their homes and retirement accounts. Many of these savers undoubtedly would have lost

their jobs or pensions (or faced increased burdens from supporting unemployed children and grandchildren)."[5]

Stepping into the spotlight led to other strange twists, including a
small uproar over Yellen's security detail in the quiet gated community
where she lived. Her search for a new home in Washington had been
the source of running jokes at Fed policy meetings during her tenure as
vice chair. Her colleagues said they were closely watching her decision
about whether to rent or buy for clues about the health of the housing
market. They also teased her about the twenty-year-old Acura she drove
to work every day.

Yellen and Akerlof ended up renting a home on a quiet cul-de-sac in
a gated community named Hillandale, 267 homes situated on the former estate of an oil heiress. Some of Washington's elites made the area
their home, including FBI Director Robert Mueller and Senator Joseph
Lieberman.

The community had its own pool and an old gatehouse where neighbors held gatherings and sometimes gave presentations to each other
about their work. Yellen once showed up with handwritten notes to
talk about the economy. She and Akerlof shopped together on weekends at a nearby Safeway, each taking their own carts in different directions, as they'd long done. She dropped Akerlof off at work at the IMF in
the morning because he didn't have a parking space for his Volvo.

After Yellen became Fed chair and started traveling with the Fed's
security detail, Akerlof hitched a ride to work in the morning. But some
neighbors weren't happy when security officers rented a home across the
street from Yellen and Akerlof and mounted a roof camera on top of it.
Neighbors filed a bill of grievances calling the security post an "armed
camp," and claiming that the police presence was "uncomfortable for
residents of various religious persuasions," such as Quakers. They also
complained that security trucks were spilling fluids in the street, which
violated local bylaws.[6]

Mueller's security was businesslike and didn't socialize, one anonymous neighbor complained to the *Wall Street Journal*. "Now we have this group, overweight, wearing the most ridiculous blue uniforms with the most ridiculous blue caps, and they have guns that are visible."

Yellen and Akerlof were bemused about the fuss. They found the security officers nice and polite, and were relieved when neighbors sent over wine to make amends for the embarrassment.

If the glare ever got to Yellen, it happened only once, in the hot lights of an evening speech she gave in Amherst, Massachusetts, in September 2015. Yellen was on medication to hold her blood pressure down and had a long day of meetings before the speech. She got dehydrated under the lights, started slurring during the speech, and lost focus on the large written words on the page in front of her. During long silences she struggled to keep herself from falling over on the stage in front of everyone. She stopped the speech, went back to Washington, and was cleared by doctors who said it was nothing more than a fainting spell. Somehow she had managed to faint without actually falling down.

Three months later the Fed raised its benchmark interest rate for the first time since pushing it down to near zero in 2008. Yellen had made a tiny move—one-quarter of a percentage point. It had taken seven years, but the economy finally looked like it was getting back on its feet. The unemployment rate finished the year at 5 percent, a low it hadn't reached in seven years.

This was good news, yet large parts of the country had seen enough. It had taken too long. Many people wanted change, and they found a man who promised to deliver it.

22

Yellen Loses Her Job

Too Short
2016–2018

When Donald Trump arrived in Hickory, North Carolina, in March 2016, people lined up hours in advance at Lenoir-Rhyne University to hear what he had to say. They came in thousands, and some camped overnight for a chance to be first in line. It was like the way students behaved for marquee college basketball games in the sports-crazed state.

"You had these great jobs twenty years ago," Trump said from a stage, sitting on a locally upholstered chair. "You don't have them anymore. Why? Because they're in different countries." He promised to bring the jobs back, and proceeded to point a finger at the national elites he blamed for losing the jobs in the first place.

"I'm supposed to say, 'Oh, no, we don't have anger, we're wonderful people, we're so happy with the way the country is run,'" Trump said. "I'm going to tell the truth. Yes, I am angry. Yes, the millions of people that are supporting Trump, and I'm supporting them, we're all angry. We're tired of a government that's run incompetently. We have incompetent people running our country."

He pressed all of their buttons. Christians were losing their voices. Gun owners were threatened with confiscation. Veterans weren't being cared for. Schools were teaching values his followers didn't like. Immigrants were bringing drugs and crime across the border. Trump was the voice of people who didn't like any of this.

The whole day was a spectacle. Protesters came too. They picketed outside and argued with Trump supporters, decrying his verbal attacks on immigrants. Police managed the tussling. Some protesters snuck inside and tried to shout Trump down. But they were outdone. When protesters shouted out, his crowd of supporters shouted the protesters down, and Trump egged them on. Reports of violence were cropping up at his gatherings, but he said they were untrue. His were peaceful, loving people, he said. The problem was the other side.

"This is not Charlotte, this is not Philadelphia. We do have our own small amount of violence here, but I don't see it happening at this school," Anna Boone, a Trump supporter, told a local television reporter.[1]

Trump won the North Carolina primary, then on Election Day took Catawba County with 67 percent of the vote. Hillary Clinton got just 29 percent, but took Charlotte's Mecklenburg County with 62 percent of the vote to Trump's 33 percent. Hickory and Charlotte, less than an hour apart, were mirror images, a microcosm of the new red-blue divide that shaped the election.

Robert Akerlof's new friends in London doubted Trump could ever win. Akerlof told them that Trump could. His research about social division suggested to him that Trump's appeal was powerful in large parts of the country.

Yellen's first instinct on election night was to call Treasury Secretary Jack Lew and prepare for market turbulence the following day. Stock futures fell that evening. Trump's brash and unpredictable persona seemed prone to unsettling markets, she thought.

Many people in Washington and in the national media had misjudged the power of Trump's message outside of thriving American cities and underestimated the likelihood of his being elected. They also misjudged how the markets would react. Yes, Trump would destabilize the cozy power structures of the Washington establishment, but investors didn't worry about that. They liked the promise of lower corporate taxes and less government regulation.

Stocks rallied.

What was a Trump presidency going to mean for Yellen and the institution she led? She and the president-elect had never met or spoken, yet Trump already seemed to have a fickle relationship with her. At times during the campaign he said he respected her. At other times he attacked her and the way the Fed managed the economy.

"She is very political and to a certain extent I think she should be ashamed of herself," Trump told CNBC two months before Election Day. He said she was keeping interest rates low to support his opponent, Hillary Clinton, and also President Obama. "We are in a big, fat, ugly bubble," he said in his first presidential debate with Clinton. He blamed the Fed for causing it.

A Trump ad in the waning days of the campaign featured Yellen's picture, among others, and lambasted what Trump called a failed and corrupt Washington establishment that had trillions of dollars at stake in the election. Some people saw it as more than an attack on Yellen. The Anti-Defamation League called it anti-Semitic because it featured a number of high-profile Jews—among them Yellen, Goldman Sachs CEO Lloyd Blankfein, and hedge-fund investor George Soros—and colored them as destructive money grabbers.

Yellen sent the ad to her friend from her days at Brown, Carol Greenwald, who was Jewish and a Trump supporter. Greenwald saw him as a strong ally of Israel and had started a group called Jews Choose Trump.[2] She didn't see a problem with the controversial ad; she had a completely different view about his association with Jewish people than his critics.

The man had a way of dividing families and friends. Yellen stopped talking to Greenwald. When contacted years later to talk about her old college friend, who had accomplished so much, Greenwald said, "I have nothing to say about Janet Yellen."

Thus began a strange new dance between the Fed and the White House that started with Yellen and intensified with her successor, Jerome Powell.

Economists learned during the Nixon years that the central bank needed to avoid political entanglements to prevent making the kind of policy mistakes that in the 1970s had led to double-digit inflation. Trump tended to cast many decisions in personal and transactional terms. In his mind, the Fed was already politically entangled with the Obama administration for the benefit of Obama and Clinton. At the very least he wanted equal treatment, meaning low interest rates to boost economic growth and stock prices during his presidency. Yellen thought policy had to respond to what was happening in the economy, not any perception of which president got what.

"Congress very wisely established the Federal Reserve as an independent agency in order to insulate monetary policy from short-term political pressures," she said, when asked about Trump's criticism at a press conference before Election Day. "I can say emphatically that partisan politics plays no role in our decisions about the appropriate stance of monetary policy."[3]

Yellen's term as Fed chair was up in early 2018. Trump would be deciding whether to replace her during his first year in office. She didn't want to be kicked out, and she also didn't want to be replaced by somebody who might break the independent culture of the institution, which she regarded as sacred.

The old economic models hadn't worked at predicting how the economy would behave as unemployment fell, but Yellen's suspicion was that the risks of inflation or a financial bubble would finally start to build if interest rates remained so low much longer. She didn't need to move aggressively, but she also couldn't ignore the risk altogether. She would need to raise rates more as the economy continued to strengthen.

In December 2016 the unemployment rate was down to 4.7 percent, two percentage points lower than when she started the job. The Fed raised rates for a second time and had plans for more hikes. She and her colleagues also wanted to begin shrinking the giant portfolio of bonds the Fed held as the economy improved.

Trump surely wasn't going to like any of it. He was looking at the Fed's behavior in personal terms, while she was looking at it as a response to economic data. The path she set out thus risked the ire of the new president, and risked putting the Fed's cherished independence at stake, and also her own job.

Trump's economic advisers became a buffer between Yellen and the bombastic new president. Gary Cohn left the number-two job at Goldman Sachs to become the director of the White House National Economic Council, making him a central intermediary between the president and the nation's top economic policy makers. Cohn's self-confidence won Trump's respect. The president called the Goldman exec one of his geniuses.

Cohn understood that political intrusions into Fed decisions could spook investors and send stocks lower or interest rates higher. Part of his job, he said, was to keep the new president from firing out attacks on Yellen or the Fed through his active Twitter account.[4]

Cohn began meeting with Yellen regularly, and a few weeks after the inauguration he arranged to introduce her to Trump. Yellen and Trump were born just two months apart in neighboring New York City boroughs, Brooklyn and Queens. But that's about where the similarities ended.

Yellen was short, modest, and driven by a sense of duty that she saw as being more important than self-interest. She kept her hair simply cut and its natural gray, and spoke in long, complex sentences. She enjoyed a drink from time to time and laughed at her own mistakes, even though she did everything she could to avoid them. Trump was tall, with dyed and carefully combed hair. He rambled, boasted, and was driven by a sense of self-interest that seemed to supersede all else. A teetotaler, he didn't admit to mistakes, even though his shoot-from-the-hip style seemed to invite them.

At first their interests seemed to be aligned. Trump wanted a fast-growing economy, and Yellen's long record suggested she did too. With inflation low, Yellen believed she could move rates up slowly.

At the meeting set up by Cohn, Trump held court with Yellen from behind the Resolute Desk in the Oval Office. She sat in a cushioned chair before him, with Cohn seated nearby. Trump did most of the talking, telling her he considered her a "low-interest-rate person" like him. Her views about interest rates were more nuanced than that; in fact, she had already started raising them. But she saw no point in getting into it with him, so she let him talk while she listened.

In public, Cohn tried to strike a neutral tone about Yellen's work, as had his White House predecessors. "The Fed will do what they need to do, and we respect the powers of the Fed," he told Fox News about the central bank.[5]

Yellen's other point of contact was Steven Mnuchin, another Goldman Sachs veteran. Mnuchin had made a fortune buying IndyMac, the failed West Coast thrift, and turning it around with the help of tough foreclosure policies for delinquent mortgage borrowers. In 2009, he became chief executive of the renamed firm, OneWest Bank, and moved his family from its Park Avenue apartment in Manhattan to a twenty-two-thousand-square-foot mansion in Los Angeles.[6]

Mnuchin was a top fundraiser for Trump during the campaign. Trump made him his Treasury secretary, and Yellen began meeting with him regularly, a long-standing Washington tradition. The Fed and the Treasury had always worked together on bank regulation, but Yellen and Mnuchin didn't see eye to eye. Mnuchin wanted to ease Obama-era bank rules, which he saw as a choke hold on economic growth, while Yellen saw them as essential to preventing another financial crisis. Their relationship was formal, cordial, and professional. As a former Wall Street banker, Mnuchin also understood that Fed independence mattered to investors, and he didn't want to create an impression that was changing.

But they tussled over regulation. Both served on a body set up by Obama called the Financial Stability Oversight Council. One of its jobs was to coordinate government oversight of the nation's biggest financial institutions, firms that were so big or entangled with each other that their failure could destabilize the whole system. Mnuchin wanted to ease federal pressure to restrain these firms. Yellen was reluctant.

During the summer of Trump's first year in office, the search for the next Fed leader heated up. Convinced that Yellen liked low interest rates, Trump became intrigued about the idea of keeping her. Yellen wanted to stay in the job. Presidents didn't tend to fire Fed leaders who were doing a good job. Clinton, a Democrat, kept Greenspan, a Republican, on board. Obama, also a Democrat, kept Bernanke, a Republican, on board. Yellen thought she deserved the same treatment. She also thought the Fed needed somebody who wasn't bound by loyalty to the president. Burns's relationship with Nixon had proven to be a disaster that she didn't want to see repeated.

Cohn led the search.

In May 2017 Yellen returned to Brown to give a speech on the role of women in the labor force. The school was marking the 125th anniversary of women being admitted to the university and asked her to give a keynote address.

Yellen was the first woman ever to lead the Federal Reserve. She had reached the top in a male-dominated field that presented challenges at almost every turn in her career—the only woman in her PhD class at Yale in the 1960s, an isolated junior professor on the faculty at Harvard in the 1970s, a working mother at Berkeley in the 1980s, a top adviser in a Clinton White House in the 1990s that was filled with energy and testosterone. Yet she didn't like to make a fuss about the challenges or her own story as a woman rising in economics. She was becoming seen as a trailblazer with a gray-haired, pop-collar style, but she didn't like to parade herself or make a cause of the barriers she broke. She wanted to be supportive of young women who saw her as a role model, but she also wanted her reputation to rest on her work.

At Brown she barely spoke about her own experiences. Instead she focused on economics. Women had made progress, she said, but still lagged in wages compared to men, were still underrepresented in some occupations, and still struggled to strike a balance between work and family. This kept some women out of the workforce, which held back economic growth. Policies aimed at addressing these issues, she said, could increase prosperity for everyone.[7]

The talk captured the interest of a powerful woman in the Trump administration, the president's daughter Ivanka Trump. She wanted to address challenges for women in the workplace from her new perch as an adviser to the president. Ivanka tweeted about Yellen's speech and asked to meet with the Fed chair. They had breakfast at the central bank and spoke politely about their children, economics, and workplace issues.

Trump's decision became an odd spectacle. He liked Yellen, but his advisers thought he should nominate a Republican who was more sympathetic to his deregulatory agenda. Trump also seemed to be of two minds about Yellen's look. "I like her; I like her demeanor," he told the *Wall Street Journal* in July, but privately, he wondered if she looked like a central banker. Looks mattered to Trump, according to people who worked with him. He wanted economic advisers who could go on television and make a convincing case for his policies.

"Is Janet Yellen tall enough to be Fed chair?" he reportedly wondered aloud in front of some dumbfounded advisers.[8] He later denied ever having said or thought such a thing. "I don't even know if she's short or not.

I really don't. I didn't notice. We have a lot of fake news out there," he said years later in an interview. "She's tall in spirit and in mind."[9]

Yellen didn't help her chances that August when she went to the Fed's annual retreat in Jackson Hole and delivered a defense of the central bank's tough postcrisis regulatory stance. "Reforms since the crisis have made the financial system substantially safer," she argued, an unsubtle counter to Trump's desire to roll them back. Trump officials argued that bank regulation was holding back growth. Yellen said there wasn't convincing evidence for that assertion, nor was there evidence to support an aggressive rollback.[10]

"Janet Yellen has too much backbone," Alan Blinder said when asked to size up her chances of being appointed for another term. "She is not going to make a loyalty pledge to Donald Trump."[11]

Trump said that summer that he was considering Cohn for the job, but Cohn's chances ended that August after the president chimed in about a right-wing rally of white nationalists and neo-Nazis in Charlottesville. A self-described neo-Nazi later sentenced to life in prison ran over and killed a young woman protesting against the rally. Trump said there was "blame on both sides" before offering an official condemnation of neo-Nazis and other right-wing extremists. He again came off looking anti-Semitic to many people. Cohn told colleagues he was disgusted by Trump's response, and then told the *Financial Times* that the White House "can and must do better" condemning hate groups.[12] "Citizens standing up for equality and freedom can never be equated with white supremacists, neo-Nazis and the KKK," he told the newspaper.

Trump saw Cohn's rebuke as an act of betrayal and crossed him off the list. He told others he didn't think Cohn was up to the job, and Mnuchin emerged as a bigger force in the search.[13]

Yellen and Mnuchin had begun sparring over the Financial Stability Oversight Council. Mnuchin wanted to roll back intense government oversight of AIG, the large insurer the United States took over during the financial crisis. Yellen slowed the process but eventually went along with Mnuchin, to the dismay of progressives in her party. Mnuchin came to see Yellen as an impediment to the deregulatory agenda.

In the weeks ahead, Trump's selection process started looking like a strange reality television special. In a meeting with Republican senators, he polled the room about its preferences. Then he spoke on Fox Business Network to Lou Dobbs and asked the TV host whom he would like to see win the job. Dobbs, flummoxed to be asked on national television, said Yellen might be worth keeping. Trump said he'd think about it, but then countered himself by saying he'd also like to make his own mark on the institution.

"He's always got somebody else in his head and he's polling everyone around him for more names," one adviser told the *Wall Street Journal*.[14]

It came down to four people: a former Fed governor named Kevin Warsh; a Stanford academic named John Taylor; Jerome Powell, then still a Fed governor; and Yellen.

Warsh had worked in the White House under George W. Bush and then became close to Bernanke at the Fed during the early days of the financial crisis. He also had ties in Republican donor circles. He was married to Jane Lauder, a descendant in the Estée Lauder cosmetics empire, and his father-in-law, Ronald Lauder, was friendly with Trump. Taylor had Republican roots and solid academic credentials. He had developed a well-known formula describing when the central bank should raise or lower interest rates, though Yellen saw his "Taylor rule" as outdated and too rigid.

Powell was closest to Yellen in temperament and also her friend. A Republican who joined the Fed in 2010 skeptical of the central bank's unconventional new programs, he came around to her view that these programs were necessary, and not nearly as damaging as critics alleged. After other governors, including Stein and Duke, moved on, Powell stayed at the Fed and took on more work governing the organization.

She appreciated his efforts to help her run the place and his easygoing style. He admired her intellect. When Powell met with Andrew Olmem, a White House official, early that year, he made the case that Yellen should get a second term, saying, "There is only one person here who has taken this team to the playoffs."

Yellen was the last of the four to be given a formal interview with the president. Trump asked Yellen why the US economy couldn't grow as fast as the economies of China or India. She explained that developing countries have more ground to make up and tend to grow faster. The United States likely couldn't reach that pace because it was already developed. Her point undermined his argument that the United States should be growing much faster, but he moved on.

He asked her what she thought of the other candidates he was considering. Yellen talked about what it takes to be a good Fed leader, turning to an analogy she liked to use about paint. One of her jobs, she explained, was to throw away bad ideas diplomatically. Suppose you have nineteen people sitting around a table, and the group has to pick a color to paint the room. Suppose you want a simple off-white, and you need to get the group on common ground. As Fed chair, she had to give the people who wanted chartreuse or hot pink a chance to air their ideas. The rest of the group would shoot down the worst ideas, saving her the trouble of shooting them down herself.

Years of experience were in Yellen's mind as she made the analogy. When she was vice chair and San Francisco Fed president, Yellen was sometimes the person shooting down the bad ideas of others. She studied their positions, sometimes taking an opponent's position against her own staff members to see how her staff reacted and what arguments they mustered against her. Then in policy meetings she picked apart her opposition in exacting detail.

As chair, she came to realize that she needed to give everyone a chance to talk and examine ideas, and the committee would do some of the work of throwing out the ideas that didn't make sense. Her approach to leadership involved debate and discussion and took preparation and patience to play out, but she believed it got the Fed to good decisions and kept the group together.

She boiled all of these thoughts down for the president with the analogy of paint.

Yellen employed paint analogies in another way as Fed leader. The economy was fragile after the financial crisis. Taking away the Fed's easy-money policies was going to be slow, like watching paint dry, she said. People would barely notice it happening. She had a way of explaining things that made sense to people.

Trump liked Yellen, but Mnuchin was convinced that she would give him and the president trouble on bank regulation.

"People are anxiously awaiting my decision as to who the next head of the Fed will be," Trump said teasingly in an Instagram video he posted. "I have somebody very specific in mind. I think everybody will be very impressed."

Trump picked Powell at Mnuchin's urging, and he didn't invite Yellen to the ceremony announcing the choice. Trump's chief of staff, John Kelly, said he had been sure all along that Yellen would never get the nod because she wasn't seen as loyal to the president and because she was associated with Obama. "Personal loyalty trumped everything," Kelly said.[15]

"I gave her serious consideration," Trump said later in an interview. "I think she's an excellent person and I think she knows what to do." In the end, he said, he chose Powell because he wanted a change and he wanted a Republican. "It had nothing to do with her," he said. "It was obvious to me that she loved our country."

Yellen had wanted the job, but still, she was relieved. She thought Powell was the one among the final candidates most likely to stand up for the Fed's independence and to make sound decisions about interest rates. She could have stayed at the Fed as a lower-level governor even after losing the top job, and she had considered doing so during the nomination drama, but after Powell landed the pick, she decided it was best to leave.

At a going-away party for Yellen at the Fed, Powell reflected on how diligently he had prepared for his meetings with her. When she was vice chair, Powell, a lawyer, regularly sought out Yellen for her views on economics. Invariably she found weaknesses in his arguments that he hadn't considered. As he spoke, Akerlof sat in the audience, nodding knowingly. He had won a Nobel Prize, and she did the same to him. Powell said the Fed would never again have a leader who came into the job with the same preparation or qualifications. "There won't be another person with that much knowledge," he said.

She was exiting the stage with a short but sterling record. During her four-year term, the unemployment rate dropped from 6.7 percent to 4.1 percent, and more than six million people entered the labor force. The jobless rate for Black people dropped from 11.8 percent to 6.8 percent. Annual incomes for American households in the middle of the earnings spectrum rose by $7,000 to $65,000 adjusted for inflation, reversing fifteen years of stagnation. The number of Americans who said they were too discouraged to look for a job dropped from 740,000 to 355,000. The number of people with disabilities who said they had jobs rose from 4.7 million to 5.6 million. The University of Michigan's measure of household confidence in the economy rose for the first time in more than a decade above precrisis levels. The Dow Jones Industrial Average rose 53 percent. The number of Americans collecting food stamps dropped by more than five million. The number living under official poverty thresholds dropped by six million. All along, inflation remained stable.

It took too long for millions of Americans to get there, and progress didn't all happen on her watch, but after a long and painful decade the US economy was finally back on its feet.

A couple of months before her departure, Yellen sat down with Lord Mervyn King, the former leader of the Bank of England, for a public interview. King likened Yellen and Akerlof to Andre Agassi and Steffi Graf, the only husband-and-wife combination ever to win individual Wimbledon tennis titles.[16]

King asked Yellen to reflect on the lessons she had learned. She said she'd learned not to be doctrinaire. "I had pretty strong views about how the economy works and how to interpret data. But one of the most important things I learned as chair and thought was important to making good policy is to keep an open mind and not to simply assume that history is repeating itself. There are always new features, things are always changing, there are always puzzles that one needs to look at objectively, to analyze and to really try to figure out what is going on, rather than what you thought should be going on."

Then he asked her how hard it was to rise in a field dominated by men. She pointed to two factors that made it possible: her study habits and her husband.

"I've had a very good career in economics," she said, "studying hard and making sure that I prepared for things, I think these are my trademarks, and they are traits that I probably had going back to my Fort Hamilton high school days, and I've found they've served me well."

Looking back, she said, many women were held back by a dearth of mentors in her world. In that respect, she had lucked out. First she met Tobin. Then she met Akerlof, whose work with her on research in the 1980s led to breakthroughs.

"My husband has in many ways been a mentor," she said.

More than that, though, he was a steadfast supporter who put her career choices first in the family.

"He has encouraged me. When I have been offered jobs in Washington, for example, his attitude has been, 'You want to do that? Absolutely, we're going to make that work.'"

After Trump let her go, she thought it would be the last time Akerlof would have to say that.

23

Professor
Robert Akerlof

Explaining a Red and Blue America
2018–2020

After Yellen left the Fed in 2018, the family traveled with her brother, John, and his wife to Provence for a getaway. John was the archaeology program director at the National Science Foundation and a researcher at the Smithsonian Institution's National Museum of Natural History.

A bookworm in his own right, even he was struck by his sister's approach to vacation in the south of France. Every morning Yellen, George, and Robby buried themselves in different rooms, where they studied, read, and wrote. Yellen worked on a speech on financial regulation that she was scheduled to deliver to the American Economic Association in eighteen months. After a morning of work, the three emerged for a relaxing lunch or a trip into town to enjoy fine food and wine. Yellen and George were geeks of a very high order, and they were well aware of it. Robby had become one too.

All those years Robby had spent hiking with George around Berkeley parks, following him to restaurants with intellects like Robert Shiller, listening from the back seat to his conversations with Rachel Kranton; all those years needling his mother about the way Angelo Mozilo dressed, chopping carrots with her in the kitchen, watching her work through crises that disrupted the lives of millions of Americans; all those years learning the rigors of math and how to use it—it had all sunk in. "My son was, I suppose, doomed to become an economist," Yellen told Mervyn King before she left the Fed.

What could Robert Akerlof possibly do to distinguish himself, with a mother who served as the world's most powerful economic policy maker and a father who took a back seat to her with his Nobel Prize?

As was the case for Summers, economics was the field where Robby's skills were sharpest. In his mind economics still needed a lot of work, and so he followed that path. George once said that his life's work was mostly about putting human beings back into economics. Conventional economics models were built upon rigid assumptions about how humans behaved in a marketplace, but George believed those assumptions didn't measure up to reality. Robert embraced his father's worldview and set out to build on what George started.

Robert and George lived in a different world than Yellen. She was a policy maker who put ideas to test in the marketplace, while they were professors who lived in a world of abstraction and theory. While Yellen made policy in Washington, they wrote research papers and books that only the most highly skilled technicians could understand. At the heart of their work was a single subversive idea: that a core premise upon which modern economics was built—the notion that people acted rationally and in their own individual self-interests to advance their welfare—was barren and incomplete.

As George and Robby saw it, behavioral economics hadn't gone far enough. It focused on just one problem in economics, individual irrationality. There was an entire world beyond that, they believed, a world driven by group dynamics.

To understand their mindset, it helps to look at another area in science. The individual was to economics as the atom was to physics, the solitary particle that drove everything. Robert and George were like chemists, adding a new dimension to this analogy. In chemistry, atoms form bonds to create a world of rich molecules that bring nature to life. Similarly, the bonds that connect humans in groups shape how people behave, driving economic, social, and political lives.

Robert wanted to trace the nature of human bonds more deeply and examine how those bonds affected broader spheres of business, family life, politics, and economic activity. In geekier terms, he wanted to unify economics with sociology, like a chemist who plumbs the workings of individual atoms to discover how life grows out of them.

His work mattered in 2018 because it helped to explain the divisiveness that was by then in full bloom across America. Group psychology was an important part of that story, and his research papers, like stepping-stones, led toward deeply disturbing conclusions about the path the nation was following.

Economics had always focused on human behavior from the perspective of "I," Robert wrote in one paper, assuming that individuals wanted to maximize their incomes, wealth, and consumption. He looked at human behavior, by contrast, from the perspective of "we," and assumed that human motivations went far beyond individual consumption. "I define 'we thinking' as a mode of thinking in which an individual takes a group's goals as his own," he said.[1]

This kind of thinking was everywhere. Clearly volunteers in the army sought something more than consumption and identified themselves with a larger cause and set of beliefs. Businesses often tried to build cultures that encouraged workers to see themselves as part of a meaningful enterprise that motivated them beyond their paychecks. New Yorkers or Bostonians likewise took a pride in their cities that went beyond the material gain of being there, and allegiances to sports teams tied people together in ways that couldn't be explained solely by economic gain.

What were the dynamics of behavior, reason, and emotion that connected people in groups? How did group identification shape individual decisions, economic and otherwise? Why did people choose to conform to certain group norms, such as the belief in some communities that only women should be in charge of child-rearing, or appeals by some businesses to patriotism from workers and customers? Where did such norms come from? How did leadership form in these groups, and how did leaders maintain their authority? What kept groups together, and what set them against each other?

Understanding "we" dynamics, he said, helped to explain how companies worked, and much more. It explained labor movements, families, class struggles, religious groups, even the ethos of an entire nation. You couldn't understand economics, he argued, without understanding the nature of "we" thinking. Yet most economists completely ignored it.

Take a very simple institution: the family. Many families are shaped by norms and narratives about what they stand for. A traditional family might see the male as the provider and the female as a caretaker and nurturer. An unconventional modern family might have a more expansive view of the roles that men or women play at home and work, or even whether the family should be defined as one male and one female at its core. These family norms, in turn, influence how people work, how they raise children, how they view education, and where they choose to live.

Looking at how family life was changing across countries, Robert saw that shifting family norms had measurable economic impacts.[2] National incomes tended to be higher in countries where women took on expansive roles in the workplace. These places were becoming more service oriented and less exposed to manufacturing. The shift was socially divisive. Some families saw the move away from their model as a threat to a whole cloth of beliefs and values they held dearly. Some believed the shift away from traditional family values caused social decay. When people in traditional families vocalized these feelings of threat, their resistance was seen by modern families as a threat to their values. Politicians capitalized on the tension, playing to one side's grievances against the other.

The example of families showed how groups sometimes defined themselves as apart from or even in opposition to others, as had happened in the Robbers Cave experiment. "Oppositional identity," as Robert and others called it, could be an especially powerful force among people who felt dispossessed. Rather than identify with a dominant group, the dispossessed sometimes defined themselves in opposition to those perceived as being in power, even when such opposition might hurt their own economic advancement.

One example was in American cities in the 1960s, 1970s, and 1980s. Starting with the book written by the Harvard sociology professor William Julius Wilson, *When Work Disappears: The World of the New Urban Poor*, he noted that factories had moved out of urban areas and that middle-income households had fled to the suburbs. In some neighborhoods, people became isolated and defined themselves in opposition to dominant mainstream culture, notably in poor Black neighborhoods. An oppositional mindset in these neighborhoods made it even harder to find scarce jobs. Akerlof said his model helped to explain the phenomenon in a broad context that, over time, applied to many different groups.[3]

A related example of identity economics was the tendency of some Black people in the 1990s to give their children distinctive names such as DeShawn or Shanice, which, among other things, distinguished them from white children with names like Connor or Molly. These name patterns were well documented by a flood of economic research in the 2000s and were prevalent for Black people living in racially isolated neighborhoods.[4] Economic research showed that men and women with distinctively "Black" names faced discrimination in workplaces.[5] Their résumés were much less likely to be selected by employers for follow-up interviews than were the résumés of people with distinctively "white" names, even when other markers on the résumés, such as education or work experience, were the same. Black parents gave their children those names despite an economic incentive to do otherwise. The power of group identification helped to explain these collisions of interests.

In chemistry, atoms are bound by the behavior of electrons. In identity economics, Robert argued, bonds are shaped between people in part by the sense of worth and value they derive from their group connections, a sense he called esteem. It was in part by being aligned with others in groups and their common norms of thinking that people gained a sense of personal esteem. Like the glue that holds atoms together in complex molecules, this sense of group esteem held people together and connected them with a wide array of behaviors and beliefs.

By 2018, new patterns of oppositional identity had emerged across red-versus-blue America. Trump mobilized his followers against what they perceived to be dominant elites by lashing out at a popular culture that many saw as overbearing, corrupt, and alienating. People signaled their group allegiances by waving big American flags from trucks (a signal of patriotism to those on the right) or attaching rainbow bumper stickers to their cars (a signal of tolerance to those on the left), or taking stands for gun rights on one side or against climate change on the other.

Blue America was concentrated in thriving, dense urban areas devoted to service jobs, while red America was concentrated in sparser rural areas with more manufacturing. Division was getting worse, Robert believed, because the economy and social norms were in such flux. Not only had manufacturing jobs been disappearing in sparser areas, so had traditional family norms common in the same places. It was a strain for many working men at a time when norms about the roles of men and women in the workplace were also in flux.

These were no longer just the abstractions of a few interesting academics. In fact, identity economics had become big business.

As Rachel Kranton saw it, while brick-and-mortar factories closed down, the nation had been building identity factories—cable news stations that produced programming that fed the belief systems of their viewers, sold advertisements, and rewarded popular anchors with lucrative contracts and book promotions for keeping their audiences strong and growing. Politicians checked in to cable news stations raise their profiles and raise money. The whole lucrative system was built to affirm the belief systems of the groups that tuned in to them. College campuses—whether it be progressive Ivy League schools in the Northeast or conservative campuses like Liberty University in Virginia—had become part of the nation's identity machinery too. Running these identity factories were identity entrepreneurs who profited from discord and from reinforcing the alliances, norms, and grievances of their groups.[6]

Donald Trump was the ultimate identity entrepreneur. In Hickory he talked about being angry at American elites. Robert wrote about the use of anger as a powerful enforcement tool in the business of identity economics. Leaders mobilized anger to keep people loyal within their groups and to focus their emotions against those on the outside.[7] The power of anger explained a wide range of behavior through history, including the challenges police faced preventing crime in cities. When people were angry at police and saw their work as illegitimate, they were less likely to cooperate with authorities against gang behavior. The gangs only lost control when people became angry at them for not protecting their own communities.

Robert's research also turned to the idea of legitimacy. Groups were held together by common beliefs in the legitimacy of their values and their leaders; Robert explored how this sense of legitimacy was shaped, and when it cracked. One example was company mergers. When two companies merged, the belief systems of two firms often collided. The leaders of merged companies, Robert found, were vulnerable during these collisions, sometimes losing the loyalty of their workers. Workers placed in direct opposition to the contrasting cultures of other firms were prone to questioning the legitimacy of their leaders.[8]

These ideas led logically toward disturbing questions about America: What were the nation's identity wars doing to the faith Americans had in their leaders, and in the institutions that held the whole country together? His research showed that powerful forces of group behavior could damage trust in institutions like merged companies or city police and that enterprising leaders could mobilize anger for their own purposes. This was happening on a grand scale. As the identity wars wore on, Americans were losing faith in the institutions that kept the nation working: The press. The courts. The federal bureaucracy. Electoral systems. The presidency. Banks. Big business. Surveys conducted by polling institutions such as Gallup found that American trust in these and other institutions had been falling for decades, and the trend had intensified.[9]

A year after Yellen left the Fed, the economy was still improving, yet the nation's internal rage was only growing worse.

24

Yellen Makes History

Cleaning Up Another Mess
2020

In mid-March 2020 Robert Akerlof was in London, unattached and watching a worsening health crisis sweep across Europe. He decided to jump on a plane and fly to Washington to be with his parents before the city of London shut down altogether. It was chaos in Heathrow Airport. After he arrived at George and Janet's Chevy Chase home, he quarantined in the family's basement for two weeks. His mother left meals she'd prepared for him at the basement door while he waited alone for a clean bill of health.

Janet Yellen and George Akerlof were enjoying a quiet but active time in their lives. Yellen was still working on her speech to the American Economic Association, which she now led as its president. The speech had occupied her mornings in the south of France, even though she had more than a year to finish it. She also had been thrust into the middle of a reckoning in the economics profession about the way it treated women, after a researcher reported vulgar and misogynist language on an economics job search website.[1] The outcry was amplified when Harvard suspended a prominent professor, Roland Fryer, after junior assistants alleged that sexual banter and bullying in a lab he ran created a work environment hostile to women, allegations he denied.[2]

The field had always drawn combative personalities—from Keynes through Friedman, Samuelson, Summers, and others—who turned seminar rooms into the intellectual equivalent of a fight club. The atmosphere turned some women off, but the problem ran deeper. Studies found that women were less likely to be promoted than men, even when they were just as productive.[3] Papers written by women also faced more grueling peer review than papers written by men.[4]

Yellen called the culture unacceptable and was working on new association rules to change it. She also started talking more openly about the challenges she'd faced as she rose through the ranks of economics. She didn't like to define her place in economics by her gender, but as she looked back on her career, she could see its imprint.

Being a woman at Harvard in the 1970s had been challenging. It was difficult to find friends and research partners, which probably slowed her publishing. Early in her career she gravitated to some subjects that weren't her main interest, such as economic development or business pricing strategies, largely because those were areas where she could find partners to work with her. When she moved to Washington after Harvard, it was partly because she thought she'd have a better chance to find friends there. She didn't say it publicly, but the locker room atmosphere of the White House later in the 1990s was also uncomfortable. Clinton wanted to advance women in top jobs, and she benefited from that, but working in the White House in his administration could be unpleasant.

After leaving the Fed, Yellen also returned to the issue of climate change. She joined a bipartisan group called the Climate Leadership Council, a mix of businesspeople, nonprofit leaders, academics, Republicans, and Democrats. There she helped author a petition that few politicians wanted to endorse and many economists saw as obvious. "A carbon tax offers the most cost-effective lever to reduce carbon emissions at the scale and speed that is necessary," it started.[5] The proposal accepted climate change as a problem and described government regulation as a relatively cumbersome and inefficient way to address it. The money raised by the tax could be returned to households in the form of rebates. The point wasn't to raise money; it was to create incentives for people and businesses to avoid the carbon-based fuels that destabilized the environment. "By correcting a well-known market failure, a carbon tax will send a powerful price signal that harnesses the invisible hand of the marketplace to steer economic actors towards a low-carbon future," the statement said. It made perfect sense to economists and more than three thousand of them signed it, but few politicians would go near it.

To Robby, Janet seemed more relaxed than she had been in years. The heavy weight of running the Fed and managing through economic crisis had been removed.

It might have helped that for the first time in their lives, Yellen was raking in money. She earned more than $7 million in fees after leaving the Fed for speaking and consulting work with Goldman Sachs, Citigroup, the Citadel hedge fund group, and other financial firms. Greenspan and Bernanke had also reaped windfalls from Wall Street speaking engagements after leaving the Fed. Yellen asked the firms for questions in advance, wrote out her answers, and memorized them so she didn't need any paper in her lap when she spoke.

Before that time, the only interesting assets in Yellen's public disclosures had been Berkeley retirement funds and a stamp collection she'd inherited from her mother that was worth somewhere between $15,000 and $50,000.[6] For years the family had driven old cars. Now Yellen bought a new Audi. They also bought the Chevy Chase home for $2 million.

By early 2020, the US economy was in a sweet spot. The expansion that had started in mid-2009 and crept along so slowly for years was now the longest period of economic growth in US history, outdistancing the decade-long period of growth of the 1990s. Slow progress had meant drawn-out suffering for millions of families, though it prevented an upsurge of inflation and destabilizing new financial bubbles. As unemployment decreased, companies were finally bidding up wages for mid- and low-income workers. Inflation-adjusted incomes for middle-class households were posting their most convincing gains in decades.

Trump was planning a reelection campaign that celebrated those economic gains, and his victory looked assured. "We were doing so well and people were coming together," Trump said, wistfully, two years later.[7]

Did his policies deserve credit for the economy's performance up to that point?[8] Perhaps a little, but Trump's economic record never fit the black-and-white narratives told by either his ardent fans or his furious foes. His detractors said his tax policies catered to the rich, yet poverty and inequality fell during his first three years in office. At the same time, Trump said he would supercharge economic growth, and while the growth rate did pick up, it didn't speed up as much or in the ways he projected.

Economic output grew at a 2.1 percent annual rate during the first six years of the expansion on Obama's watch. It grew at a 2.5 percent rate during Trump's first three years as president. But his agenda of tax cuts, deregulation, and tough trade policies didn't spark the economy in the ways he said it would. Business investment actually slowed during his first three years, and trade became a drag on growth; other countries retaliated against tariffs that Trump had imposed on their products, and export growth slowed.

Along the way, Trump turned on the person he chose to replace Yellen, lashing out repeatedly at Powell for raising interest rates and lambasting Mnuchin privately for talking him into choosing Powell. He saw Powell's interest-rate decisions as foolish and an impediment to his promise of faster economic growth, though they were an extension of a policy the Fed had been telegraphing for years. "He never forgave Mnuchin," Lawrence Kudlow, an economist and television host turned White House adviser, would later say.[9]

One of the faster-growing parts of the economy during the Trump years was federal spending, which expanded at an inflation-adjusted

3 percent annual rate during his first three years in office. During Obama's last six years, by contrast, federal spending contracted at an inflation-adjusted 1 percent annual rate, the result of budget battles with Republicans who lost their devotion to spending restraint once they controlled the White House. They pushed for more military spending, and Democrats pushed for more social spending, and both got what they wanted; at the same time, growth in tax revenues slowed. Trump had said he would shrink the budget deficit and eliminate debt, but instead the deficit expanded from $585 billion before he took office to $984 billion in 2019, and the debt soared by $3 trillion along the way.

Democrats and Republicans didn't get into the nuance of any of these points. Nuance didn't suit political debate that was about bludgeoning and humiliating opponents.

The truth was that the best medicine for the economy was simple to state: keep it out of recession. During the previous twenty years, downturns had been so damaging and taken so long to clean up, the best policy was to avoid getting into them in the first place. When they were avoided and the unemployment rate fell, many people on the fringes of the economy—minorities, college dropouts, and disabled people—benefited the most. After recessions hit, it often took years for them to get back on their feet.

Obama and Trump, archrivals with mutual contempt, shared the distinction of presiding over the longest US expansion on record, and early in 2020 it was hard to see what would knock it off course. Then, as Robert Akerlof sat in his family's basement, the United States tumbled into a recession unlike anything it had ever before experienced.

The whole world was a sitting duck when the Covid-19 virus emerged in Wuhan, China, in early 2020.[10]

During the previous half century, people all over the world had been moving into cities in search of jobs and social connections. Between 1960 and 2018, the share of the world's population living in cities had risen from 34 percent to more than 55 percent. Packed closely together, people were more prone to transmit bugs to each other. In addition, globalization meant more international travel, which facilitated the spread of disease elsewhere. China had long been a hotspot for viruses, in part because of its widespread use of open markets for animal meat. Then, after China entered the World Trade Organization in 2001, it became more connected to the rest of the world. Passenger traffic between the United States and China grew from 700,000 in 2003 to more than 8.5 million in 2018.

An old rule of thumb in pandemic research was that global disease outbreaks happened about three times every century. But in the twenty years before 2020 the world had already confronted outbreaks of SARS in 2002 and 2003, the swine flu (also known as H1N1) in 2009 and 2010, MERS in 2012, Ebola from 2014 to 2016, Zika in 2015 and 2016, and Dengue fever in 2016. Then, in March and April 2020, Covid-19 struck.

Business closures tied to Covid in early 2020 devastated the world economy. But Covid was more than a health and economic shock. It was also a social and political disaster. By 2020 American cities had become the hotbeds of US economic life, centers for fast-growing technology and other service-sector jobs. Their perimeters were the dividing lines between red and blue America: young, diverse, and progressive on the inside; older, whiter, slower-growing, and more conservative on the outside.[11] Hickory and Charlotte were examples.

Covid upended city life.[12] With schools closed and police departments depleted by the pandemic, violent crime started rising. People fled to less populated terrain. Then urban areas boiled over during the summer, after the killing in May 2020 of George Floyd, a Black man, by police officers in Minneapolis sparked protests across the nation.

Instead of being a referendum on Trump's handling of the long economic expansion, the 2020 election became a looking glass through which an already divided population stepped and made judgments about streets in pain and chaos, empty restaurants, grounded airplanes, policing, and hospital wards overrun by death. A red-blue divide now defined almost every corner of American life and the election that loomed ahead.

Yellen largely stayed out of it.

Economists often advised political campaigns. Yellen hadn't involved herself in Clinton's run for president in 1992. When she joined his White House in 1997, she was an outsider compared to others. Nor had she tried to help Obama get elected, outside of the thirty-minute phone call Austan Goolsbee arranged for her to explain the Fed's bailout of Bear Stearns to the candidate in 2008. Yellen was a Democrat. She was progressive in her worldview and cared about policies, but she didn't like political maneuvering; nor did she aspire to political appointments outside the Fed, the economic policy monastery where she felt most comfortable.

The 2020 campaign was little different.

Joe Biden's top economic advisers were Jared Bernstein, an aide from Biden's days as vice president, and Heather Boushey, president of a liberal think tank named the Washington Center for Equitable Growth. They advocated a more progressive brand of economics than the Larry Summers camp of the Democratic Party.

Yellen did participate in a videoconference with Biden in August, and urged him to support broad government action to combat the pandemic and crisis. Austerity after the 2009 downturn had slowed the expansion after an initial burst of spending, she said. With interest rates so low, she told Biden the government could borrow at low cost and avoid a repeat of the mistakes she thought the government made after the previous recession. Later that month she and Bernstein wrote an opinion piece in the *New York Times*, making a similar argument.

She wasn't gunning for a job in Biden's administration should he win. That was evidenced by the fact that she kept speaking out publicly in the weeks before the election on a range of issues. Advisers in hope of work often lie low to avoid getting into trouble by straying from campaign messages. In an October interview with the *Wall Street Journal*, Yellen acknowledged that the low levels of unemployment reached during Trump's first three years in office had produced benefits for many low-income workers, not the kind of thing a person would say if she were campaigning for a job with Trump's opponent.[13]

When Biden was elected, he wanted a person who would appeal to the progressive and more moderate wings of the Democratic party. With the economy in chaos, he also needed somebody whom the public and financial markets regarded as a trusted hand. Progressives wanted Elizabeth Warren, the Massachusetts senator who pushed for aggressive government spending programs and tough regulations against banks. Biden asked Warren whom she favored, and she urged him to ask Yellen to take the job.

When Biden's adviser Jeffrey Zients reached out to Yellen, she wasn't expecting an offer. She told him she wasn't interested. She enjoyed her quieter life. She enjoyed being in bed by eight thirty. She was seventy-four years old.

A few days later another Biden adviser, Mark Gitenstein, reached out to Yellen's brother and asked if she could be talked into it. John reached out to his sister, and she discussed it with George and Robby in their kitchen. If the president asked, they agreed, she had a duty to take the job. A little more than two weeks after the election, Biden and Yellen talked by Zoom. He offered and she accepted.

Yellen was about to become the only person in American history to serve as Fed chair, Treasury secretary, and chair of the White House Council of Economic Advisers. She would be the longest-serving senior economic adviser of her generation, putting in more years in top policy roles than any person since Greenspan. More than Bernanke. More than Summers. She disliked politics, and still had managed to become the most trusted economic hand in Washington. Along the way she'd broken through every barrier there was for women in her field.

25

Yellen Leads the Treasury

Trillions
2021

Janet Yellen dressed in a dark, hooded parka and covered her lap with a thick blanket for Joe Biden's inauguration. It was a cold winter day on the back steps of Congress. Two weeks earlier the same ground had been overrun by thousands of riotous supporters of President Trump who were trying to stop Congress's certification of Biden's election.

Yellen covered her face with a white mask, arrived early, and sat waiting all alone, like a solitary figure you might meet on a park bench in Brooklyn. George stayed home. Another Covid surge hadn't been tamed. Why risk the health of both of them in the frigid January weather?

The image of Yellen sitting there could hardly convey the enormity of money at the fingertips of this lone and still little-known Washington figure. The Treasury managed the government's $22 trillion debt, adding to it when the government ran budget deficits and needed to raise money to make up for shortfalls between tax revenues coming in and spending going out. The debt had risen by more than $4 trillion during President Trump's last year in office, as the government borrowed money and pumped it out to households and businesses to carry them through pandemic closures. After all of that borrowing, Washington was inflamed by disagreement over how much further to go with the pandemic still raging.

A day earlier, Yellen had testified remotely from her home to the Senate Finance Committee for her confirmation hearing. From there she uttered two words that would define her first year in office, and in many ways defined the first year of the new president and the mindset of the party he led.

"The best thing we can do is act big," she told lawmakers.

Act big. In those two words were packed years of shifting economic thinking and political gamesmanship. Should government budgets be managed with restraint after crises, as happened after an initial spurt of support following the 2008 financial crisis? Or should the government press hard to bring down unemployment rapidly? The two words encapsulated where Yellen came down, and where Washington was going.

Biden had announced a few days earlier that he wanted quick passage of a $1.9 trillion relief bill dubbed the American Rescue Plan, more money on top of the trillions already borrowed and spent by his predecessor. That would include checks of $1,400 sent directly to most American adults to spend or save as they saw fit.[1]

Biden's team of advisers hatched the program during a chaotic transition into power. Impeachment of Trump loomed after the Capitol riot that he helped stir up; control of the Senate was in flux after runoff elections in Georgia; face-to-face contact between Biden and his advisers was limited by the Covid surge. Yellen spent much of the transition taking part in video meetings at the computer at home, her shelves neatly arrayed behind her with books and photos.

She once again found herself an outsider, just as she had been in Clinton's White House. Biden's team included advisers who had worked for him during his vice presidency in the Obama administration. Some went back decades in Congress with Biden, a former senator. Ron Klain,

who became his chief of staff, had worked on Biden's failed 1988 presidential campaign.

Yellen thought the economic implications of the $1.9 trillion pro-
gram hadn't been carefully thought through, but events were moving
too fast to slow or hone it. When Biden and his closest advisers settled
on the $1.9 trillion plan in mid-January before his inauguration, she
wasn't in the meeting. Then she had little choice but to support it. "Act
big" was her implicit and unavoidable endorsement.

The size and scope of the program was partly a political choice, not an
economic formulation. Congress had approved $600 payments to house-
holds in December, and Trump said those payments were too small. He
wanted to send $2,000 checks. Before the Georgia Senate runoffs on Jan-
uary 5, Biden said he would get another round of $1,400 checks through
Congress to make up the difference if Democrats took the Senate. Progressives in the House and Senate were eager to match Trump's number.
This bumped up the size of the plan at the last minute.

In Washington, choices are often defined by what is possible, not by
what is best or right. With Biden in the White House and Democrats in
control of the House and Senate, another $1,400 in payments was possi-
ble. They had promised it, so they did it. It was that simple.

"We have got to move as aggressively as we can," Vermont progressive
Bernie Sanders said soon after Democrats took the Senate. "We don't
have months and months to argue about this thing."[2]

"We have to deliver $2,000 survival checks to the American peo-
ple. Not anything less," chair of the House progressives Pramila Jayapal
wrote on Twitter.[3]

On March 11, 2021, in his first big move as president, Biden signed
the package into law. He brought in Gene Sperling, the economic policy
veteran from the Clinton and Obama years who had sometimes frustrated Yellen, to manage implementation.

One problem was that the breadth of the program meant that many individuals who didn't need the money would get it anyway. Yellen blessed the deal in part because of lessons she'd learned after the previous recession. It had taken nearly a decade to get the jobless rate back under 5 percent after the 2008 financial crisis. For the millions of people who went without jobs during this long period of economic repair, it added up to more than four hundred million months of collective joblessness and all of the dislocation that came with it.

Time was the true villain of the post-financial-crisis economy, and Yellen was always fighting against it. That recovery took too long. Time is also the hidden ingredient in the world of credit in which the Federal Reserve operates. The bond programs Yellen championed at the Fed, and the promises of long periods of low interest rates, boiled down to an effort to convince people and businesses to move faster, to borrow money and put it to work today rather than wait.

Economists used the phrase "time value of money" when they talked about credit. The most important years of Yellen's career were essentially an effort to speed up events and actions to beat the crushing costs of prolonged joblessness. She told Biden that if his administration was going to make a mistake, it should be by doing too much and not too little, as she believed had happened before. She thought a smaller stimulus program might be appropriate, but she wasn't going to resist a push for more.

Her successor at the Fed had learned the same lessons. As a Fed governor in the early 2010s, Jerome Powell shuddered at the thought of increasing Fed bond holdings to $5 trillion. As Fed chairman, he set the central bank on a course to increase those holdings to nearly $9 trillion. He pushed interest rates back to zero after raising them in the face of Trump's ire. He had come to believe that these Fed policies had worked before, and this new crisis necessitated taking them off the shelf.[4]

There was another reason Yellen and Powell were willing to go big. Many of the worries that restrained policy makers during the previous expansion had never materialized into actual problems. Critics of Bernanke and Yellen—in Congress and on Wall Street, in editorial pages and on cable news channels, even inside the Fed—had said inflation was inevitable. Instead, inflation routinely came up short of the central bank's 2 percent goal during the preceding decade and central bankers worried that the United States was heading toward a Japan-style deflation.

The critics had also said that the US dollar would collapse. It didn't. It routinely got stronger. They said another financial bubble would bring down Wall Street, but that hadn't happened either. Instead, during the long, grim postcrisis expansion, Wall Street's calculus about debt and deficits flipped.

During the 1990s investors had worried about large federal budget deficits. Who was going to buy all of the government bonds the Treasury was issuing to raise money to cover these shortfalls? Back then, investors demanded high interest payments from the government as compensation for those perceived risks, and Washington came to know the people on Wall Street who traded government debt as "bond vigilantes." Then when the government cut deficits, the market's reward was lower interest rates, which helped to spur the economic boom of the 1990s.

During the 2000s everything changed. Wall Street's worries about deficits disappeared. Even as government borrowing grew, interest rates remained low. This was what Keynes said happened during periods when the economic engine stalled, as happened during the Great Depression. China's emergence as an economic power also changed inflation and interest-rate trends. When China ushered hundreds of millions of workers into the global workforce, inflation and wages were restrained all over the world. China also soaked up trillions of dollars from its export machine and used that money to buy US government bonds, holding down the US government's cost of borrowing.

Powell and Yellen reasoned that they still had room to go big. Interest rates were low, inflation was low, and the critics who warned otherwise had been wrong.

As for Democrats in Congress, they damn well weren't going to hold back now that they had control of the House, Senate, and White House. This was a chance to advance their social-spending priorities. Moreover, they were angry. As they saw it, Republicans had slowed the recovery with their push for smaller budget deficits when Obama was in office. Then they widened deficits with tax cuts and military spending when Trump was in office. To some Democrats, a $1.9 trillion spending package was an act of vengeance against a Republican Party they believed had acted in bad faith.

Much of Washington was proceeding with a road map and drawing on analysis and emotions that had built up during the previous decade. But was it the right map for the moment? Watching all of this from a distance, Lawrence Summers thought he saw a recipe for disaster.

For many years Summers had been a leading proponent of the arguments Democrats were now mustering to justify their efforts to revive a post-Covid economy. In this new era of sluggish economic growth, inflation and interest rates were bound to stay low, and the government had leeway to launch investment programs. China had built roads and bridges during its boom. The United States could too, he had been arguing.

But Summers believed this was all too much and too fast. Trump had already poured trillions of dollars into the economy during the early stages of the Covid crisis. The economy was already recovering as lockdowns associated with Covid receded. The government needed to move more slowly and more deliberately, Summers believed, and not just send households another $1,400 in checks, as Biden had signed on to do.

In one calculation, Summers estimated that households during the Covid economy were running about $25 billion to $30 billion a month short of the income they would generate in a normally functioning economy. But Washington was pouring about $200 billion a month into that hole. Something was bound to spill.

"What was kindling is now ignited," Summers said. For years he had argued that inflation was unlikely. Now he said it was inevitable. This debater had a knack for seeing two sides of an argument, and now he was on another side. "These are the least responsible fiscal macroeconomic policies we've had in the last 40 years," he said. "I think fundamentally it's driven by intransigence on the Democratic left and intransigence and completely unreasonable behavior in the whole of the Republican Party. It has driven us to the kind of political deals that we are seeing."[5]

To his detractors—and there were many—it looked like a shot from a man out of power toward those who had jobs he wanted. Yellen thought otherwise. She had known Summers for nearly fifty years, and took his argument seriously. He could be rough and argumentative, but when Summers spoke he often made a good point, and she thought he was making a reasonable one now.

On the outside, they might have looked like bitter rivals. In fact, Summers and Yellen spoke regularly during her first year as Treasury secretary. The man she had vanquished became her behind-the-scenes confidant on other issues even after he challenged her publicly on the new spending program.

They talked about cleaning up an Internal Revenue Service that had been drained of funds and unable to enforce the tax code. Mail coming into the IRS was taking a year to open. The institution was broken and needed fixing.

They also talked about corporate tax reform. Yellen set out to forge an agreement with countries around the world to stick to a common minimum tax rate of 15 percent for businesses. She hoped that would put an end to the beggar-thy-neighbor policies that were driving business taxes everywhere toward zero. Mnuchin had taken a step in this direction as part of Trump's tax cuts, creating a version of a minimum US business tax, but Yellen wanted something more comprehensive. A new international tax would also help raise needed revenue to fund

Biden's spending proposals. Yellen still believed that deficits needed to be reduced in the long run.

Her staff prepared weekend briefings for her on the tax code that were as much as three hundred pages long. By Monday she had read them and come back with questions. At the Fed, she had to bring together nineteen policy makers from around the country, with varying views on interest rates. In international tax negotiations, she set out to bring together more than a hundred countries with varying interests.

She zeroed in on the UK and Ireland as keys to a breakthrough. If the British joined, others would likely follow. Among them would be Ireland. Its corporate tax rate, at 12.5 percent, was one of the world's lowest, which made it a draw to foreign CEOs. Yellen had to convince her Irish counterparts that it was in their interest to raise their rate and be part of a global agreement, rather than forge a path on their own. "It was like trying to find keys for a bunch of different locked doors," David Lipton, one of her Treasury advisers, said of the negotiations. "Each door was different. Each lock was different." Yellen's strategy was to master the details, hear out the other side, and find a way forward, in contrast to Trump's go-it-alone bravado.

After forging an agreement with 136 countries, Yellen turned her attention to Congress; it was time to hold up the US end of the bargain. But by midyear problems were brewing, not only in Congress but across the broader economy.

The government's all-out efforts to stimulate demand had begun to push up inflation, as Summers predicted would happen. The other part of the problem was the supply bottlenecks that had built up after the economy shut down during the Covid crisis. Restarting the engines of commerce proved to be hard and complicated. Businesses scrambled to get lettuce to reopened restaurants or computer chips to automobile manufacturers. Many jacked up prices on materials in short supply.

Workers were also in short supply. As it was, many baby boomers were already on course to retire. The Covid crisis accelerated that demographic shift. Those people who did come back to work wanted wage increases to keep up with the rising cost of living, and were in a better position to get those raises than they'd been in years.

The United States hadn't seen anything like this since the 1970s. The government had stimulated consumer and business demand, and then shocks to the economy constrained the supply of goods and services that businesses offered to the public. More demand and less supply was a textbook recipe for higher prices, and that's exactly what happened.

As inflation marched higher, Powell came to see that it would be mostly his responsibility to stop it. The Labor Department's consumer price index signaled 5 percent inflation by June 2021 and was heading toward 9 percent, the highest readings in decades. Powell slowly realized he was going to have to pull back the flood of money sooner than expected. As for Yellen and Biden, they faced political blowback that altered his agenda. Biden's bid to pass a second spending program to rebuild the nation's digital and physical infrastructure was slowed, scaled back, and eventually passed. A third spending bill on climate and social programs stalled. Yellen's international business tax plan was part of that bill, and it stalled too.

Biden's first year in office was defined in part by his early gamble on a big short-term stimulus program and debates about whether the federal government could afford to go any further. He chose to act big and it appeared to backfire. There was important good news: the jobless rate fell rapidly toward pre-pandemic levels, as Yellen hoped would happen, and the United States averted the slow recovery that defined the previous expansion. But the job recovery was accompanied by inflation flames that would have to be doused. Household confidence fell, as measured in surveys by the University of Michigan, even as the economy recovered.

Biden's White House advisers were reluctant to concede any ground to a Republican Party that was eager to trumpet any of the new president's perceived missteps, thus the White House didn't want to acknowledge that the American Rescue Plan had anything to do with the inflation outbreak. The reality was nuanced; it was the final part of a flood of stimulus, provided not just by Biden but also by the Federal Reserve and Trump, that likely did contribute to broad and unusual supply-and-demand imbalances in the economy. In Yellen, White House officials found they had an economic spokeswoman interested in nuance and hesitant to bend her words to score political points. They rarely trotted her out at the White House briefing room to make the administration's case on economic policy.

Complicating matters that summer, a new debt-ceiling battle with Republicans in Congress loomed in the fall of 2021. If Democrats and Republicans didn't agree to raise the debt ceiling, the government might miss payments on promised Social Security checks, bills coming due with military contractors, or interest on the debt. It was the same problem that had dogged Obama.

Yellen became consumed in preparations to avoid a financial catastrophe. She pressed her staff for regular updates on the government's cash position, dissecting on a daily basis what was going in and out. Then she warned the White House and leaders of both parties in Congress that they were flirting with another disaster.

The Treasury and White House had different mindsets about how to deal with the issue. White House officials close to Biden wanted to assign blame to Republicans for causing the problem, while Yellen's team at Treasury wanted to warn everybody about the pain that would occur if the problem wasn't addressed. "Their obstruction and irresponsibility know absolutely no bounds," Biden said in October of the opposition party whose cooperation he needed to avert another disaster.[6]

Yellen hadn't asked for this stress at this stage of her life, yet she had learned over the years not to take herself too seriously. In the realm of economic policy making, there was always a new problem to resolve. History always led toward some new defining moment and then barreled right through it to the next. At home in Berkeley for a break in the summer of 2021, Yellen joked she might be the first US Treasury secretary to default on the debt and die of a heart attack. Then she went back to work.

26

Janet at War

Causing Bank Runs in the
Streets of St. Petersburg
2021–2022

Shortly before Thanksgiving 2021, Yellen made her way to a secure basement complex just under the West Wing of the White House. The Situation Room was equipped with high-tech computer systems and monitors that had allowed US officials to watch in real time back when US forces hunted down Osama bin Laden in 2011 and Islamic State leader Abu Bakr al-Baghdadi in 2019.

Jake Sullivan, Biden's national security adviser, gathered the administration's top intelligence and national security officials to discuss developments on the border of Ukraine, where Russia was massing troops. Sullivan's team believed Vladimir Putin was preparing to invade his neighbor.

Ukraine was not a member of the North Atlantic Treaty Organization (NATO), which meant the United States wasn't obliged to intervene. Exhausted by twenty years of war in Afghanistan and Iraq, the American public was hardly prepared for another one in Ukraine. Moreover, military intervention in Ukraine would mean direct conflict with a nuclear-armed power domineered by a man—Putin—who was unpredictable and bent on restoring the aura of might once exuded by the Soviet Union.

Despite those obstacles, the United States couldn't let an invasion go unchallenged. Ukraine was a nation of more than forty million people, with a democratically elected president and four NATO members—Poland, Hungary, Romania, and Slovakia—on its western border that the United States was obliged to defend. Putin had already taken Crimea, in Ukraine's south. The United States couldn't ignore an even more outrageous act of aggression.

The United States would send arms to Ukraine to help its people defend themselves. It would also share intelligence. But to really punish Putin, officials wanted to marshal the global economy against him. This is why Yellen was in this meeting. The US Treasury ran American sanctions programs. She would be central to the effort.

Back in 1991, after the Berlin Wall collapsed and the United States reversed Saddam Hussein's invasion of Kuwait, President George H. W. Bush had dreamed of a new chapter in human history, a "new world order" defined by economic integration and cooperation among peace-loving nations. Putin had long since rejected US dominance of the global order, yet the country he led was intimately woven into that world.

While China had become a manufacturing power in the world economy, Russia had become one of the globe's major suppliers of raw materials. Its oil and natural gas coursed through pipelines or by boat to Europe. Germany was finalizing an $11 billion pipeline project called Nord Stream 2 that would double the flow of gas from Siberia directly to Russia's former World War II enemy. Russia was also the world's largest wheat producer, accounting for 18 percent of global supplies, and it was a major supplier of palladium, an element critical for the catalytic converters used in car manufacturing.

In all, exports accounted for more than 25 percent of Russia's annual economic output. That made it more dependent on business from the rest of the world than the United States, in which exports accounted for 10 percent of economic output.

Russian oligarchs controlled the companies that dominated the country's export industries. They pulled from the land and got rich from what it produced. Russian bankers financed their operations and got rich too. They traveled the world in private jets and supersized yachts.

The United States could punish Putin by squeezing his economy and the people who benefited from his rule. Few benefited more than Putin himself. The Kremlin claimed he earned an annual salary of $140,000 and lived in an eight-hundred-square-foot apartment, but *Fortune* magazine estimated he could be worth as much as $200 billion, allegedly thanks to kickbacks from the oligarchs.[1]

The problem was that sanctions had a long history of mixed results. When Union forces blockaded the South during the Civil War, cutting off its cotton exports and driving up the cost of imported goods, like lead for bullets and saltpeter for gunpowder, it hurt the South but didn't stop the bloodshed. After World War I, the League of Nations tried blockades to enforce peace, but they turned out to be something of a damp squib. When Benito Mussolini's Italy invaded Ethiopia in 1935, weakly implemented sanctions merely drove Mussolini into an alliance with Adolf Hitler.

Sanctions in the 1980s did help end apartheid in South Africa. However, sanctions didn't curb North Korea's pursuit of nuclear arms and didn't dislodge Venezuelan autocrats from power. Sanctions had induced Iranian leaders to negotiate an agreement with the West to curb their nuclear production plans. Then Trump abandoned the Iranian nuclear agreement that sanctions helped to bring about, and he redeployed sanctions instead.

Economic warfare sometimes imposed collateral damage on its enforcers. In 2018 the US Treasury sought to cut off Russian aluminum producer United Company Rusal and its billionaire president Oleg Deripaska. The Treasury alleged that Deripaska was involved in money laundering, illegal wiretapping, extortion, racketeering, and bribery and had links to Russian organized crime. The sanctions that Treasury Secretary Steven Mnuchin imposed caused aluminum prices to soar, hurting American manufacturers. They were reversed after Deripaska stepped down and sold his majority stake in Rusal; he also accused the US Treasury of unfairly smearing him and denying him due process.[2]

But what alternatives did the United States have? Russia needed to be punished for the invasion, and this was the best way to do it without risking an even bigger war—and perhaps even nuclear confrontation—through direct armed intervention.

History showed that countries needed to work together to make sanctions stick.[3] Without that cooperation, a sanctioned country could find ways around blockades. Mussolini undermined the League of Nations by playing France, the United States, and UK for business. North Korea survived with the help of China. Iran preyed on divided economic interests in the United States and Europe.

Yellen wasn't a sanctions expert, but she was well prepared for the task of building an international coalition. She had spent more than a decade at the Fed, four of those years as its leader, navigating divided policy-making committees in search of consensus. She learned to listen to opponents, master the details of policy, and use that knowledge to find common ground. She had also spent years traveling to international finance meetings to compare notes on the economy and coordinate policies with officials outside the United States.

One regular meeting place was in Basel, Switzerland, where central bankers congregated every couple of months in a large cylindrical building called the Bank for International Settlements. From the outside it looked like the rook on a chessboard; on the inside it hosted debates on bank regulation and grand banquets for the modern lords of global finance. Yellen had milled with central bankers in an eighteenth-floor ballroom there, scented by white orchids and framed by white walls, a black ceiling, and panoramic views of the Rhine River below.[4]

Every April, as cherry blossoms bloomed, finance ministers met in
Washington for annual meetings of the International Monetary Fund. In
the fall, the same ministers held meetings in rotating locations, including Marrakesh, Bali, Lima, Istanbul, and Dubai. Many of these ministers had been alienated by Trump. They welcomed Yellen's presence
after Biden was elected. When she reached out to them to build a global
corporate tax plan in 2021, they were eager to collaborate and surprised to be able to come together on an issue that had divided them
for decades.

Yellen told the generals and intelligence officials in the Situation
Room in November 2021 that she would start contacting counterparts
in Europe and elsewhere to urge them to prepare a coordinated economic response to looming Russian aggression. They agreed to share
intelligence that showed the seriousness of the threat.

She started making calls shortly after the holiday. Then before the
year ended, Yellen carved out time to write personal thank-you notes
to different teams at the Treasury for the hard work they had done in
her first year leading the place. By then her worries about a debt-ceiling
crisis were receding. Republican Senate minority leader Mitch McCon-
nell wasn't interested in repeating the fights of the past; he agreed with
Democrats to legislation averting a showdown. Instead, the even bigger
threat of an actual war in 2022 loomed.

The November meeting at the White House marked the launch of an
unprecedented financial sanctions program by the West, aimed at one of
the largest economies in the world and marked by uncharacteristic cooperation between the United States and its European allies. The drama
reached a crescendo during a fraught weekend in late February 2022,
when Western officials set their sight on the biggest economic target
of all, Russia's central bank.

Women and men at the US Treasury, White House, and Commerce
Department had already spent years honing financial tactics against

Russia after its 2014 seizure of Crimea and in rounds of sanctions aimed at Iran, North Korea, and Venezuela.

Yellen's deputy secretary, Wally Adeyemo, was a cool-headed Nigerian American raised in California who oversaw the day-to-day sanctions operation at the Treasury Department. The Treasury's assistant secretary on terrorist financing issues, Elizabeth Rosenberg, was a former journalist described by one former US Department of the Treasury official as the government's financial sniper, the soldier who homes in on targets and takes them out. Their central point of contact at the White House was Daleep Singh, deputy national security adviser and a familiar face who had spent time working at Treasury and the Fed.

Among the hurdles they faced with Russia: sanctions could blow back differently on the United States and the European Union's twenty-seven individual national economies. They needed to find common ground, and also places where they were willing to put collective effort over national interest.

Yellen and her team wanted to use export controls to cut off Russian businesses from global suppliers, but many EU officials were hesitant. The EU had exported about $100 billion of goods to Russia in the past year, while the United States had directly exported less than $10 billion. Unless all EU members were on board, Russian companies could ship a product that was on one country's export-control list to a second country where it wasn't controlled, and import it from there.

US and European officials had squabbled in the past when the United States imposed sanctions on Iran and North Korea and threatened European companies with repercussions if they didn't comply. Seeking consensus this time, the sides agreed to pick their targets together, but the United States would enforce export controls with US companies while the EU, alongside member states, would oversee Europeans. It took EU specialists three days just to translate US export codes for local European jurisdictions.

In early February 2022, three US officials—all women—flew to Brussels to finalize a plan with the Europeans. Rosenberg was accompanied by Thea Rozman Kendler and Molly Montgomery, officials in the Commerce Department and State Department, respectively. The US export restrictions they produced ran thirty-eight pages long. The EU produced a complementary sixty-three-page list of products.

One example of their targets was aviation and avionics. At least 80 percent of Russia's aircraft fleet was made by Boeing Corporation or Airbus SE. State carrier Aeroflot had ambitious expansion plans, and even Russian-made planes used Western equipment. As such, imposing export controls could eventually ground Russian planes. When war broke out, "we kind of understood what plays we were going to call," Adeyemo said.[5]

On February 24, hours after Russia invaded Ukraine, EU national leaders met in Brussels and quickly approved the package of export controls, in addition to restrictions on the global operations of Russian banks. Ukrainian president Volodymyr Zelenskyy then addressed them by video link, telling the leaders it might be the last time they saw him alive. It was a galvanizing moment that focused the attention of European officials on what they could do next. "Looking around in the room, people were genuinely in shock," said Estonian prime minister Kaja Kallas.

Almost overnight, the Europeans began calling for aggressive action. They turned their attention to Russia's biggest force in finance. The Central Bank of the Russian Federation had a $630 billion stockpile of foreign assets, a portfolio of foreign bonds, gold, and deposits with commercial banks and central banks around the world. It was a reserve for Russia during times of financial distress. If Russian firms needed dollars or assets denominated in other currencies to conduct business outside the country or to pay foreign debts, they could turn to the Russian central bank when others cut them off.

Soon after the February 24 meeting in Brussels, European officials learned that the central bank was making plans to shift its portfolio from the West in a high-stakes financial cat-and-mouse game. Yellen and her colleagues in Washington heard similar murmurings.

If they moved swiftly, the United States and Europe could deny access to the funds in the same way that an ordinary bank might shut its ATMs. Blocking access was a powerful way to isolate the country and raise its cost of doing business, a strike at the heart of Russia's financial system. The West had sanctioned central banks on a smaller scale in Iran and North Korea, but never against an economy so large.

Since its earlier invasion of Crimea, Russia had been moving its central bank assets away from the United States, but it was still exposed. As of June 2021, the Russian central bank had 16.4 percent of its reserves in US dollar assets, 32.3 percent of its reserves in euro-denominated assets, and much else in China, gold, and other places. By working together, US and EU officials could block Russia's access to nearly half of its global funds. The Europeans, alarmed by Putin's aggression, wanted to move fast.

But there were long-term implications to consider. Yellen worried that if she took this step, other central banks might come to doubt the United States was a reliable place to hold reserves. That could undermine the dollar's status as the financial system's bedrock currency, a linchpin of American power since the end of World War II.

Yellen again found herself out of step with Biden's White House advisers. On Saturday morning, February 26, two days after the Russian invasion, Yellen met with Biden and his national security staff at the White House. The national security team—led by Sullivan and Singh—told Biden they were ready to move against Russia's central bank, however they hadn't yet told Yellen of their plan to make that case to the president. She said she wanted more time to study the issue. She went back to the Treasury and was meeting with Powell and a team of staffers later that day when Italian prime minister Mario Draghi called her cell phone and interrupted the discussion. Draghi was an economist and former central banker and went back years with Yellen. He told her it was imperative to act.

Yellen and her team agreed they would set out to block an impending Russian move of reserves before trading resumed Monday: If Russia wouldn't play by global norms, it shouldn't be allowed to participate in the global economic system, and this was a stockpile of assets that allowed the country to operate.

The United States and Europe agreed on the text of a blocking order at around 3:30 a.m. Brussels time on February 28, hours before financial markets opened. They announced it alongside plans to cut off some of Russia's biggest banks from the SWIFT global financial messaging system, another move to isolate the country financially.

With the central bank freeze, the ruble dropped 20 percent overnight against the dollar. Russia's stock market closed. Its central bank blocked residents from sending money to foreign accounts and ordered Russian companies that earned foreign income to turn over 80 percent of their proceeds to the central bank in exchange for rubles.

Many of the central players in this economic war were women. Elvira Nabiullina, the governor of Russia's central bank, and Yellen had circled around each other at meetings in Basel and Jackson Hole, though they never became close. Now the Russian central banker was on the outside of the system looking in. "Russia's financial system and economy are facing a totally abnormal situation," she said.

Visa and Mastercard further isolated Russia by announcing they were shutting down operations in the country. Exxon, Microsoft, Oracle, and others added to the exodus, amplifying the isolating economic effects of government sanctions. The moves rippled from the streets of St. Petersburg—where people lined up to withdraw savings from local banks—to factories along the Volga River. Within a few days, Russia's largest automaker, AvtoVAZ, shut down production at plants in Togliatti and Izhevsk because it couldn't get electronic parts for its cars.

"The atrocities that they're committing against civilians seem to be intensifying," Yellen told the *Washington Post* on March 10. "It's certainly appropriate for us to be working with our allies to consider further sanctions."[6]

Yet Putin was not defenseless. Russia had become so entwined with the global economy after the Soviet empire fell that it couldn't be cut off completely without repercussions in the West.

Russia's presence in commodities markets—including natural gas sales to Europe and wheat sales to poor countries such as Egypt—was a source of foreign income. The world also depended on it. Shutting Putin out of these markets would worsen inflation problems in the West by curtailing global supplies, and threatened famine in poor countries.

The ruble recovered. The economic war, like the war on the ground in Ukraine, would soon turn into a war of attrition.

Conclusion

Bonds

By mid-2022, the inflation problem showed few signs of receding. It was a stinging development for Yellen. She had built a reputation as a prescient forecaster but had incorrectly predicted that the upsurge of 2021 would be transitory. Then, in June, she did something that rarely happens in Washington; she admitted she'd been wrong. Yet as inflation and war in Ukraine moved toward unknown conclusions, lessons of a turbulent past were coming into clearer light.

In Janet Yellen's story was the story of two special marriages. One was the marriage of a market economy to democratic government. The second was Yellen's marriage to George Akerlof. Both of these marriages fueled and defined her. They also defined the epoch of upheaval in which she was formed and flourished.

When the new millennium dawned with great fanfare in 2000, many of the nation's leaders had looked back on a turbulent twentieth century with the conviction that democracy and market economics had emerged triumphant. The rest of the world would follow the better path that the United States had chartered.

The last quarter century proved this union was neither inevitable nor easy.

One of the reasons Bill Clinton ushered China into the World Trade Organization was that he believed welcoming the world's most populous nation into a global trade club would help transform it into a cooperative and democratic country. This was also the nation's hope for the Soviet Union and the Eastern European countries that the United States had vanquished during the Cold War. However, it is now clear that China and Russia have moved toward authoritarian rule, not democracy, and that their entry into the market-driven global economy was incomplete and more disruptive, for the United States and others, than most expected. The next quarter century may well be defined by a pulling apart or reconfiguration of the global order that looked so promising back in 2000.

China's resistance to the American order is particularly shocking because no nation has benefited more from its economic ties to the West. In 1990, two-thirds of China's people lived below official poverty measures created by the World Bank. By 2016 that count had fallen to less than 1 percent, nearly eight hundred million people lifted from destitution, malnutrition, and disease. China's entrance into the world economy, in short, was the greatest poverty reduction program in human history, formulated with America's help, encouragement, and goodwill. Yet neither democracy nor a full embrace of free markets grew out of it.

All the while, the United States struggled to keep its own marriage of democracy and markets vibrant and healthy. The big economic challenges of Janet Yellen's lifetime, and also the big theoretical debates, were almost always about striking some balance between unruly markets and a raucous, imperfect, democratically elected government. The great modern economists—Keynes, Hayek, Friedman, Samuelson, Tobin, Sen, Summers, Bernanke, Akerlof, Yellen, and on—had different views about where to strike that balance. History shows pretty clearly that none of them could claim perfection in either idea or execution. It shows, instead, that changing circumstances require adaptation. Government intrusion into markets in the 1970s was a disaster. If the government had not gotten involved when Lehman Brothers collapsed in 2008, that likely would have been a disaster, too.

Economists are sometimes blamed for their ideology. But the biggest mistakes made by modern economists were often mistakes driven by hubris, insularity, or a failure of imagination, more than devotion to any ideology. When Dani Rodrik warned in the 1990s that globalization might go too far, he was mostly dismissed by the profession because his ideas didn't fit with conventional thinking of the time. Raghuram Rajan received similar blowback in 2005 when he warned that financial innovation might be going too far. But the skeptics were right; the China trade shock and the mortgage meltdown turned out to be two of the most disruptive events of modern times.

George Akerlof often stood among the skeptics. His genius was his imagination and his willingness to challenge conventional thinking. He spent a lifetime tracing the capricious and unpredictable behavior of individuals and groups in markets. Many of his warnings about the imperfections of markets proved prescient and foreboding. Markets were unruly and unpredictable, and not always self-correcting when left to their own devices.

Did that mean more government was always the right answer? Not necessarily. Perhaps the best rejoinder to Akerlof's work came from his friend Gary Becker, the free-market advocate at the University of Chicago. When contacted the day Akerlof won his Nobel Prize, Becker observed to a reporter: "Governments face asymmetric information too."[1] This was prescient in its own way. Regulators were in their own fog when they badly misjudged the makings and consequences of a mortgage boom in the 2000s. The Biden administration, too, was in a hurry to act during a chaotic moment when it launched another $1.9 trillion economic rescue plan in 2021, which contributed to inflation.

The behavioral economists had advanced the idea of "recency bias," a human tendency to overemphasize recent events in making judgments about the future. The economists had shown how markets were prone to this mistake. It turned out that government officials and economists were, too. Having seen the United States manage import incursions from Japan and Mexico, US officials in the 1990s believed they could also manage one from China. Greenspan had seen the benefits of derivatives after Enron collapsed in 2001, then failed to see their risks building as the housing market boomed. Yellen, Powell, and many others had lived through two decades of low inflation, and probably because of that, underestimated the risk of an inflation resurgence.

Democratic government and free markets, in short, may be the best system for governing free men and women, but both are imperfect and in flux because humans are at their core. Work, attention, and some imagination are required to keep the systems functioning properly.

This is where the research of George and Robert Akerlof became especially important during the past decade. As social division in the United States worsened, the Akerlofs' theories suggested that this division, if taken to further extremes, could erode the workings of American democracy itself.

Many of the nation's founders, during their own age of upheaval, understood that their most profound task was to create institutions that could be trusted to fairly and effectively manage the unruly behavior that drove markets and also moved government to extremes and misjudgments. If those institutions—the Constitution, the rule of law, trusted courts, a fair and reliable system of national commerce, a free and unaligned media, reliable elections, effective bureaucracy—failed, then the causes of free markets and free people would fail too.[2]

"Vigor of government is essential to the security of liberty," observed Alexander Hamilton in his first Federalist Paper. Failure in the endeavor of building these institutions, he said, was the road to despotism. His mentor George Washington warned in his farewell address of the "designing men" who sowed the seeds of public division that threatened to pull the young nation apart.

A line ran from Hamilton to Yellen, the first woman to run the big economic institutions he fashioned. More than two centuries after Hamilton wrote his first Federalist Paper, perhaps the most disturbing findings of George Akerlof's career, and that of his son, Robert, lurked in their research into social division. The perceived legitimacy of institutions and their leaders could fall apart in moments of intense social division, Robert Akerlof found. George Akerlof's friend Amartya Sen saw in India that such fissure could happen suddenly and without warning and spent his life examining how democracy could be made to work for everybody.

One lesson that emerges from the Akerlofs' work is that trust is an essential glue; it holds together the institutions that govern imperfect markets and imperfect democracy, and keeps this hopeful marriage working. Robert and George Akerlof explained how some movement leaders mobilized anger to break trust and erode the common values of communities and replace them with personal power.

Today, two decades of economic and social upheaval have fueled the fires of national anger: Rising inequality. A sense in large parts of the population that the nation's leaders have betrayed working people. Tremors unleashed by global trade. Serial financial disruption. Changing social mores about family and culture. The mind-numbing blare of social media in a new information age. This puts a wide array of American institutions in a dangerous place.

Real patriots will take measure of this moment—as the founders did—and look more deeply into the work of building and repairing the institutions that hold the country and the economy together, rather than capitalizing on the friction that pulls them apart, as George Washington warned people were prone to do. Both sides of the red-blue divide now blame the other for getting the country to this unstable place, and both often employ dangerous hyperbole to prove their points. Patriots can draw on the roots of a common identity. This is perhaps the most important first step to building a new path to prosperity.

The work of building a good society was never finished. Hamilton said: "Is it not time to awake from the deceitful dream of a golden age, and to adopt as a practical maxim for the direction of our political conduct that we, as well as the other inhabitants of the globe, are yet remote from the happy empire of perfect wisdom and perfect virtue?"[3]

Market-driven democracy, this story shows, is not inevitable, nor are its systems ever complete. It is an endeavor.

Why did Janet Yellen rise during this age of reckoning? Why was she the person to break through so many ceilings for women? What blame did she deserve for problems that emerged as she rose, and what credit does she deserve for fixing them?

Yellen wasn't perfect. Though she was correct in many of her judgments about the economy, she made mistakes too. History may yet prove that encouraging Biden to "act big" was among the biggest of those mistakes. But that doesn't define her. Nor does it explain her rise.

Yellen became the nation's top economic policy maker during the decade after the 2008 financial meltdown because she saw high unemployment as a crisis and tried to do something about it when many others wouldn't. Until Covid hit and rocked the economy, she was correct that the warnings of her critics about inflation and another financial bubble and a collapsing dollar during that decade were wrong. She helped to drive the longest economic expansion in US history, and in the process she showed grit and a sense of purpose. She drew on this sense of grit when challenging Vladimir Putin and his underlings.

Yellen was motivated, more than anything, by an almost obsessive desire to examine questions fully and get as close as she could to answers that stood up to thorough and honest analysis. She adapted as circumstances changed, and updated her beliefs when they fell apart under serious scrutiny.

Yellen saw in her work a duty to contribute to some larger purpose, like a lighthouse keeper watching the shoreline. She didn't set out to break gender barriers or win top jobs. When she leaned into debates, it wasn't to be heard over anyone; it was usually because she thought her arguments were right, and she had the conviction and the knowledge to defend them.

"I am just driven by trying to do the best job I can at whatever it is that I'm doing," she said from her home in early 2022. "If you ask me why I have broken glass ceilings, it is really because at whatever job I was at, I asked myself, 'What can I do to make a contribution here?'"

Her mother taught her to do her homework and get her answers right. Tobin taught her to act with moral passion. Her father taught her to have a heart. She lived by the lessons they taught her, and ultimately those lessons defined her. Yellen battled hardest when the stakes were highest and when she had mastered the subject, but she tried not to be nasty about it, because nasty wasn't in her nature.

Some readers might not agree with Yellen's political views or economic prescriptions, but it's hard not to be impressed that decency, honesty, and a sense of duty got her somewhere at a time and in a town where those traits seemed in increasingly short supply.

Of course something else propelled Janet Yellen. She made one remarkably fortuitous choice, in a manner that was most unlike her; when George Akerlof made a case that she should make a snap judgment to spend a lifetime with him, she agreed.

Akerlof's research helped to reshape modern economics. He changed the way his profession thought about Adam Smith's invisible hand. It is thus somewhat astounding that one of the most historic contributions of his lifetime was the style of husband and father he chose to become. When traditional marriages were still the norm in America, he and Yellen independently conceived their own marriage and forged a partnership that ensured she had as much opportunity to flourish in her work as he, and that he had as much opportunity to participate in family life as she.

The partnership worked. They formed a modern family that traveled together with four suitcases, one for each parent, one for their child, and one for all their books.

In August 2021 Janet Yellen sat at a white table in their Berkeley kitchen, reflecting on her story.

A debt-ceiling crisis was at the top of her mind; legislative battles loomed; a US troop pullout from Afghanistan was going terribly wrong; inflation nagged. The perfectionist had many reasons to worry, and she did.

As for her own story, Yellen said she lived happily after choosing George as her partner. They had set out to do something larger than either of them and had worked at it together.

As she spoke, Akerlof wandered into the room, looking flabbergasted. "What's the matter, sweetie?" Yellen asked her husband kindly.

George had put his phone down somewhere and couldn't find it.

"I'll call it, and you can see where it's ringing," she suggested, as if she hadn't been through that exercise with her absentminded husband before.

He wandered off, and she dialed. A few moments later he called back into the kitchen.

"I found it," he said.

Author's Note

If you've gotten this far in the story, then perhaps at this point you'd like to know a little bit more about the author and the reporting and writing that went into the book.

I will start with my mother, Elaine Hilsenrath. When I was young, my mom went back to school to earn her master's degree in history at Queens College, part of the City University of New York. As a teen, I often found her tapping at typewriter keys in her study or folding over pages in the books of ancient scholars such as Josephus or the historian Edward Gibbon. Along the way, she developed a theory that history turned like a kaleidoscope. Events, ideas, conflicts, culture, and norms all configured at some point in time and then turned, giving new shape that was connected to the past—even apparent in it—but wholly different in the next moment. New colors and configurations emerged as the old dropped away. This kaleidoscope of history was always in flux and always connected to the past.

As I moved from chapter to chapter in this writing, I envisioned my mother's kaleidoscope turning. The achievements and misfortunes of our time grew out of a past with structure and inevitability, in addition to elements of chance. But it takes a careful eye and an open mind to see these configurations take shape, and to recognize which are fleeting, which will last, and what might follow. My mother passed away from breast cancer in 2007. I was working on stories on a brewing crisis in the US mortgage market when my family lost her.

The other mother of this story is the *Wall Street Journal*. This is where

I learned about economics. It is also where I learned a value system for reporting and writing that shapes how I see the world, how I try to conduct myself, and how I tried to develop the book.

I spent very little time studying economics as an undergraduate student at Duke University. In fact, I took one economics course as a freshman and it was a disaster. The classes met early on Tuesday and Thursday mornings, when I was barely awake. The professor's abstractions about supply-and-demand curves didn't sink in. I got a C and figured that was the end of economics for me.

I became an economics writer by accident. I wanted to be a war correspondent and traveled the Middle East, Eastern Europe, and the Soviet Union after graduating from college. After returning to the United States, I needed a paycheck and was offered a spot transcribing numbers from monthly government economics releases into real-time stories that the newswire services pumped out to Wall Street. It was rote work and sounded boring and I hoped not to do it for very long. Instead, I discovered that economics was interesting in the real world and mattered to an awful lot of people. I also discovered a newspaper, the *Wall Street Journal*, which dominated this terrain and was inhabited by a great many down-to-earth and talented people. I set out to work there because I wanted to be at a place that excelled and I wanted to work with people I liked.

At the *Wall Street Journal* I was given opportunities to write about economics and finance for more than two decades, and I discovered battlefields I hadn't imagined in my youth. From Hong Kong I witnessed a financial crisis up close in 1997 and 1998, starting in Bangkok and spreading all the way to Moscow. I saw how giant financial institutions could turn to dust overnight and what drove miscreants and rogues to push their luck too far. Back in the United States, I discovered that even advanced economies weren't immune from such misfortune. Along the way, I learned the history and met the central characters, including Janet Yellen and George Akerlof.

The *Journal* also taught me a value system that goes something like this:

Stories are not black-and-white. There are gray areas that give stories life and nuance. It is my responsibility to understand those gray areas and lay them out for readers. I shouldn't be so arrogant as to think I know the answers before I'm done reporting. I have a responsibility to hear a person out before I write about that person, and that person has a right to a heads-up about what I'm going to say before I tell the rest of the world. I must never lie to sources, readers, or colleagues. My credibility is enhanced when I write in neutral tones and respect the intelligence of readers enough to give them space to draw their own conclusions. The best stories are those that surprise, not those that confirm some prior belief. I am not to be for or against any person or group, and certainly not for or against any political party.

That value system became my worldview. I dwell on it here because I think it requires emphasis, and also because I employed this value system in the book. I reached out to every person who figures into the narrative and tried to hear their stories from their perspectives. For those characters who had died, I drew on their own words to get closer to their thoughts and sometimes I spoke to people who knew them.

Reporters don't always reveal all their sources of stories, and I don't in this text. Some people are more comfortable speaking anonymously to protect their careers or relationships. Reporters sometimes offer some form of anonymity in order to learn stories more fully, though such agreements depend on the situation and also the nature of a character's role in the story. Sometimes people will speak to reporters only if they can clear direct quotes before publication. In these and other cases, it is my responsibility to ensure that I'm not being played by sources and that any agreement before an interview is put to work for one simple purpose: to get readers closer to the truth, not further from it. The *Wall Street Journal* takes that responsibility seriously and has a team of standards editors who work behind the scenes to instill and enforce it. We depend on the trust of our readers to believe it. We aren't perfect in our execution, but this is how we orient ourselves and we've built systems to enforce the values.

Unlike a *Wall Street Journal* story, I don't attribute every idea or every scene you read in the text of this book. It's too cumbersome, but I try to use endnotes as much as possible and use attributions where they don't slow the narrative too much.

I see this all as good journalism. I hope it also makes for good book writing. Thank you for coming this far with me. I hope it was worth your effort.

Gratitude

Jay Mandel reached out to me in September 2020 after reading a story I wrote in the *Wall Street Journal*. An agent at WME, he asked if I'd like to meet and talk about a book, which we did at a bar in Brooklyn, and I told him I didn't have any burning ideas for a project that big.

Several few weeks later, after Joe Biden was elected president and asked Janet Yellen to be his Treasury secretary, the idea of this book popped into my head in the shower: an economics book disguised as a love story. I called Jay, he liked it, and off we went. Jay is thoughtful, patient, curious, and a good listener. I'm grateful for his help on this project and his friendship.

Jay connected me to Hollis Heimbouch at HarperCollins. Hollis immediately got what I was trying to do and she was the easy choice for a partnership with a publisher and editor. In addition to providing me with important advice to stay hydrated and exercise, Hollis's frank editorial input was essential in shaping the narrative and the tone of the story, from beginning to end. More than that, her embrace of this idea and her encouragement at every step were necessary fuel. She helped make the whole thing fun. I'm grateful that I've had a chance to work with her and become her friend, too.

My father, Joseph, is a retired physician, ninety-two at the time of publication, and my hero in life. He is fearless and wakes up every day with purpose. He taught me to try to do the same, though I can't say I've yet come near to matching his energy or consistency. I discovered in this project that he's also a damn good editor. He read early drafts and encouraged me to stick to my guns when I wavered on certain sections.

Like Hollis, he also saw what I was trying to do and helped me buy into my own idea at every step in a long process. Thanks, Pop!

I found Janet Byrne when I went searching for a fact-checker, and discovered that she was so much more than that. In fact-checking she was assiduous and relentless, but more than that, as a reader, she was astute and insightful. She saved my rear end with some excellent catches, and we had a great time talking about the world beyond this project. Rachel Kambury, at HarperCollins, also provided crucial perspective on the subject, the audience, and the process of writing a book. Thank you to you both.

I owe the *Wall Street Journal* a great deal of gratitude, and my bosses, for teaching me how to report and write and then allowing me to do meaningful stories. This gratitude stretches over a long list of editors and reporters too great in number to name. But I should mention a few: Mike Miller and John Bussey gave me helpful advice on getting started on this book; Matt Murray, Paul Beckett, and Jay Sapsford gave me the latitude to go off and do the project; Nell Henderson has been a friend and sounding board throughout; Emily Glazer provided detailed feedback on an early draft.

Bob Davis, who retired from the *WSJ* in 2021, became like a big brother to me over the years. Like a big brother, he handed out tough love when needed. Bob read early drafts and straightened out some organizational issues and also my annoying habit of slipping into a passive voice. David Wessel, now at the Brookings Institution, is another big brother to me and many others at the *WSJ*. He is wise, talented, and more than anything, enormously generous. The third of these wise men is Greg Ip. I like to joke that when I have lunch with Greg, it feels as if there are two and a half brains at the table, and mine is the half. Greg also read an early draft and provided essential feedback and encouragement.

Doug Elmendorf and Karen Dynan, both Harvard professors and former Fed economists, were enormously generous, too. They read the manuscript and provided feedback, which helped assure that I got my economics straight. (If I didn't, that's my fault.) David Skidmore, a former Fed official and Associated Press writer, read the manuscript, too, and provided valuable feedback and input.

I would like to thank the Wilson Center and Robert Litwak, its senior vice president for scholars, for taking me in as a visiting scholar during the pandemic and helping to fund my research. The Wilson Center's support was essential for me to have the time I needed to complete my reporting and writing. I am very grateful.

Duke University was also a valuable resource throughout this process. The David M. Rubenstein Rare Book and Manuscript Library's "economists' papers" section houses a treasure trove of documents for anyone interested in economic history. (Thank you, Kate Collins, for helping me dig up one of George Akerlof's early rejection letters, in addition to Sara Seten Berghausen and Alyssa Russell for additional research.) Duke students were a resource, too: Abigail Ullendorff, Sophia Li, Claire Neushul, Veronica Hineman, Clare Abboud, Connor Booher, and Michael Legesse, all undergraduates, read early manuscripts and provided feedback, as did their professor and my friend Emma Rasiel.

A great many people who appear in this book spent so much time with me, and I thank you all. I learned from everybody and appreciate your generosity. Among these people were Janet Yellen, George Akerlof, and Robby Akerlof. They spent many hours talking to me. Their only condition was that they be given a chance to review direct quotes taken from the interviews, which in the end I used sparingly. I learned so much from each of them and consider it a privilege to have gotten a chance to document their story. I think it is fair to say, having spent this time with them, that these are decent people, and I suspect most people who know them would agree with that assessment.

Finally, my family. Alex, Hope, and Lucas: writing this book was fun, but there is no joy in my life greater than the joy of being a part of yours, and there is no story I relish seeing unfold more than the ones you are writing for yourselves. Thank you. Cristina, my partner over all these years. Janet and George use the metaphor of a lighthouse for their lives. You have been our lighthouse, shining light and never wavering when we are soaked, lost, or tumbling about. Thank you for everything you have been to me and our children. I love you all.

Notes

Introduction

1. Case and Deaton, *Deaths of Despair*.
2. Quotes from Fed meetings here and elsewhere in the text are taken from Federal Reserve meeting transcripts, which are released with a five-year delay and made available on the Federal Reserve Board website, federalreserve.gov.
3. George A. Akerlof, "The Market for 'Lemons': Quality Uncertainty and the Market Mechanism." *Quarterly Journal of Economics* 84, no. 3 (1970): 488–500, https://doi.org/10.2307/1879431.
4. George A. Akerlof, "Behavioral Macroeconomics and Macroeconomic Behavior," Nobel Prize lecture, December 8, 2001, https://www.nobelprize.org/uploads/2018/06/akerlof-lecture.pdf.

1: Yellen's Youth

1. Reflections and quotes in this section are based largely on personal letters among the people mentioned, and the author's interviews with them.
2. "Joe Biden Announces Economic Team, Janet Yellen Press Briefing," December 1, 2020, transcript, https://www.rev.com/blog/transcripts/joe-biden-announces-economic-team-janet-yellen-press-briefing-transcript-december-1.
3. National Center for Education Statistics, Digest of Education Statistics, Department of Education, https://nces.ed.gov/programs/digest/d19/tables/dt19_325.92.asp.
4. George Boehm, "The New Uses of the Abstract," *Fortune*, 1958.
5. Binyamin Appelbaum, "Yellen's Path from Liberal Theorist to Fed Voice for Jobs," *New York Times*, October 9, 2013.
6. "A Fed Duet: Janet Yellen in Conversation with Ben Bernanke," Brookings Institution, February 27, 2018, https://www.brookings.edu/events/a-fed-duet-janet-yellen-in-conversation-with-ben-bernanke/.
7. Stephanie Grace, "Banker to the Nation," *Brown Alumni Magazine*, February 2014.
8. Janet Yellen, interview by Gregory Mankiw, Radcliffe Institute, Harvard, May 2016, https://www.wsj.com/articles/wsj-pro-transcript-janet-yellen-interviewed-at-harvards-radcliffe-institute-1464383609.

2: Akerlof's Youth

1. R Byron Bird, Charles Curtiss, and Phillip Certain, "Joseph Oakland Hirschfelder," *Biographical Memoirs* 66 (2002): 190–205.
2. Recollections from this chapter come largely from George Akerlof and also his Nobel Prize biography, https://www.nobelprize.org/prizes/economic-sciences /2001/akerlof/biographical/. These biographies are rich in personal detail for many acclaimed economists. See also *National Academy of Sciences of the United States of America: Biographical Memoirs*, vol. 66, for a section on Joseph Hirschfelder and the family's history; and "Gosta C. Akerlof, Textile Chemist," obituary, *New York Times*, May 11, 1966.
3. George Akerlof and Monroe Price, "Montgomery, Tension in the Heart of Dixie," *Yale Daily News*, March 23, 1960.
4. George Akerlof, "Agile Akerlof tops Overeager Odenweller in Invitational Event," *Yale Daily News*, April 17, 1961.
5. Paul Anthony Samuelson, *Foundations of Economic Analysis* (New York: Atheneum, 1965).
6. Robert Solow, email message to author.
7. Joseph Stiglitz, Bob Hall, and George Akerlof, interviews by author.

3: Yellen at Yale and Harvard

1. Elmus Wicker, *Banking Panics of the Gilded Age* (New York: Cambridge University Press, 2008).
2. Bureau of Economic Analysis, National Income and Product Accounts, table 2.1.
3. Robert A. Margo, "Employment and Unemployment in the 1930s," *Journal of Economic Perspectives*, Spring 1993. This draws on data developed by Stanley Lebergott in *Manpower in Economic Growth* (New York: McGraw Hill, 1964).
4. Kennedy Center, "Brother Can You Spare a Dime? The Story behind the Song."
5. Irving Fisher, "The Debt-Deflation Theory of Great Depressions," *Econometrica* 1, no. 4 (1933): 337, https://doi.org/10.2307/1907327.
6. Robert Formaini, "Irving Fisher: Origins of Modern Central Bank Policy" (Dallas, TX: Federal Reserve Bank of Dallas, 2005).
7. There are many authoritative accounts of Keynes's life. This is a composite that leans on Nasar, *Grand Pursuit*; Heilbroner, *Worldly Philosophers*; and Skidelsky, *John Maynard Keynes*, among others.
8. Sylvia Nasar, *Grand Pursuit: The Story of the People Who Made Modern Economics* (London: Fourth Estate, 2012). 199.

9. For a full display of Keynes's writings, see *The Collected Writings of John Maynard Keynes* (Cambridge, England: Cambridge University Press for the Royal Economic Society, 2013).

10. Peter Temin, "The German Crisis of 1931: Evidence and Tradition," *Cliometrica* 2, no. 1 (2007): 5–17.

11. Nina Paulovicova, "The Immoral Moral Scientist: John Maynard Keynes," *Past Imperfect* 13 (2008): 24–55. See also Anand Chandavarkar, "Was Keynes Anti-Semitic?," *Economic and Political Weekly* 35, no. 19 (May 2000); E. Roy Weintraub, "Keynesian Historiography and the Anti-Semitism Question," *History of Political Economy* 44, no. 1 (2012): 41–67; David Felix, *Keynes: A Critical Life* (1921; repr. Westport, CN: Greenwood Press, 1999); and Kent Puckett, "J. M. Keynes and the Visible Hands," Public Books, https://www.publicbooks.org/j-m-keynes-and-the-visible-hands/.

12. Keynes, *General Theory of Employment*.

13. John Maynard Keynes to George Bernard Shaw, January 1935, in *John Maynard Keynes, The Collected Writings of John Maynard Keynes*, vol. 28, ed. Donald Moggridge (London: Macmillan, 1982), 42.

14. Hayek, *Road to Serfdom*.

15. James Tobin, speech at the Nobel Banquet, December 10, 1981, https://www.nobelprize.org/prizes/economic-sciences/1981/tobin/speech/. See also Spencer and Macpherson, *Lives of the Laureates*.

16. See Nobel Prize biography.

17. Karen W. Arenson, "Tobin Always 'Ahead of Field,'" *New York Times*, October 14, 1981.

18. President and Council of Economic Advisers, *Economic Report of the President*, 1962, https://fraser.stlouisfed.org/title/45/item/8133.

19. Robert S. Goldfarb, "Remembering James Tobin: Stories Mostly from His Students," *Eastern Economic Journal* 29, no. 4 (Fall 2003).

20. Jon Hilsenrath, "A Top Contender at the Fed Faces Test over Easy Money," *Wall Street Journal*, May 12, 2013.

21. David M. Rubenstein Rare Book and Manuscript Library, Duke University, Durham, NC, Economists' Papers Archive, American Economic Association records, Committee on the Status of Women in the Economics Profession (CSWEP), 1971–1996, historical data files and correspondence, 1971–1974.

22. Ylan Mui, "New Fed Chief Janet Yellen Lets a Long Career of Breaking Barriers Speak for Itself," *Washington Post*, February 2, 2014.

23. Boyne, *Red Rose Crew*. See also sobermom, "Feminisms: Women Under Way," DailyKos, June 25, 2008, https://www.dailykos.com/stories/2008/6/25/5398

75/-.; and Dan Levin, "Revel of Oars and Shells," *Sports Illustrated*, November 1974.

24. Lawrence Summers, interview by author.

4: Akerlof's Early Voyages

1. This section is a composite from a range of public sources.
2. Dave Newhouse, "The 1968 Golden Bears," *Bear Insider*, November 2013.
3. See 1970 Census, table 45, Employed Persons by Hours Worked, Detailed Occupation, and Sex, for detailed breakdown by occupation.
4. Amartya Sen, "Biographical," https://www.nobelprize.org/prizes/economic-sciences/1998/sen/biographical/. See also Amartya Sen, *Home in the World: A Memoir* (London: Allen Lane, 2009).
5. Amartya Sen, interview by author.
6. Gurley to Akerlof, David M. Rubenstein Rare Book and Manuscript Library, Duke University, Durham, NC, rejection letters from the *American Economic Review* in the American Economic Association collection, July 10, 1967. Akerlof threw away his rejections many years ago while cleaning his office.
7. George Akerlof, "Writing 'The Market for "Lemons"': A Personal Interpretive Essay," https://www.nobelprize.org/prizes/economic-sciences/2001/akerlof/article/.
8. Akerlof, *Economic Theorist's Book of Tales*.
9. George Akerlof and Pascal Michaillat, "Beetles: Biased Promotions and Persistence of False Belief," National Bureau of Economic Research, June 19, 2017, https://www.nber.org/papers/w23523.

5: Yellen and Akerlof Meet

1. Jon Hilsenrath, "When Americans Took to the Streets over Inflation," *Wall Street Journal*, June 11, 2021.
2. "Food: Behind the Boycotts: Why Prices Are High," *Time*, November 4, 1966.
3. *Richard Nixon and Arthur F. Burns on 19 March 1971*, Miller Center, University of Virginia, Presidential Recordings, Digital Edition.
4. Burns and Ferrell, *Inside the Nixon Administration*.
5. Sebastian Mallaby, *The Man Who Knew: The Life and Times of Alan Greenspan* (London: Bloomsbury, 2017), 143; see also Burton Abrams, "How Richard Nixon Pressured Arthur Burns: Evidence from the Nixon Tapes," *Journal of Economic Perspectives* 20, no. 4 (2006); Miller Center, University of Virginia, for recordings and transcripts of the actual tapes.
6. Jeffrey E. Garten, *Three Days at Camp David: How a Secret Meeting in 1971 Transformed the Global Economy* (New York: Harper, 2021). This is one of the best accounts of Nixon's fateful decision and his relationship with Burns.

7. Edward Cowan, "Nixon Sets Meat Price Ceilings," *New York Times*, March 30, 1973.

8. This calculation is based on the meat category in the consumer price index, produced by the Bureau of Labor Statistics. See BLS.gov, consumer price index databases for more detail.

6: Redefining Keynes

1. Yellen, memorial remarks for James Tobin, Battelle Chapel, Yale University, April 27, 2002.

2. Milton Friedman, "Biographical," https://www.nobelprize.org/prizes/economic-sciences/1976/friedman/biographical/. See also Friedman and Friedman, *Two Lucky People*; and Spencer and Macpherson, *Lives of the Laureates*.

3. Ryan Masse, "UW Erred, Lost Vital Economist," *Badger Herald*, November 30, 2006. See also John Allen, "2 Who Got Away," *OnWisconsin*, Winter 2017, https://onwisconsin.uwalumni.com/features/2-who-got-away/.

4. Milton D. Friedman and George J. Stigler, "Roofs or Ceilings? The Current Housing Problem," FEE Freeman Article, Foundation for Economic Education, February 21, 2011, https://fee.org/resources/roofs-or-ceilings-the-current-housing-problem/. First published in pamphlet form in September 1946.

5. Bruce Caldwell, *Mont Pelerin 1947*, CHOPE Working Paper No. 2020-02, Hoover Institution and Duke University, January 2020, https://hope.econ.duke.edu/sites/hope.econ.duke.edu/files/Caldwell%20Chapter%201%20Mont%20Pelerin.pdf. See also Friedman and Friedman, *Two Lucky People*.

6. Mont Pelerin Society, "Statement of Aims," April 1947, https://www.montpelerin.org/statement-of-aims/.

7. For a detailed account of Strong's life and the role his death played in the Great Depression, see also Ahamed, *Lords of Finance*.

8. Friedman and Schwartz, *Monetary History of the United States*.

9. Friedman and Friedman, *Two Lucky People*.

10. Rose and Milton Friedman, "Our Early Years," interview by Peter Robinson, *Hoover Digest*, no. 2 (1996): 126–35, https://miltonfriedman.hoover.org/internal/media/dispatcher/215060/full, reprinted in *The Collected Works of Milton Friedman*, ed. Robert Leeson and Charles Palm (Stanford, CA: Hoover Institution, 2017).

11. David Glasner, "Milton Friedman and the Chicago School of Debating," *Uneasy Money* (blog), September 11, 2017, https://uneasymoney.com/2017/09/11/milton-friedman-and-the-chicago-school-of-debating/. See also Perry Mehrling, *Fischer Black and the Revolutionary Idea of Finance* (Hoboken, NJ: Wiley and Sons, 2012); and Emmett Ross, "Sharpening Tools in the Workshop: The

Workshop System and the Chicago School's Success," September 2007, reprinted in *Building Chicago Economics: New Perspectives on the History of America's Most Powerful Economics Program*, ed. Robert van Horn, Philip Mirowski, and Thomas Stapleford (Cambridge, England: Cambridge University Press, 2011), 93–115.

12. Deirdre McCloskey, interview by author.
13. Spencer and Macpherson, *Lives of the Laureates*.
14. Spencer and Macpherson, *Lives of the Laureates*.
15. Paul Anthony Samuelson, *Foundations of Economic Analysis* (New York: Atheneum, 1965).
16. From written correspondence between author and Solow.
17. Roger E. Backhouse, "Paul A. Samuelson's Move to MIT," *History of Political Economy* 46 (December 1, 2014): 60–77, https://read.dukeupress.edu/hope/article-abstract/46/suppl_1/60/38734/Paul-A-Samuelson-s-Move-to-MIT.
18. Spencer and Macpherson, *Lives of the Laureates*.
19. Paul A. Samuelson Papers, David M. Rubenstein Rare Book and Manuscript Library, Duke University, Durham, NC, folder on Milton Friedman.
20. Samuelson to Summers, box 71, Paul A. Samuelson Papers, 2006. See also Lawrence H. Summers, "The Great Liberator," *New York Times*, November 19, 2006.

7: Yellen and Akerlof at Berkeley

This chapter is based on Nobel Prize biographies, reflections from individual interviews by author, and other sources.

1. See Bureau of Labor Statistics, current population survey database, available at: https://www.bls.gov/cps/.
2. Jay Cocks, "How Long Till Equality?," *Time*, July 1982.
3. Akerlof and Yellen later published an analysis that concluded that abortion and birth control also led to a decrease of "shotgun" marriages and an increase in single motherhood. See G. A. Akerlof, J. L. Yellen, and M. L. Katz, "An Analysis of Out-of-Wedlock Childbearing in the United States," *Quarterly Journal of Economics* 111, no. 2 (1996): 277–317.
4. Rachel McCulloch and Janet L. Yellen, "Technology Transfer and the National Interest," *International Economic Review* 23, no. 2 (1982): 421, https://doi.org/10.2307/2526449; Rachel McCulloch and Janet Yellen, "Can Capital Movements Eliminate the Need for Technology Transfer?" *Journal of International Economics* 12, no. 1–2 (1982): 95–106, https://doi.org/10.1016/0022-1996(82)90077-0.
5. Friedrich Hayek, "The Use of Knowledge in Society," *American Economic Review* 35, no. 4 (September 1945): 63–68.

6. Akerlof and Yellen, "Fair Wage-Effort Hypothesis." See also Yellen, "Efficiency Wage Models"; and Akerlof and Yellen, "Unemployment through the Filter of Memory."

7. Akerlof, *Economic Theorist's Book of Tales.*

8. Arthur Burns, "The Anguish of Central Banking," Per Jacobsson Lecture, Belgrade, Yugoslavia, September 30, 1979.

8: Behavioral Economists

1. Alan Murray, "Jobless Puzzle: Why Unemployment Sometimes Lingers On Stirs Renewed Interest," *Wall Street Journal*, December 26, 1985.

2. George A. Akerlof and Janet L. Yellen. "A Near-Rational Model of the Business Cycle, with Wage and Price Inertia." *Quarterly Journal of Economics* 100 (1985): 823. See also George A. Akerlof and Janet L. Yellen, "Can Small Deviations from Rationality Make Significant Differences to Economic Equilibria?" *American Economic Review* 75, no. 4 (1985): 708–20.

3. Michael Lewis, *The Undoing Project* (New York: W. W. Norton, 2017).

4. Daniel Kahneman, Jack L. Knetsch, and Richard H. Thaler, "Fairness as a Constraint on Profit Seeking: Entitlements in the Market," *American Economic Review* (September 1986): 728–41.

5. Based on an interview with Thaler.

6. Jon E. Hilsenrath, "As Two Economists Debate Markets, the Tide Shifts," *Wall Street Journal*, October 18, 2004.

7. Robert J. Shiller, "Stock Prices and Social Dynamics." *Brookings Papers on Economic Activity 1984*, no. 2 (1984): 457.

8. Robert J. Shiller, "Do Stock Prices Move Too Much to Be Justified by Subsequent Changes in Dividends?" *American Economic Review* 71, no. 3 (1981): 421–36.

9. This section is based on interviews with Shiller and his Nobel biography.

10. Andrei Shleifer and Lawrence H. Summers, "The Noise Trader Approach to Finance," *Journal of Economic Perspectives* 4, no. 2 (1990): 19–33, https://doi.org /10.1257/jep.4.2.19.

11. Quote from Shiller's Nobel biography.

9: Yellen, Akerlof, and Socialism's Failure

1. Francis Fukuyama, "The End of History?" *National Interest*, no. 16 (Summer 1989): 3–18.

2. Based on International Monetary Fund, World Economic Outlook database, adjusted for inflation.

3. Carla Anne Robbins, "Harvard Settles Suit Over Profit In Russian Aid," *Wall*

Street Journal, August 4, 2005, https://www.wsj.com/articles/SB11231164766970 4561.

4. Akerlof et al., "East Germany in from the Cold," 1.

5. Paul Hemp, "THE M.I.T. Connection: University's Graduates Dominate Clinton Economic Policy Team," *Boston Globe*, January 24, 1993.

6. Clay Chandler, "Administration's Economic Voice of Reason; Laura Tyson's Straightforward Style Helps Win Over Detractors," *Washington Post*, April 25, 1994. See also Paul Krugman, "Incidents from My Career," https://www.princeton.edu/~pkrugman/incidents.html.

7. Peter Behr, "Tyson Willing To Confront Rivals of U.S.," *Washington Post*, December 12, 1992.

10: Yellen Becomes a Central Banker

1. Mallaby, *The Man Who Knew*, 69. See also Nathaniel Branden, *My Years with Ayn Rand* (San Francisco: Jossey-Bass, 1999); and John Cassidy, "The Fountainhead," *New Yorker*, April 24, 2000.

2. David Wessel, "Clearly, the Chairman Tries to Obfuscate or Maybe He Doesn't," *Wall Street Journal*, June 24, 1995.

3. Alan Murray, "Fed Chief Sees No Acceleration in Inflation Rate," *Wall Street Journal*, September 22, 1987..

4. Alan Greenspan. *The Age of Turbulence: Adventures in a New World* (New York: Penguin, 2007), 176.

5. Federal Reserve, "Meeting of the Federal Open Market Committee, November 15, 1994," transcript, https://www.federalreserve.gov/monetarypolicy/files/FOMC19941115meeting.pdf.

6. Laura Jereski et al., "Bitter Fruit: Orange County, Mired in Investment Mess, Files for Bankruptcy," *Wall Street Journal*, December 7, 1994.

7. Sarah Lubman and John R. Emshwiller, "Before the Fall: Hubris and Ambition In Orange County; Robert Citron's Story," *Wall Street Journal*, January 18, 1995.

8. There are many histories of this period. A good one is Federal Deposit Insurance Corporation, *History of the 80s: Lessons for the Future*, vol. 1, *An Examination of the Banking Crises of the 1980s and Early 1990s* (Washington, DC: Federal Deposit Insurance Corporation, 1997).

9. George A. Akerlof and Paul M. Romer, "Looting: The Economic Underworld of Bankruptcy for Profit," *Brookings Papers on Economic Activity* 2 (1993): 1–73.

10. Federal Reserve, "Meeting of the Federal Open Market Committee, January 31–February 1, 1995," transcript, https://www.federalreserve.gov/monetarypolicy/files/FOMC19950201meeting.pdf.

11. Federal Reserve, "Meeting of the Federal Open Market Committee, July 2–3, 1996," transcript, https://www.federalreserve.gov/monetarypolicy/files/FOMC 19960703meeting.pdf.

12. Jon Hilsenrath, "Janet Yellen, a Top Contender at the Fed, Faces Test Over Easy Money," *Wall Street Journal*, May 12, 2013, with additional reporting from author's notes.

11: Yellen in the Clinton White House

1. Remarks by Alan Greenspan, "Technological Advances and Productivity," at the 80th Anniversary Awards Dinner of The Conference Board, New York, October 16, 1996.

2. Federal Reserve, "Meeting of the Federal Open Market Committee on September 24, 1996," transcript, 22.

3. Bowmaker, *When the President Calls*, 326.

4. Bowmaker, *When the President Calls*, 327.

5. Birnbaum, *Madhouse*.

6. Bowmaker, *When the President Calls*, 329.

7. Bowmaker, *When the President Calls*, 330.

8. Bowmaker, *When the President Calls*, 331.

9. Yellen, statement before the Senate Committee on Environment and Public Works, July 17, 1997.

10. Yellen, testimony before House Commerce Subcommittee on Energy and Power, March 4, 1998.

11. See Akerlof's Nobel autobiography, https://www.nobelprize.org/prizes/economic -sciences/2001/akerlof/biographical/.

12. The cat was named after Chelsea Clinton, who babysat one of Robby's friends. Robby admired the president's daughter from afar but never got to meet her.

13. Joshua Cooper Ramo, "The Three Marketeers," *Time*, February 15, 1999.

14. David Wessel and Bob Davis, "Markets under Siege—Crisis Crusaders: Would-Be Keyneses Vie Over How to Fight Globe's Financial Woes," *Wall Street Journal*, September 25, 1998.

12: Trade in the Twilight of a Golden Age

1. Krugman, "Incidents from My Career."

2. For a copy of the letter, see *Congressional Record*, November 10, 1993, submission by Senator Pete Domenici of New Mexico.

3. See Akerlof's Nobel autobiography, https://www.nobelprize.org/prizes/economic -sciences/2001/akerlof/biographical/.

4. Remarks by Bill Clinton on signing the North American Free Trade Agreement Implementation Act, December 8, 1993, US Government Publishing Office, www.gpo.gov.
5. See chapter 7 of the report, titled, "The Benefits of Market Opening."
6. Rodrik, *Has Globalization Gone Too Far?*
7. Dani Rodrik, interview by author.
8. Roxanne Roberts, "The Clintons Host a Historic Fete," *Washington Post*, January 1, 2000.
9. Yellen, remarks on Senate Action on Permanent Normal Trade Relations with China, September 19, 2000, US Government Publishing Office, www.gpo.gov.
10. Yellen, remarks at the First Session of the White House Conference on the New Economy, Washington, DC, April 5, 2000, https://www.federalreserve.gov /boarddocs/speeches/2000/20000405.htm.
11. Yellen, remarks at the White House Conference on the New Economy, Washington, DC, April 5, 2000. https://www.federalreserve.gov/boarddocs/speeches /2000/20000405.htm.

13: Akerlof Wins a Nobel, Yellen Returns to the Fed

1. Peter Gosselin, "Three Americans Share Nobel Economics Prize Research," *Los Angeles Times*, October 11, 2001.
2. See George A. Akerlof, "Behavioral Macroeconomics and Macroeconomic Behavior," Nobel Prize lecture, December 8, 2001, https://www.nobelprize.org /uploads/2018/06/akerlof-lecture.pdf.
3. John Emshwiller and Rebecca Smith, "Bad Bets," *Wall Street Journal*, October 12, 2021.
4. Accounts of this legendary transaction vary slightly. Kindleberger's latest edition cites Simon Schama, *The Embarrassment of Riches: An Interpretation of Dutch Culture in the Golden Age* (New York: Alfred A. Knopf, 1987). See also, Charles Mackay, *Memoirs of Extraordinary Popular Delusions and the Madness of Crowds* (London: Richard Bentley, 1841). The Mackay version included oxen and beer and specified that all of the animals were to be "fat."
5. Lorraine Boissoneault, "Thank the Erie Canal for Spreading People, Ideas and Germs Across America," *Smithsonian Magazine*, July 2017.
6. Edward Glaeser, "A Nation of Gamblers: Real Estate Speculation and American History," National Bureau of Economic Research, May 2013, https://www.nber .org/papers/w18825.
7. See Mallaby, *The Man Who Knew*, 501–5. See also Greenspan, *The Age of Turbulence*, 176.
8. Shiller's ventures included the Shiller Barclays CAPE indexes, based on stock

market valuations he designed. They also included the S&P CoreLogic Case-Shiller Home Price Indexes, originally designed with economists Allan Weiss and Karl Case. Shiller's father was an inventor, and in addition to his academic ventures, Shiller always wanted to follow in those footsteps.

9. Owen A. Lamont and Richard H. Thaler, "Can the Market Add and Subtract? Mispricing in Tech Stock Carve-outs," *Journal of Political Economy* 111, no. 2 (2003): 227–68, https://doi.org/10.1086/367683.

10. Lawrence Summers, remarks at the New York Economic Club, September 8, 1999, https://www.econclubny.org/documents/10184/109144/1999Summer sTranscript.pdf.

11. Randall Smith, Susanne Craig, and Deborah Solomon, "Wall Street Firms to Pay $1.4 Billion to End Inquiry," *Wall Street Journal*, April 29, 2003.

12. Financial Crisis Inquiry Commission, *Inquiry Report*.

13. John Emshwiller, Rebecca Smith, and Alan Murray, "Lay's Legacy: Corporate Change—But Not the Kind He Expected," *Wall Street Journal*, July 6, 2006.

14. For an excellent discussion of this issue, see Financial Crisis Inquiry Commission, *Inquiry Report*, chapter 4, "Deregulation Redux."

15. Remarks by Chairman Alan Greenspan before the Council on Foreign Relations, Washington, DC, November 19, 2002.

16. Speech by Roger W. Ferguson Jr. at the Future of Financial Services Conference, University of Massachusetts, Boston, October 8, 2003.

17. Based on Bureau of Labor Statistics, current population data, ratio of those unemployed twenty-seven weeks or longer to all unemployed.

18. Jon Hilsenrath and Sholnn Freeman, "Affluent Advantage: So Far, Economic Recovery Tilts To Highest-Income Americans," *Wall Street Journal*, July 20, 2004.

19. See Census income table H-2, "Share of Aggregate Income Received by Each Fifth and Top 5 Percent of All Households: 1967 to 2020." Census.gov.

20. Jon E. Hilsenrath, "Junk Bond: How U.S. Trash Helps Fuel China's Economy," *Wall Street Journal*, April 9, 2003.

21. This is based on Bureau of Labor Statistics consumer price databases.

22. Hilsenrath, "91-Year-Old."

23. Alan S. Blinder and Janet L. Yellen. *The Fabulous Decade: Macroeconomic Lessons from the 1990s* (New York: The Century Foundation Press, 2001), overview panel.

24. Jackson Hole Policy Symposium, 2001, "Economic Policy for the Information Economy," overview panel.

25. Jackson Hole Policy Symposium, 2003, "Monetary Policy and Uncertainty: Adapting to a Changing Economy," overview panel.

26. James R. Hagerty and Joann S. Lublin, "Countrywide Directors' Dilemma,"

Wall Street Journal, November 3, 2007, https://www.wsj.com/articles/SB1194 04440821681023.

14: Yellen as a Regulator

1. Accounts of Mozilo's life are abundant. One thorough account is Connie Bruck, "Angelo's Ashes: The Man Who Became the Face of the Financial Crisis," *New Yorker*, June 22, 2009.

2. Federal Reserve's "Flow of Funds" database, https://fred.stlouisfed.org/series /HMLBSHNO.

3. Shawn Tully, "Meet the 23,000% Stock," *Fortune*, September 15, 2003.

4. Financial Crisis Inquiry Commission, *Inquiry Report*.

5. John Emshwiller, "Key Lawmaker Received Countrywide Loans—Democratic Panel Chief Resists Move to Subpoena 'VIP' Records," *Wall Street Journal*, August 7, 2009. Dodd was later cleared of wrongdoing by a Senate ethics committee, though the panel did say in a letter to the senator that he should have exercised better judgment by asking more questions about how Countrywide was treating his business. Dodd acknowledged he could have handled the situation better. Later, as chairman of the Senate Banking Committee, he played a leading role in rewriting the nation's banking regulatory rules after the crisis. The legislation became known as the Dodd Frank Act. See also Michael Crittenden and Jessica Holzer, "Senate Ethics Clears Dodd, Conrad on Countrywide Loans," *Wall Street Journal*, August 7, 2009.

6. James R. Hagerty, "Countrywide Writes Mortgages for the Masses—Dwarfed by Its Big-Bank Rivals, Company Manages to Grab Lead In White-Hot Home-Loan Market," *Wall Street Journal*, December 21, 2004. See also Countrywide Financial Corporation 2004 form 10-4, filed with the Securities and Exchange Commission.

7. Financial Crisis Inquiry Commission, *Inquiry Report*.

8. Janet Yellen, "Housing Bubbles and Monetary Policy," presentation to the Fourth Annual Haas Gala, San Francisco, October 21, 2005.

9. See Jackson Hole Symposium, hosted by the Federal Reserve Bank of Kansas City, "The Greenspan Era: Lessons for the Future," https://www.kansascityfed.org /research/jackson-hole-economic-symposium/the-greenspan-era-lessons-for -the-future/.

10. Akerlof and his son were especially interested in Jeff Bailey's article "The Mortgage Maker vs. the World," *New York Times*, October 16, 2005.

11. San Francisco Fed supervisory letter, September 8, 2005, signed by Robert Johnson, director of large-institution supervision, Financial Crisis Inquiry Commission database, Stanford Law School, https://fcic.law.stanford.edu/.

12. Financial Crisis Inquiry Commission database.

13. "San Francisco Fed Launches FedVille, an Online Educational Resource for Kids 9–12; Fun and Learning on Your Own PC," *Business Wire*, January 22, 2004.

14. Public discussion with Ben Bernanke at the Brookings Institution, February 27, 2018; "A Fed Duet: Janet Yellen in Conversation with Ben Bernanke."

15. Deposition with the Securities and Exchange Commission, released by the Financial Crisis Inquiry Commission, October 3, 2008.

16. "Meeting with Office of Thrift Supervision," Countrywide briefing paper, Financial Crisis Inquiry Commission, July 13, 2006.

17. Public discussion with Ben Bernanke at the Brookings Institution, February 27, 2018; "A Fed Duet: Janet Yellen in Conversation with Ben Bernanke."

15: Yellen and Akerlof See Storms from the Lighthouse

1. Federal Reserve, "Charge-Off and Delinquency Rates on Loans and Leases at Commercial Banks."

2. Bernanke, *Courage to Act*.

3. Federal Reserve, "Meeting of the Federal Open Market Committee on June 27–28, 2007," transcript, 37.

4. For a good overview, see Financial Crisis Inquiry Commission, *Financial Crisis Inquiry Report*. See also Carrick Mollenkamp, Edward Taylor, and Ian McDonald, "Global Scale: Impact of Mortgage Crisis Spreads—How a Subprime Mess Ensnared German Bank," *Wall Street Journal*, August 10, 2007.

5. See Countrywide Financial Corporation, Form 10-Q, for the quarterly period ending June 30, 2007 (from Securities and Exchange Commission).

6. Financial Crisis Inquiry Commission, *Inquiry Report*.

7. James R. Hagerty, Jonathan Karp, and Serena Ng, "Countrywide Airs Plan to Weather Credit Squeeze," *Wall Street Journal*, August 17, 2007.

8. Geithner, *Stress Test*.

9. Federal Reserve, "Conference Call of the Federal Open Market Committee on August 16, 2007," transcript, https://www.federalreserve.gov/monetarypolicy /files/FOMC20070816confcall.pdf.

10. Federal Reserve, "Meeting of the Federal Open Market Committee on September 18, 2007," transcript, https://www.federalreserve.gov/monetarypolicy /files/FOMC20070918meeting.pdf.

11. Federal Reserve, "Meeting of the Federal Open Market Committee on December 11, 2007," transcript, https://www.federalreserve.gov/monetarypolicy /files/FOMC20071211meeting.pdf.

12. Federal Reserve, "Conference Call of the Federal Open Market Committee on

January 21, 2008," transcript, https://www.federalreserve.gov/monetarypolicy/files/FOMC20080121confcall.pdf.

13. Countrywide Financial Corporation earnings conference call, July 24, 2007.

14. Angelo Mozilo, interview by author, 2022.

15. Yellen interview with Financial Crisis Inquiry Commission, November 15, 2010, https://fcic.law.stanford.edu/interviews/view/201.

16: Financial Panic

1. Bernanke, *Courage to Act*.

2. Ben Bernanke, *Essays on the Great Depression* (Princeton, NJ: Princeton University Press, 2004).

3. See Federal Reserve primer at https://communitybankingconnections.org/articles/2020/i2/federal-reserve-discount-window-what-it-is-and-how-it-works.

4. Ben Bernanke, "On Milton Friedman's Ninetieth Birthday," remarks before the Conference to Honor Milton Friedman, University of Chicago, November 8, 2002, https://www.federalreserve.gov/boarddocs/speeches/2002/20021108/.

5. Federal Reserve, "Bear Stearns, JPMorgan Chase, and Maiden Lane LLC," for a brief explanation of the arrangement, https://www.federalreserve.gov/regreform/reform-bearstearns.htm.

6. Federal Reserve, "Meeting of the Federal Open Market Committee on March 18, 2008," transcript, https://www.federalreserve.gov/monetarypolicy/files/FOMC20080318meeting.pdf.

7. Remarks at the Economic Club of New York, April 8, 2008, https://www.econclubny.org/documents/10184/109144/2008VolckerTranscript.pdf.

8. As formerly stated in section 13(3) of the Federal Reserve Act.

9. Federal Reserve, "Conference Call of the Federal Open Market Committee on March 10, 2008," transcript, https://www.federalreserve.gov/monetarypolicy/files/FOMC20080310confcall.pdf.

10. Federal Reserve, "Meeting of the Federal Open Market Committee on March 18, 2008."

11. Federal Reserve, "Conference Call of the Federal Open Market Committee on July 24, 2008," transcript, https://www.federalreserve.gov/monetarypolicy/files/FOMC20080724confcall.pdf.

12. IndyMac was later purchased out of bankruptcy by an investor team managed by Steven Mnuchin, the future Treasury secretary.

13. For a good summary, see Financial Crisis Inquiry Commission, *Inquiry Report*, chapter 17, "September 2008: The Takeover of Fannie Mae and Freddie Mac."

See the section titled, "Wasn't Done at My Pay Grade," for details on compensation.

14. See Financial Crisis Inquiry Commission, *Inquiry Report*; and Paulson, *On the Brink*.

15. This quote is from the speaking notes of New York Fed general counsel Thomas Baxter, according to FCIC documents.

16. Matthew Karnitschnig, Carrick Mollenkamp, and Dan Fitzpatrick, "Bank of America to Buy Merrill," *Wall Street Journal*, September 15, 2008.

17. Paulson, *On the Brink*.

18. Paulson, *On the Brink*.

19. "Report on the Troubled Asset Relief Program," Congressional Budget Office, July 2021.

20. See Federal Reserve, "Meeting of the Federal Open Market Committee on October 28–29, 2008," transcript, https://www.federalreserve.gov/monetary policy/files/FOMC20081029meeting.pdf.

17: "These Are Fucking People!"

1. Jeanna Smialek, "Dropout-Turned-Ph.D. Informs Yellen's Job Market Outlook at Fed," Bloomberg, June 25, 2015, https://www.bloomberg.com/news/articles /2015-06-25/dropout-turned-ph-d-informs-yellen-s-job-market-outlook-at-fed. (Hat tip to my competitor for the scoop on a really good profile.)

2. Federal Reserve, "Meeting of the Federal Open Market Committee on December 15–16, 2009," transcript, https://www.federalreserve.gov/monetarypolicy /files/FOMC20091216meeting.pdf

3. Akerlof and Shiller, *Animal Spirits*.

4. The *Wall Street Journal* has traditionally kept a discrete separation between its news pages and its editorial pages. This author has worked in the *Journal*'s newsroom for many years and had no input into editorial page decisions or interaction with its writers.

5. "Perry's Public Service," *Wall Street Journal*, August 18, 2011, https://www.wsj .com/articles/SB10001424053111903639404576514672642520978. The opinion page seemed particularly interested in the politics of the moment, welcoming Perry's remarks into a 2012 presidential election that was still more than a year away.

6. Hearing before the Senate Committee on Banking, Housing, and Urban Affairs, December 3, 2009, https://www.govinfo.gov/content/pkg/CHRG-111 shrg54239/html/CHRG-111shrg54239.htm.

7. Sanders accepted a compromise on the matter and Paul called him a sellout. See

Meredith Shiner, "Sanders Defends Fed Deal," Politico, May 7, 2010, https://www.politico.com/story/2010/05/sanders-defends-fed-deal-036940.

8. Bernanke, *Courage to Act*.

9. John King, "Towering Expectations: S.F.'s New Federal Building Challenges Ideas of What a Government High-Rise Should Look Like—Its Humane Design Is Green, Dazzling," *San Francisco Chronicle*, February 25, 2007.

10. "Promoting Beautiful Federal Civic Architecture," White House Executive Order 13967, December 21, 2020, https://www.federalregister.gov/documents/2020/12/23/2020-28605/promoting-beautiful-federal-civic-architecture.

11. Federal Reserve, "Meeting of the Federal Open Market Committee on December 15–16, 2009."

12. Federal Reserve, "Meeting of the Federal Open Market Committee on August 10, 2010," https://www.federalreserve.gov/monetarypolicy/files/FOMC20100810meeting.pdf.

18: Yellen as #2

1. Elizabeth Duke, interview by author.

2. Kristina Peterson, "Who Is Ben Bernanke's Mystery Visitor?" *Wall Street Journal*, September 21, 2012.

3. Carl Robinson, interview by author.

4. Andrew Levin, interview by author.

5. Federal Reserve, "Meeting of the Federal Open Market Committee on August 9, 2011," transcript, https://www.federalreserve.gov/monetarypolicy/files/FOMC20110809meeting.pdf.

6. Jon Hilsenrath, "How Bernanke Pulled the Fed His Way," *Wall Street Journal*, September 28, 2012.

7. Federal Reserve, Office of Inspector General, Investigation File Report I2013 0013-HQO.

8. This author was the reporter who wrote the *WSJ* article that triggered Bernanke's first letter to colleagues on the matter. The Fed's investigation of the leak correctly pointed out, as the article stated, that I talked to many officials to piece together the narrative that I had written in 2013. I didn't cover any of the subsequent investigations for the paper to avoid any conflict of interest.

9. Redacted investigation files have been released to different organizations under Freedom of Information Act requests. Some of these files can be reviewed online here: https://www.governmentattic.org/40docs/FRBoigInvFOMCleak_2012-2017.pdf; one investigation file dated July 1, 2014, under the title, "Investigation File Report, 120130013-HQO," said that board delays in reporting the case

to the OIG "may have impacted the ability of the OIG to thoroughly pursue this matter." See also Binyamin Appelbaum, "Fed Deflects Outside Aid to Investigate Data Leaks," *New York Times*, June 5, 2015.

10. Statement of Dr. Jeffrey Lacker, April 4, 2017.

11. Letter to Jeb Hensarling, House Committee on Financial Services, May 4, 2015, obtained through Federal Reserve freedom of information files, www.federal reserve.gov/foia/files/hensarling-duffy-letter-20150504.pdf.

12. Federal Reserve, "Meeting of the Federal Open Market Committee on March 19–20, 2013," transcript, https://www.federalreserve.gov/monetarypolicy/files /FOMC20130320meeting.pdf.

13. Bernanke, *Courage to Act*.

14. Jeremy Stein, interview by author.

15. Jerome Powell, "Audit the Fed and Other Proposals," speech, Catholic University of America, Columbus School of Law, February 2015.

19: Yellen Becomes Leader

1. This section is based on interviews with Summers, and also a range of profiles written about him over time. See, for example, Ryan Lizza, "Inside the Crisis," *New Yorker*, July 14, 2014.

2. Jon Hilsenrath, "Letters Show Little-Known Side of Summers," *Wall Street Journal*, September 15, 2013. See also Lawrence Summers, "Kenneth Arrow Commemoration at the Institute for Advanced Studies," speech, Tel Aviv, July 5, 2017, http://larrysummers.com/2017/07/15/kenneth-arrow-commemoration-at-the -institute-for-advanced-studies/.

3. Lawrence Summers, "In Memory of Paul Samuelson," remarks at MIT memorial service, April 10, 2010, http://larrysummers.com/wp-content/uploads/2015/07 /In-Memory-of-Paul-Samuelson_4.10.10.pdf.

4. William Cohan, "Endless Summers," *Vanity Fair*, December 2009.

5. Summers, "Paul Samuelson."

6. David Wilcox, interview by author.

7. Lawrence Summers, "A Conversation with Lawrence H. Summers and Laurie H. Glimcher, MD," Dana-Farber Cancer Institute, November 5, 2017, YouTube video, https://www.youtube.com/watch?v=5nOcWN_qe3s&ab.

8. "Toxic Memo," *Harvard Magazine*, May 2001. See also John Rosenberg, "A Worldly Professor," *Harvard Magazine*, May 2001.

9. Rubin and Weisberg, *In an Uncertain World*.

10. Sarah Wright, "Alumnus Summers Sworn In as Secretary of the Treasury," MIT News Office, July 14, 1999.

11. Morgenson and Rosner, *Reckless Endangerment*.

12. Samuelson to Summers, David M. Rubenstein Rare Book and Manuscript Library, Duke University, Durham, NC, Summers file in the Samuelson collection among economist letters. See also Hilsenrath, "Letters Show Little-Known Side of Summers."

13. Cornel West, *Brother West: Living and Loving Out Loud: A Memoir* (Carlsbad, CA: SmileyBooks, 2010).

14. Hilsenrath, "Letters Show Little-Known Side of Summers."

15. Obama, *Promised Land*, 213

16. Obama, *Promised Land*, 213.

17. Geithner, *Stress Test*, 456.

18. Hilsenrath and Peterson, "Federal Reserve 'Doves' Beat 'Hawks' in Economic Prognosticating."

19. Bernanke, *Courage to Act*, 562.

20. Bernanke, discussion with Liaquat Ahamed, Brookings Institution, January 16, 2014, transcript, https://www.brookings.edu/wp-content/uploads/2014/01/20140116_bernanke_remarks_transcript.pdf.

20: Identity Crisis

1. Rick Brooks, Greg Jaffe, and Martha Brannigan, "Merger Has Rocky Start, with Bicoastal Friction," *Wall Street Journal*, October 23, 1998.

2. This is based on Bureau of Labor Statistics, Quarterly Census of Employment and Wages database, county level.

3. Davis and Hilsenrath, "China Shock."

4. This calculation is based on Bureau of Labor Statistics metro area employment statistics for the Hickory-Lenoir-Morganton area. Employment dropped from 185,200 to 146,300 from December 2000 to December 2014, seasonally adjusted, not including employment on farms.

5. Based on Census Bureau, American Community Survey, comparative county level statistics.

6. Warren Wood, interview by author.

7. The following is a sobering summary of the effects of Trade Adjustment Assistance programs: Ronald D'Amico and Peter Schochet, "The Evaluation of the Trade Adjustment Assistance Program: A Synthesis of Major Findings," Mathematica, December 2012, https://wdr.doleta.gov/research/FullText_Documents/ETAOP_2013_08.pdf.

8. Davis and Hilsenrath, "China Shock."

9. David H. Autor, David Dorn, and Gordon H. Hanson, "The China Shock: Learn-

ing from Labor-Market Adjustment to Large Changes in Trade," *Annual Review of Economics* 8, no. 1 (2016): 205–40.

10. Paul Krugman, "What Economists (Including Me) Got Wrong about Globalization," Bloomberg, October 10, 2019, https://www.bloomberg.com/opinion/articles/2019-10-10/inequality-globalization-and-the-missteps-of-1990s-economics.

11. Based on Census Bureau estimates, Quick Facts and American Community Survey.

12. M. Sherif et al., *Intergroup Conflict and Cooperation: The Robbers Cave Experiment* (Norman: University of Oklahoma, 1954).

13. Henri Tajfel et al., "Social Categorization and Intergroup Behaviour," *European Journal of Social Psychology* 1, no. 2 (1971): 149–78.

14. George A. Akerlof and Rachel E. Kranton, "Economics and Identity," *Quarterly Journal of Economics* 115, no. 3 (2000): 715–53.

15. Akerlof and Kranton, *Identity Economics*.

21: Yellen Leads the Fed

1. "This is the essence of secular stagnation—sick recoveries which die in their infancy and depressions which feed on themselves and leave a hard and seemingly immovable core of unemployment," Hansen said in a 1939 paper, "Economic Progress and Declining Population Growth," *American Economic Review* 29, no. 1 (1939): 1–15.

2. Janet Yellen, "Perspectives on Inequality and Opportunity from the Survey of Consumer Finances," at the Conference on Economic Opportunity and Inequality, Federal Reserve Bank of Boston, October 17, 2014.

3. Binyamin Appelbaum, "House Republicans Intensify Attacks on Federal Reserve," *New York Times*, February 25, 2015.

4. Open letter to Yellen, October 30, 2015, https://www.huffpost.com/entry/an-open-letter-to-chairwo_b_8438486?1446247344=.

5. Yellen letter to Nader, November 23, 2015, https://www.federalreserve.gov/foia/files/nader-vidal-letter-20151123.pdf.

6. Elizabeth Williamson, "Security Detail for Fed Chairwoman Irks Neighbors," *Wall Street Journal*, June 30, 2014.

22: Yellen Loses Her Job

1. Joe Bruno and Dave Faherty, "Thousands Gather to Hear Donald Trump in Hickory," WSOC-TV, March 12, 2016, https://www.wsoctv.com/news/local/trump-campaign-contacts-lenoir-rhyne-university-about-monday-event/158546825/.

2. See a commentary Greenwald coauthored in the *Forward* titled, "Two Reasons

Trump Deserves the Jewish Vote," August 12, 2016, https://forward.com /community/347562/two-reasons-trump-deserves-the-jewish-vote/.

3. Federal Reserve press conference, September 21, 2016, https://www.federal reserve.gov/mediacenter/files/fomcpresconf20160921.pdf.

4. Nick Timiraos and Kate Davidson, "Wall Street Veteran Leads Search for Next Fed Chief," *Wall Street Journal*, June 13, 2017.

5. "Trump Economic Adviser: Fed Doing 'Good Job,' Respects Independence," Reuters, March 12, 2017, https://www.reuters.com/article/us-usa-trump-fed/trump -economic-adviser-fed-doing-good-job-respects-independence-idUSKBN16J0NF.

6. Nick Timiraos, *Trillion Dollar Triage: How Jay Powell and the Fed Battled the White House and Saved the Economy* (New York: Little, Brown, 2022).

7. Janet Yellen, "So We All Can Succeed: 125 Years of Women's Participation in the Economy," speech at Brown University, May 5, 2017.

8. Timiraos, *Trillion Dollar Triage*. See also Kate Davidson, "Cohn and Yellen Are among Trump's Contenders to Lead Fed," *Wall Street Journal*, July 25, 2017.

9. Donald Trump, interview by author.

10. Janet Yellen, "Financial Stability a Decade after the Onset of the Crisis," speech at symposium sponsored by the Federal Reserve Bank of Kansas City in Jackson Hole, Wyoming, August 25, 2017.

11. Damian Paletta and Philip Rucker, "Top Adviser Condemns President's Va. Remark," *Washington Post*, August 26, 2017.

12. Michael Bender and Harriet Torry, "Cohn Now Seen as Unlikely Pick to Be Fed Chairman," *Wall Street Journal*, September 7, 2017.

13. Peter Nicholas, Kate Davidson, and Michael Bender, "Inside Trump's Search for a Fed Leader," *Wall Street Journal*, November 2, 2017.

14. Nicholas, Davidson, and Bender, "Inside Trump's Search for a Fed Leader."

15. John Kelly, interview by author.

16. NYU Stern's "In Conversation with Mervyn King," with Janet Yellen, November 21, 2017, https://www.stern.nyu.edu/experience-stern/news-events/nyu -stern-s-conversation-with-mervyn-king-series-presents-janet-yellen.

23: Professor Robert Akerlof

1. Robert Akerlof, "'We Thinking' and Its Consequences," *American Economic Review* 106, no. 5 (2016): 415–19.

2. Robert Akerlof and Luis Rayo, *Narratives and the Economics of the Family*, December 15, 2020, http://www.robertakerlof.com/download/akerlofrayo-families -12-15-20.pdf.

3. Robert Akerlof, "Value Formation: The Role of Esteem," *Games and Economic Be-*

havior 102 (2017): 1–19. It is important to note that there is a long and rich literature on the idea of oppositional identity in Black communities during the 1970s and 1980s, with a wide range of views on the causes and consequences of behavior. I don't fully delve into this literature here. I use the example to show how this area of research may fit into a much wider model of human behavior.

4. One example is Roland Fryer and Steven Levitt, "The Causes and Consequences of Distinctively Black Names," *Quarterly Journal of Economics* 119, no. 3 (2004): 767–805.

5. Marianne Bertrand and Sendhil Mullainathan, "Are Emily and Greg More Employable than Lakisha and Jamal? A Field Experiment on Labor Market Discrimination," *American Economic Review* 94, no. 4 (2004): 991–1013.

6. Other researchers have been exploring this idea. See, for example, Nancy Leong, "Identity Entrepreneurs," *California Law Review* 104, no. 6 (December 2016): 1333–99.

7. Robert Akerlof, "Anger and Enforcement," *Journal of Economic Behavior and Organization* 126 (2016): 110–24.

8. Robert Akerlof, "The Importance of Legitimacy," *World Bank Economic Review* 30, suppl. 1 (March 2016): 157–75, https://academic.oup.com/wber/article/30/Supplement_1/S157/2897349 .

9. See, for example, Gallup, "Americans' Confidence in Major U.S. Institutions Dips," July 14, 2021, https://news.gallup.com/poll/352316/americans-confidence-major-institutions-dips.aspx.

24: Yellen Makes History

1. Alice Wu, "Gendered Language on the Economics Job Market Rumors Forum," *AEA Papers and Proceedings* 108 (May 2018): 175–79, https://scholar.harvard.edu/files/alicewu/files/gendered_language_2018.pdf.

2. Ben Casselman and Jim Tankersley, "Harvard Suspends Roland Fryer, Star Economist, after Sexual Harassment Claims," *New York Times*, July 10, 2019.

3. John M. McDowell, Larry D. Singell, and James P. Ziliak, "Gender and Promotion in the Economics Profession," *Industrial and Labor Relations Review* 54, no. 2 (2001): 224–44.

4. Erin Hengel, "Publishing While Female: Are Women Held to Higher Standards? Evidence from Peer Review," January 18, 2022, https://www.erinhengel.com/research/publishing_female.pdf.

5. "Economists' Statement on Carbon Dividends," *Wall Street Journal,* January 17, 2019. It had 3,623 signatories, including twenty-eight Nobel laureates, fifteen

former leaders of the Council of Economic Advisers from both political parties, and four former leaders of the Federal Reserve, also of both parties. https://cl council.org/economists-statement/.

6. Natalie Andrews and Nick Timiraos, "Yellen Earned Millions in Speaking Fees after Leaving Fed, Disclosures Show," *Wall Street Journal*, December 31, 2020.

7. Donald Trump, interview by author.

8. Jon Hilsenrath, "The Verdict on Trump's Economic Stewardship, before Covid and After," *Wall Street Journal*, October 14, 2020.

9. Lawrence Kudlow, interview by author.

10. Jon Hilsenrath, "Global Viral Outbreaks like Coronavirus, Once Rare, Will Become More Common," *Wall Street Journal*, March 6, 2020.

11. Janet Adamy and Paul Overberg, "Rural America Is the New 'Inner City,'" *Wall Street Journal*, May 26, 2017.

12. Jon Hilsenrath, "Homicide Spike Hits Most Large U.S. Cities," *Wall Street Journal*, August 2, 2020.

13. Hilsenrath, "Verdict on Trump's Economic Stewardship."

25: Yellen Leads the Treasury

1. "President Biden Announces American Rescue Plan," White House statement, January 20, 2021.

2. Kristina Peterson, "Schumer to Take the Reins with Bumpy Road Ahead," *Wall Street Journal*, January 11, 2021.

3. Eliza Collins and Richard Rubin, "Biden Pursues $1.9 Trillion In Pandemic, Economic Relief," *Wall Street Journal*, January 15, 2021.

4. The Fed's role during Covid is thoroughly covered in Timiraos, *Trillion Dollar Triage*.

5. Andrew Davis, "Summers Sees 'Least Responsible' Fiscal Policy in 40 Years," Bloomberg, March 20, 2021, https://www.bloomberg.com/news/articles/2021-03-20/summers-says-u-s-facing-worst-macroeconomic-policy-in-40-years.

6. This is based on interviews with several people involved.

26: Janet at War

1. Mahnoor Khan, "Putin Claims He Makes $140,000 and Has an 800-Square Foot Apartment. His Actual Net Worth Is a Mystery No One Can Solve," *Fortune*, March 3, 2022.

2. Ian Talley, "U.S. Gives Rusal Path to Escape Sanctions," *Wall Street Journal*, May 2, 2018. See also "Treasury Designates Russian Oligarchs, Officials, and Entities in Response to Worldwide Malign Activity," US Department of the Treasury, No-

vember 6, 2018; and Kenneth P. Vogel and Alan Rappeport, "Russian Oligarch Sues the U.S. Over Sanctions." *New York Times*, March 15, 2019.

3. For a good review of the history of sanctions, see Nicholas Mulder, *The Economic Weapon: The Rise of Sanctions as a Tool of Modern War* (New Haven, CT: Yale University Press, 2022).

4. Jon Hilsenrath and Brian Blackstone, "Inside the Risky Bets of Central Banks," *Wall Street Journal*, December 12, 2012.

5. Much of this account is based on reporting by me and my colleagues in the following story: Ian Talley, Daniel Michaels, and Jon Hilsenrath, "How the U.S. and EU Cut Russia Off from the Global Economy," *Wall Street Journal*, March 18, 2022.

6. "Transcript: The Path Forward: U.S. Treasury Secretary Janet L. Yellen," *Washington Post*, March 10, 2022, https://www.washingtonpost.com/washington-post-live/2022/03/10/transcript-path-forward-us-treasury-secretary-janet-l-yellen/.

Conclusion

1. Jon E. Hilsenrath, "Three Americans Win Nobel for Economics for Challenging Theory of Efficient Markets," *Wall Street Journal*, October 11, 2001.

2. I considered taking a detour at this point into the work of Daron Acemoglu and James Robinson on institutions and how they shape the fate of nations. It is essential work, but at this point in the story, you're probably ready to stop. So I will just recommend the following: Daron Acemoglu and James A. Robinson, *Why Nations Fail: The Origins of Power, Prosperity, and Poverty* (New York: Crown Business, 2013). Also see Acemoglu and Robinson's book *The Narrow Corridor*.

3. Alexander Hamilton, "Concerning Dangers from Dissensions between the States," Federalist Paper no. 6, https://guides.loc.gov/federalist-papers/text-1-10.

Selected Bibliography

Ahamed, Liaquat. *Lords of Finance: 1929, the Great Depression, and the Bankers Who Broke the World*. New York: Penguin, 2009.

Akerlof, George A. *An Economic Theorist's Book of Tales: Essays That Entertain the Consequences of New Assumptions in Economic Theory*. Cambridge, MA: Cambridge University Press, 1984.

———. "The Market for 'Lemons': Quality Uncertainty and the Market Mechanism." *Quarterly Journal of Economics* 84, no. 3 (1970): 488–500.

Akerlof, George A., and Rachel E. Kranton. *Identity Economics: How Our Identities Shape Our Work, Wages, and Well-Being*. Princeton, NJ: Princeton University Press, 2011.

Akerlof, George A. Andrew K. Rose, Janet L. Yellen, and Helga Hessenius. "East Germany in from the Cold: The Economic Aftermath of Currency Union." *Brookings Papers on Economic Activity* 1 (1991): 1–87.

Akerlof, George A., and Robert J. Shiller. *Animal Spirits: How Human Psychology Drives the Economy, and Why It Matters for Global Capitalism*. Princeton, NJ: Princeton University Press, 2010.

———. *Phishing for Phools: The Economics of Manipulation and Deception*. Princeton, NJ: Princeton University Press, 2016.

Akerlof, George A., and Janet L. Yellen. "The Fair Wage-Effort Hypothesis and Unemployment." *Quarterly Journal of Economics* 105, no. 2 (1990): 255–83.

———. "A Near-Rational Model of the Business Cycle, with Wage and Price Inertia." *Quarterly Journal of Economics* 100, supplement (1985): 823–38.

———. "Unemployment through the Filter of Memory." *Quarterly Journal of Economics* 100, no. 3 (1985): 747–73.

Akerlof, George A., Janet L. Yellen, and Michael L. Katz. "An Analysis of Out-of-Wedlock Childbearing in the United States." *Quarterly Journal of Economics* 111, no. 2 (1996): 277–317.

Akerlof, Robert. "Anger and Enforcement." *Journal of Economic Behavior and Organization* 126 (2016): 110–24.

———. "The Importance of Legitimacy." *World Bank Economic Review* 30, suppl. 1 (March 2016): 157–75. https://academic.oup.com/wber/article/30/Supplement_1/5157/2897349.

———. "'We Thinking' and Its Consequences." *American Economic Review* 106, no. 5 (2016): 415–19.

Bernanke, Ben. *The Courage to Act: A Memoir of a Crisis and Its Aftermath*. New York: W. W. Norton, 2017.

———. *Essays on the Great Depression*. Princeton, NJ: Princeton University Press, 2004.

Birnbaum, J. H. *Madhouse: The Private Turmoil of Working for the President*. New York: Times Books, 1996.

Blinder, Alan S., and Janet L. Yellen. *The Fabulous Decade: Macroeconomic Lessons from the 1990s*. New York: Century Foundation Press, 2001.

Bowmaker, Simon W. *When the President Calls: Conversations with Economic Policymakers*. Cambridge, MA: MIT Press, 2019.

Boyne, Daniel J. *The Red Rose Crew: A True Story of Women, Winning, and the Water*. Guilford, CT: Lyons Press, 2005.

Burns, Arthur F. *Reflections of an Economic Policy Maker: Speeches and Congressional Statements, 1969–1978*. Washington, DC: American Enterprise Institute for Public Policy Research, 1978.

Burns, Arthur, and Robert H. Ferrell. *Inside the Nixon Administration: The Secret Diary of Arthur Burns, 1969–1974*. Lawrence: University Press of Kansas, 2010.

Case, Anne, and Angus Deaton. *Deaths of Despair and the Future of Capitalism*. Princeton, NJ: Princeton University Press, 2020.

Clinton, Bill. *My Life*. New York: Random House, 2004.

Davis, Bob, and Jon Hilsenrath. "How the China Shock, Deep and Swift, Spurred the Rise of Trump." *Wall Street Journal*, August 11, 2016.

Davis, Bob, and Lingling Wei. *Superpower Showdown: How the Battle between Trump and Xi Threatens a New Cold War*. New York: Harper Business, 2020.

Federal Reserve. "FOMC: Transcripts and Other Historical Materials." https://www.federalreserve.gov/monetarypolicy/fomc_historical.htm.

Financial Crisis Inquiry Commission. *The Financial Crisis Inquiry Report: Final Report of the National Commission on the Causes of the Financial and Economic Crisis in the United States*. Washington, DC: Government Printing Office, 2011.

Friedman, Milton, and Rose Friedman. *Two Lucky People: Memoirs*. Chicago: University of Chicago Press, 1999.

Friedman, Milton, and Anna Jacobson Schwartz. *A Monetary History of the United States, 1867–1960*. Princeton, NJ: Princeton University Press, 1993.

Geithner, Timothy. *Stress Test: Reflections on Financial Crises*. New York: Crown Publishers, 2014.

Greenspan, A. *The Age of Turbulence: Adventures in a New World*. London: Penguin Group, 2007.

Hayek, Friedrich A. *The Road to Serfdom*. Chicago: University of Chicago Press, 2007.

Heilbroner, Robert L. *The Worldly Philosophers: The Lives, Times, and Ideas of the Great Economic Thinkers*. New York: Touchstone, 1999.

Hilsenrath, Jon. "Fed Chief Yellen Seeks Interest-Rate Consensus." *Wall Street Journal*, September 15, 2014. https://www.wsj.com/articles/fed-chief-yellen-seeks-interest-rate-consensus-1410748205.

———. "How Bernanke Pulled the Fed His Way." *Wall Street Journal*, September 28, 2012.

———. "Janet Yellen, a Top Contender at the Fed, Faces Test over Easy Money." *Wall Street Journal*, May 13, 2013.

Hilsenrath, Jon E. "A 91-Year-Old Who Foresaw Selloff Is 'Dubious' of Stock-Market Rally." *Wall Street Journal*, July 25, 2002.

Hilsenrath, Jon, and Kristina Peterson. "Federal Reserve 'Doves' Beat 'Hawks' in Economic Prognosticating." *Wall Street Journal*, July 29, 2013.

Keynes, John Maynard. *The General Theory of Employment, Interest and Money*. New York: Harcourt, Brace, 1936.

Kindleberger, Charles Poor. *Manias, Panics and Crashes: A History of Financial Crises*. Basingstoke, UK: Palgrave Macmillan, 2001.

Mallaby, Sebastian. *The Man Who Knew: The Life and Times of Alan Greenspan*. London: Bloomsbury, 2017.

Morgenson, Gretchen, and Joshua Rosner. *Reckless Endangerment: How Outsized Ambition, Greed, and Corruption Led to Economic Armageddon*. New York: St. Martin's Griffin, 2012.

Mulder, Nicholas. *The Economic Weapon: The Rise of Sanctions as a Tool of Modern War*. New Haven, CT: Yale University Press, 2022.

Nasar, Sylvia. *Grand Pursuit: The Story of the People Who Made Modern Economics*. London: Fourth Estate, 2012.

"Nobel Prize Biographies." NobelPrize.org. https://www.nobelprize.org/prizes/economic-sciences/.

Obama, Barack. *A Promised Land*. New York: Crown, 2020.

Paulson, Henry M. *On the Brink: Inside the Race to Stop the Collapse of the Global Financial System*. New York: Business Plus, 2011.

Rodrik, Dani. *Has Globalization Gone Too Far?* Washington, DC: Institute for International Economics, 1997.

————. *Straight Talk on Trade: Ideas for a Sane World Economy*. Princeton, NJ: Princeton University Press, 2019.

Rubin, Robert Edward, and Jacob Weisberg. *In an Uncertain World: Tough Choices from Wall Street to Washington*. New York: Random House, 2004.

Samuelson, Paul A., and William A. Barnett, eds. *Inside the Economist's Mind: The History of Modern Economic Thought, as Explained by Those Who Produced It*. Malden, MA: Blackwell, 2007.

Shiller, Robert J. "Stock Prices and Social Dynamics." *Brookings Papers on Economic Activity 1984*, no. 2 (1984): 457.

Shleifer, Andrei, and Lawrence H. Summers. "The Noise Trader Approach to Finance." *Journal of Economic Perspectives* 4, no. 2 (1990): 19–33.

Skidelsky, Robert. *John Maynard Keynes*. New York: Penguin, 2002.

Spencer, Roger W., and David A. Macpherson. *Lives of the Laureates: Thirty-Two Nobel Economists*. Cambridge, MA: MIT Press, 2020.

Thaler, Richard H. *Misbehaving: The Making of Behavioral Economics*. New York: W. W. Norton, 2016.

Timiraos, Nick. *Trillion Dollar Triage: How Jay Powell and the Fed Battled the White House and Saved the Economy* (New York: Little, Brown, 2022).

Warsh, David. *Knowledge and the Wealth of Nations: A Story of Economic Discovery*. New York: W. W. Norton, 2007.

Wessel, David. *In Fed We Trust: Ben Bernanke's War on the Great Panic*. New York: Three Rivers Press, 2010.

Yellen, Janet L. "Efficiency Wage Models of Unemployment." *American Economic Review* 74, no. 2 (1984): 200–205.

Index

About the Author

JON HILSENRATH is a senior writer for the *Wall Street Journal*, where he has been since 1997, reporting from Hong Kong, New York, and Washington, DC. He was a Pulitzer Prize finalist in 2014 for his coverage of the Federal Reserve; part of a team of 2009 Pulitzer finalists for coverage of the global financial crisis; and contributed on-the-scene reporting from the World Trade Center on September 11, 2001, which helped the *WSJ* win a Pulitzer in 2002. His 9/11 coverage also was featured in the book *September Twelfth*, by Dean Rotbart. Hilsenrath's colleagues twice voted him among the nation's most influential financial journalists. A nonpartisan, he has been a contributor to Fox News, Fox Business, CNBC, ABC, CBS, PBS, NPR, MSNBC, and C-SPAN. He graduated from Duke University and was a Knight-Bagehot Fellow at Columbia University.